The *Sams Teach Yourself in 24 Hours* Series

Sams Teach Yourself in 24 Hours books provide quick and easy answers in a proven step-by-step approach that works for you. In just 24 sessions of one hour or less, you will tackle every task you need to get the results you want. Let our experienced authors present the most accurate information to get you reliable answers—fast!

Sams Teach

Yourself Office 2000 SBE

in 24 Hours

SAMS

Greg Perry

SAMS

Teach Yourself

Microsoft® Office 2000
Small Business Edition

in 24 Hours

SAMS

A Division of Macmillan Computer Publishing
201 West 103rd St., Indianapolis, Indiana, 46290 USA

International Standard Book Number: 0-672-31568-8

Library of Congress Catalog Card Number: 98-89231

Printed in the United States of America

First Printing: May 1999

01 00 99 4 3 2 1

Trademarks

All terms mentioned in this book that are known to be trademarks or service marks have been appropriately capitalized. Sams Publishing cannot attest to the accuracy of this information. Use of a term in this book should not be regarded as affecting the validity of any trademark or service mark.

Warning and Disclaimer

Every effort has been made to make this book as complete and as accurate as possible, but no warranty or fitness is implied. The information provided is on an "as is" basis. The author and the publisher shall have neither liability or responsibility to any person or entity with respect to any loss or damages arising from the information contained in this.

Executive Editor
Angela Wethington

Acquisitions Editor
Stephanie J. McComb

Development Editor
Ben Milstead

Managing Editor
Tom Hayes

Project Editor
Damon Jordan

Copy Editor
Keith Cline

Proofreader
Carl W. Pierce
Sheri Replin

Indexer
Cheryl Jackson

Technical Editor
Kyle Bryant

Production
Lisa England

Overview

Table of Contents

PART II PROCESSING WITH WORD 2000 — 55

About the Author

Greg Perry is a speaker and a writer on both the programming and the application sides of computing. He is known for his skills at bringing advanced computer topics to the novice's level. Perry has been a programmer and a trainer since the early 1980s. He received his first degree in computer science and a master's degree in corporate finance. Perry has sold more than 1.5 million computer books, including such titles as *Sams Teach Yourself Windows 98 in 24 Hours*, *Absolute Beginner's Guide to C*, and *Sams Teach Yourself Visual Basic 6 in 21 Days*. He also writes about rental-property management and loves to travel. His favorite place to be when away from home is either at New York's Patsy's or in Italy because he enjoys only the best pasta!

Acknowledgments

The people at Macmillan Computer Publishing all take their jobs seriously. They want readers to have the best books possible. They accomplish that goal. Among the MCP editors and staff who produced this book, I want to send special thanks to Stephanie McComb who nurtured this book. Ben Milstead and Kyle Bryant honed my writing and turned a mediocre manuscript into one we can be proud of. Damon Jordan and Keith Cline also added their excellent editing skills to my work. Finally, without Richard Swadley leading the pack, I may not have had the offer to write this book. To each of them I am most grateful.

Although they did not have a direct hand in this book, I must thank MCP's two most outstanding members, Rosemarie Graham and Grace Buechline. Rosemarie and Grace are friends I made when working on previous books and I want them to know I appreciate the jobs they do.

My lovely and gracious bride stands by my side night and day. Thank you once again. You, precious Jayne, are everything that matters to me on earth. The best parents in the world, Glen and Bettye Perry, continue to encourage and support me in every way. I am who I am because of both of them.

—Greg Perry

Tell Us What You Think!

As the reader of this book, *you* are our most important critic and commentator. We value your opinion and want to know what we're doing right, what we could do better, what areas you'd like to see us publish in, and any other words of wisdom you're willing to pass our way.

As the Executive Editor for the Desktop Applications team at Macmillan Computer Publishing, I welcome your comments. You can fax, email, or write me directly to let me know what you did or didn't like about this book—as well as what we can do to make our books stronger.

Please note that I cannot help you with technical problems related to the topic of this book, and that due to the high volume of mail I receive, I might not be able to reply to every message.

When you write, please be sure to include this bookís title and author, as well as your name and phone or fax number. I will carefully review your comments and share them with the author and editors who worked on the book.

Fax: 317-817-7070

Email: awethington@mcp.com

Mail: Angie Wethington
          Executive Editor
          General Desktop Applications
          Macmillan Computer Publishing
          201 West 103rd Street
          Indianapolis, IN 46290
          USA

Introduction

Microsoft Corporation's Office products have an installed base of more than 20 million licensed users. More than 90 percent of the Fortune 500 companies use Microsoft Office. When developing Office 2000, Microsoft conducted thousands of hours of customer research and beta testing. Based on that research and user feedback, Micosoft designed Office 2000 to be more user friendly as well as more integrated among applications and the Internet. You won't regret your decision to learn and use Office 2000. With the Office 2000 skills that you master in these 24 lessons, you will know the most popular application software on earth.

Who Should Read This Book?

This book is for both beginning and advanced Office 2000 users. Readers rarely believe that lofty claim for good reason, but the design of this book and the nature of Office 2000 make it possible for this book to address such a wide audience. Here is why: Office 2000 is a major improvement over the previous Office products.

Readers unfamiliar with the Windows-style of windowed environments will find plenty of introductory help here that brings them quickly up to speed. This book teaches you how to start and exit Office 2000 as well as how to manage many of the Internet-based Office 2000 elements that you need to use Office 2000 in today's online world. If you are new to the Internet, this book helps you get started and shows how to make the most of the Internet and Office 2000. This book talks to beginners without talking down to them.

This book also addresses those who presently use a Microsoft Office product. Here is how: Step-Up sidebars contained in this book explain how a specific Office 2000 feature improves on or replaces a previous Office feature. With your fundamental Office understanding, you will appreciate the new features and added power of Office 2000. Keep in mind that Office 2000 is similar to previous Office versions but includes plenty of new features, improvements, and Web-based add-ons to keep Office gurus intrigued for a long time. This book teaches the Office 2000 Professional Edition, the edition that includes all the Office 2000 products and the one that sells the best.

What This Book Does for You

Although this book is not a complicated reference book, you learn almost every aspect of Office 2000 from the user's point of view. Office 2000 includes many advanced technical details that most users never need, and this book does not waste your time with those.

You want to get up to speed with Office 2000 in 24 hours, and this book helps you fulfill that goal.

Those of you tired of the plethora of quick-fix computer titles cluttering today's shelves will find a welcome reprieve here. This book presents both the background and descriptions that a new Office 2000 user needs. In addition to the background, this book is practical and provides more than 100 step-by-step tasks that you can work through to gain practical hands-on experience. The tasks guide you though all the common Office 2000 actions you need to make Office 2000 work for you.

Can This Book Really Teach Office 2000 in 24 Hours?

Yes. You can master each chapter in one hour. (By the way, chapters are referred to as *hours* in the rest of this book.) The material is balanced with mountains of tips, shortcuts, and methods that make your hours productive and hone your Office 2000 skills.

Conventions Used in This Book

Each hour ends with a question-and-answer session that addresses some of the most frequently asked questions about that hour's topic.

This book uses several common conventions to help teach the Office 2000 topics. Here is a summary of those typographical conventions:

- Commands, computer output, and words you type appear in a special monospaced computer font.
- To type a shortcut key, such as Alt+F, press and hold the first key, and then press the second key before releasing both keys.
- If a task requires you to select from a menu, the book separates menu commands with a vertical bar. For example, File, Save As is used to select the Save As option from the File menu. All menus in this book are shown in full even though Office 2000 users can elect to display only menu options they use most.

In addition to typographical conventions, the following special elements are included to set off different types of information to make them easily recognizable:

Special notes augment the material you read in each hour. These notes clarify concepts and procedures.

 You find numerous tips that offer shortcuts and solutions to common problems.

 The warnings are about pitfalls. Reading them saves you time and trouble.

STEP-UP

Users of previous Office products, such as Office 97, advance quickly by reading the Step-Ups provided for them.

 Each hour contains new-term definitions to explain important new terms. New-term icons make those definitions easy to find.

PART I

Gearing Up for Business

Hour

HOUR 1

Reviewing Windows Fundamentals

If the Office 2000 Windows environment is new to you, this hour briefly covers some of the fundamentals you need to know to use Office 2000 Small Business Edition effectively. This hour does not give you an in-depth Windows tutorial. Instead, it reviews the tasks and features that directly relate to Office 2000.

Although the Windows interface has been around for awhile, many companies are slow to upgrade from older Windows interfaces (such as Windows for Workgroups 3.11) to Windows 95, Windows 98, or Windows NT (the required Office 2000 operating environments). Therefore, even if you have used previous versions of Windows, you might need this hour's refresher so that you can hit the ground running with Office 2000.

The highlights of this hour include the following:

- What the Windows interface provides
- What improvements Office 2000 brings to the Windows interface

- How to access the Start menu
- Why the Open dialog box is so crucial to your Office 2000 work
- Where to find ToolTips
- How to use dialog box tabs
- How to preview your documents before printing to save time and paper
- Why you should master consistent Windows terminology while learning Office 2000 with *Sams Teach Yourself Microsoft Office 2000 Small Business Edition in 24 Hours*
- How Windows and the Internet combine to give you worldwide data access

Basic Windows Elements

Although this book does not assume you are a Windows guru and teaches Office 2000 from the ground up, it does assume you possess those basic Windows skills that you can pick up in less than an hour with the Windows Tour (available from the Start menu's Help option). Therefore, you won't find any instructions for using the mouse except where the mouse specifically works in a unique way with Office 2000.

Just to keep terminology straight throughout the book, take a moment to study the callouts in Figure 1.1. When this book mentions the Control menu or the window's Close button, you'll know exactly what is meant.

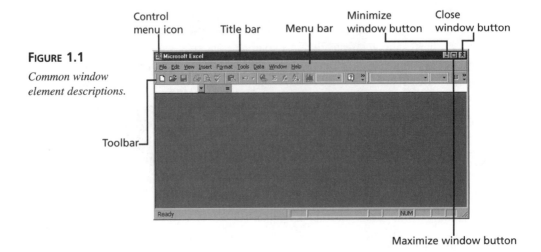

FIGURE 1.1

Common window element descriptions.

When you maximize a window's size by clicking the Maximize window button, that button changes to the Resize window button.

You might save time by skimming through this material if you're already familiar with many of this hour's topics, such as ToolTips. By presenting all the required Windows interface elements in one hour, the remaining hours are devoted to Office 2000 without Windows reviews. You'll be better able to concentrate on the differences and improvements in Office 2000.

The Windows Interface

If you use Windows NT, Windows 95, or Windows 98, the interface that your Windows version uses is called the *Windows 95 interface* because it has been around since the first version of Windows 95. The most prominent features of the Windows 95 interface are the *Start button* and the *Start menu* (see Figure 1.2).

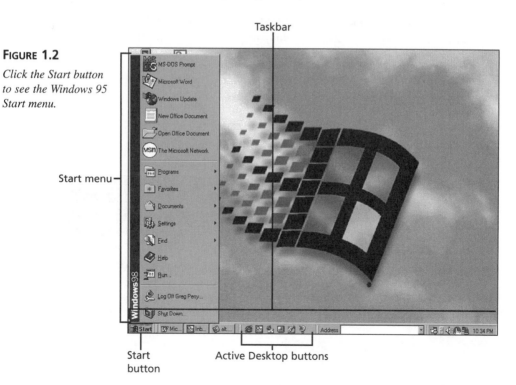

FIGURE 1.2

Click the Start button to see the Windows 95 Start menu.

Taskbar

Start menu

Start button

Active Desktop buttons

NEW TERM The *Windows 95 interface* is the user interface all versions of Microsoft operating systems have used since Windows 95 was released. The interface makes Windows simple to learn and use.

NEW TERM The *Start button* is the button labeled Start from which you display the Windows Start menu. The *Start menu* is the menu from which you can start any Windows program or shut down your PC.

Your Windows screen might differ slightly from Figure 1.2 because of the programs and icons you have installed on your computer. In addition, the *wallpaper*—the screen's background picture—might differ from the figure's. Two things should be similar: You should see the Start menu when you click the Start button, and you should see two commands, New Office Document and Open Office Document, at the top of your Start menu.

NEW TERM *Wallpaper* is the graphic background on your Windows 95 interface.

The Start menu provides access to all your computer's programs. If you want to start any program, click the Start button, select Programs, and follow the Start menu path to the program. You can start more than one program if you want to share work between two or more programs, such as between Word 2000 and Access 2000. As you start and run programs, the Windows *taskbar* displays all the program icons on task buttons. Click the task buttons to switch between running programs just as you click the remote control to switch between television programs.

NEW TERM The *taskbar* at the bottom of your screen displays all programs currently running.

> You can also switch between running programs by pressing Alt+Tab.

Office 2000 provides you with a shortcut to all the Office 2000 programs. Select New Office Document if you want to create a new Office 2000 *document* (as you'll learn in Hour 2, "Getting Acquainted with Office 2000 Small Business Edition," an Office 2000 document is any data file you create or edit with Office 2000) by using any of the Office 2000 programs. Select Open Office Document if you want to work on an existing Office 2000 document. To *open* a document means that you want to work with the document somehow, just as when you open a file cabinet drawer you want to work with a file from the cabinet.

NEW TERM To *open* a document is to load it into your program workspace so that you can work with it.

When you open an Office 2000 document, a window such as the one in Figure 1.3 appears.

FIGURE 1.3

The Office 2000 Open dialog box.

The Open dialog boxes in Office 2000 differ somewhat from other Open dialog boxes you'll find in Windows. The Office 2000 Open dialog boxes are customized to give you quicker access to Office 2000 documents.

As you use Office 2000 more, you'll learn which *icons* (pictures that represent items on your screen) go with which Office 2000 products. When you display the Open dialog box, the icons indicate which Office 2000 program created the document listed. For example, the flying W icon represents documents created by Word 2000.

NEW TERM *Icons* are small colorful pictures that represent items on your Windows screen.

The Open dialog box is simple or complex, depending on what you need to do with it. Most of the time, you see the Office 2000 document that you want to open and you double-click the document's name to load it. The Open dialog box is smart enough to know which Office 2000 product created the document; therefore, if you click a PowerPoint 2000 document, the Open dialog box starts PowerPoint 2000 and loads the selected document into PowerPoint 2000 for you.

Each time a new Office 2000 product is introduced in an hour in this book, that hour introduces the program's initial screens and describes how you can begin to create documents from within that product. For now, concentrate on getting an overall feel for the Windows interface.

Following is a summary of other common tasks you can perform from the Open dialog box:

- If you want to open a document located in a folder or disk drive other than the one showing, or even on a different computer on a network across the Internet, click the Look In drop-down list box and select the location.

- You can limit the files shown to specific Office 2000 programs by selecting from the Files of Type drop-down list box. For example, the Open dialog box displays only Web pages if you select Web Pages.

- The toolbar buttons across the top of the Open dialog box display the files in a different format, giving you more or less detail about the documents that appear. (Rest your mouse pointer on each toolbar button to see what that tool does.)

ToolTips

As you work with the Office 2000 products and dialog boxes, such as the Open dialog box, you'll need to use the toolbar buttons across the top (and sometimes the bottom and sides) of your screen. Office 2000 fully supports ScreenTips (also called ToolTips). Figure 1.4 shows an Excel 2000 ToolTip describing the button to which it is pointing.

FIGURE 1.4

ToolTips indicate what the buttons do.

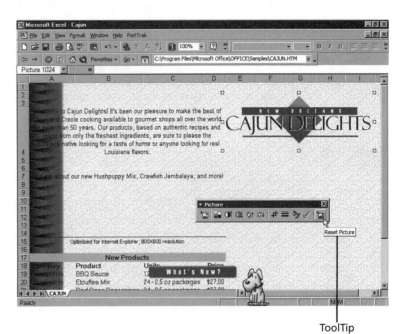

ToolTip

NEW TERM *ToolTips* are floating toolbar button descriptions that appear when you rest your mouse pointer over any toolbar button.

As you read this book, you won't find long boring tables that describe every toolbar button. Let the ToolTips guide you! Although many of the buttons are obvious, you might need to use ToolTips to locate a particular button.

Dialog Boxes

You've probably worked with dialog boxes before. Earlier in this hour, you saw the Open dialog box. Dialog boxes give you access to a set of related *controls* and selection options that not only let you issue commands, select items, and set options, but also display information.

NEW TERM Windows contains *controls* such as buttons, labels, and scrollbars that display data values, prompt you for information, enable you to enter new information, and manage the windows.

Starting with Windows 95, many dialog boxes took on an added dimension. Instead of containing a single set of controls, such as command buttons and text boxes, *tabbed dialog boxes* contain several sets of controls. Each set appears on a tabbed page in the dialog box. Figure 1.5 shows one such dialog box. Notice the tabs across the top of the dialog box.

Click a tab to see a
different dialog box page.

FIGURE 1.5

Windows dialog boxes often contain several pages.

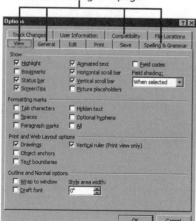

When you click one of the tabs, you display a different page that contains an additional set of dialog box controls within the dialog box. The use of the tabbed pages in dialog boxes gives you access to much more information from a single menu command.

 Tabbed dialog boxes contain pages that hold a set of controls and are common in Office 2000 and other Windows programs.

Printing from Office 2000

Because it is a Windows program, Office 2000 uses the Windows printer subsystem for printing, so you'll always see the same print options throughout the Office 2000 suite of products. Windows controls all printing from Windows programs. Therefore, no matter what kind of printer you connect to Windows, Office 2000 requires only that you inform Office 2000 of the print type or location of the printer.

Windows lets you direct printed output to any printer device, including fax/modems that you might have connected to your computer. Windows always defaults to your system's primary printer, but you can override the default printer by selecting a different target printer.

The most common way to initiate the print process is to select File, Print. Office 2000 opens the Print dialog box shown in Figure 1.6.

FIGURE 1.6

The Print dialog box controls all Office 2000 printing.

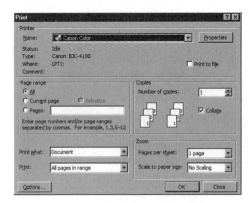

Your Print dialog box might look different depending on your printer hardware.

1

With the exception of FrontPage 2000, the Office 2000 products always contain a Print toolbar button that you can use to print, but the Print toolbar button does not display the Print dialog box. Therefore, if you want to select a printer that differs from your usual Windows default printer, or if you want to select different print options, you'll need to use the Office 2000 File, Print menu command to display the Print dialog box before you print.

From the Print dialog box, you can change several options, including

- The number of copies
- The range you want to print, such as selected pages or only a portion of text from a single page
- The collation selection of output papers
- The target printer

Before printing, you'll almost always want to preview your printed output on the screen. Although Office 2000 products are generally *WYSIWYG*-based (What You See [on the screen] Is What You Get [on the page]), you rarely see an entire page at once unless you use an extremely high-resolution monitor and graphics adapter. Therefore, when you click the Preview button in the Print dialog box (or select File, Print Preview from the menu bar), Office 2000 displays the printed page on your screen, as shown in Figure 1.7. If your output looks correct, you can send it to paper.

NEW TERM *WYSIWYG* (pronounced *wizzy-wig*) is an acronym for *What You See Is What You Get*, and refers to the concept that your screen shows your output as it will look when printed on paper.

When previewing any Office 2000 document, your mouse pointer changes to a magnifying glass. If you click the glass over any portion of the preview, Office 2000 magnifies the preview to make the text more readable (at the expense of displaying less of the preview). Click the magnifying cursor once again, and the preview reverts back to its original full-page state.

FIGURE 1.7

Preview your output before printing it.

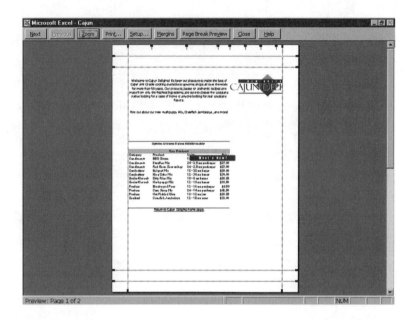

A Word on Shortcut Keys

Often, a menu option or toolbar button has an associated *shortcut key* (sometimes called an *accelerator key*) that you can press to trigger the same operation. For example, if you display Word 2000's File menu, you see that Ctrl+S is an equivalent shortcut key for the File, Save option. The Office 2000 suite of applications uses a consistent shortcut key interface across all programs. Therefore, Ctrl+S saves a document in every Office 2000 program. When you learn one Office 2000 program's shortcut key, you know the other programs' equivalent keys as well.

 A *shortcut key* is a keystroke, often combined with the Ctrl key, that enables you to access a menu option without having to use the menu. *Accelerator key* is another name for shortcut key.

The primary goal of this book is to acquaint you with Office 2000 as quickly as possible, showing you the basics as well as useful shortcuts and tricks to make your Office 2000 life simple. Generally, Office 2000 offers several ways to accomplish the same task. This book does not discuss a lot of the shortcut-key equivalents. You'll see shortcut-key equivalents when selecting from Office 2000 menus, and you'll learn those shortcut keys as you use Office 2000.

If a shortcut key seems obvious (for example, Ctrl+S for the Save operation) and generally easier to use (as opposed to an equivalent menu option or toolbar button), this book teaches you the shortcut key for the task. If, however, the shortcut key is not the best way to trigger a task, this book does not waste your time with the shortcut-key description.

As you use Office 2000, you'll discover the shortcut keystrokes that you prefer. Everybody has different preferences.

Windows and the Internet

Microsoft is moving toward integrating Windows and the Internet. The Internet's slow speed (for dial-up modem-based users) is keeping the Internet from truly integrating into your Windows desktop, but the day is not far off when quick Internet access will be available. Microsoft is preparing for that day by making the Windows operating system, as well as products such as Office 2000, as compliant and compatible with the Internet as possible.

If you are a PC user who has not yet worked on the Internet, this book discusses the Internet throughout these 24 hours. You never have to access the Internet to use Office 2000 because Office 2000 is standalone software designed to be used on a PC whether or not that PC is connected to the Internet. Nevertheless, the presence of the Internet runs throughout Office 2000; you don't have to use the Internet features, but if you want them, you'll be surprised at how easily Office 2000 helps bridge the Internet-to-PC connection.

With every copy of Windows sold today, as well as with Office 2000, Microsoft gives you a free Internet *browser* called Internet Explorer. In addition, you'll probably run across a competitor to Internet Explorer named Netscape Navigator. After you locate a provider for Internet access, you'll be able to *surf* the Web like a pro.

 A *browser* is a program that lets you traverse the Internet and view graphical and textual content that you find.

 To *surf* the Internet means to view Web pages that you find while you use the Internet. Browse is another word for surf in Internet terminology.

 If you want to learn more about Windows, check out *Sams Teach Yourself Windows 95 in 24 Hours, Second Edition*; *Sams Teach Yourself Windows 98 in 24 Hours*; *Using Windows 98, Second Edition*; and *Easy Windows 98*.

HOUR 2

Getting Acquainted with Office 2000 Small Business Edition

Microsoft Office 2000 Small Business Edition improves your work environment by offering integrated software tools that are powerful yet easy to learn and use. Offices large and small can use Office 2000–based applications for many of their day-to-day computer needs, as can home-based businesses and families who want simple but robust writing and analysis tools for their computers.

If you have used previous versions of Office, you'll see that Office 2000 Small Business Edition takes you to the next step by offering more products, automation, and Web-based tools than previous versions. Office 2000 automates many of your computing chores and provides products that work in unison by sharing data between them. This hour shows you how Office 2000 tackles many of the standard software requirements of today's offices.

The highlights of this hour include the following:

- What Office 2000 Small Business Edition contains
- Which Office 2000 Small Business Edition products you use for the various tasks
- When to use an Office 2000 product
- How Office 2000 complies with year 2000 dates
- What the document-centric concept means to all Office 2000 products

What's in Office 2000?

Office 2000 contains Microsoft's most powerful applications—such as Word, Excel, Outlook, and Internet Explorer—in a single package. The programs work well together now that Microsoft has combined them in the Office 2000 collection of programs. Program collections such as Office 2000 are often called *suites of programs*. You can still purchase the Office programs individually, to build a suite of products on your own, but the Office 2000 package offers the best deal.

 A *suite of programs* is a collection of programs that work well together and have a similar interface. It is usually less expensive to purchase the suite than to purchase each product separately.

The following is a quick overview of each Office 2000 program:

- Word 2000 is a word processor with which you can create notes, memos, letters, school papers, business documents, books, newsletters, and even Internet Web pages.
- Excel 2000 is an electronic worksheet program with which you can create charts, graphs, and worksheets for financial and other numeric data. After you enter your financial data, you can analyze it for forecasts, generate numerous what-if scenarios, and publish worksheets on the Web.
- Outlook 2000 is a personal information manager (PIM) that organizes your contact addresses, phone numbers, and other information in an address-book format. You can use Outlook 2000 to track your appointments, schedule meetings, generate to-do lists, keep notes, manage all your Internet email, and keep a journal of your activities.
- Publisher 2000 takes document publishing past the word processing stage and into the publication arena. With Publisher 2000, you can easily combine graphics and text into multicolumned professional publications and put those publications on the Web.

All the Office 2000 products share common features and common menu choices. Figure 2.1 shows the Word 2000 screen, for example, and Figure 2.2 shows the Excel 2000 screen. Both screens display the File menu. As you can see, the two program interfaces look virtually identical, even though the programs accomplish entirely different tasks. Also, information created in one program can be inserted into another program. If you create a financial table with Excel 2000, for instance, you can put that table in a Publisher 2000 publication that you send to your board of directors, or embed the table in a Web page for stockholders to view online. After you learn one program in the Office 2000 suite, you will be comfortable using all the others because they have many similarities.

2

FIGURE 2.1

The Word 2000 interface looks very similar to that of Excel 2000.

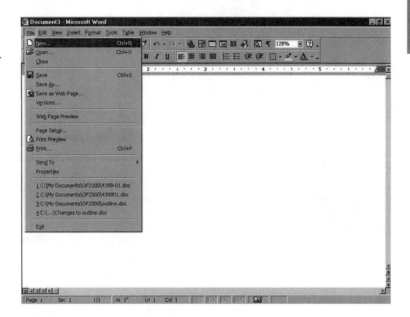

One of the most helpful features of Office 2000 is its capability to adjust menus and toolbars for you. For example, after you work with Word 2000 for a while, Word 2000 learns your habits. It does not display all the menu commands on the File menu when you choose the File menu, but only those commands you use most often. The less often you use a menu option, the more likely Word 2000 will be to remove that option from the menu that first appears. All the commands are there, however—you can click the arrows at the bottom of a menu to see all of the menu's commands. The Office 2000 products thus attempt to keep your screen as free of clutter as possible. As you use menus and toolbars, Office 2000 analyzes the menu options and buttons you use most; the options and buttons you use infrequently will begin to be hidden, so that only your common choices remain. You can always access these hidden menu options and toolbar buttons, but Office 2000 puts them out of the way until you need them.

FIGURE 2.2

*The Excel 2000 inter-
face looks very similar
to that of Word 2000.*

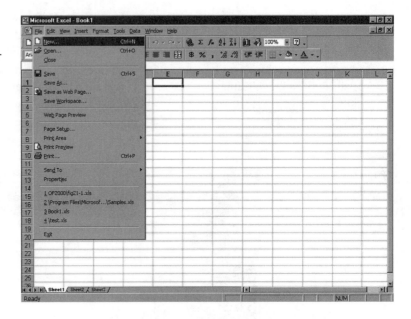

The figures in this book always display all menu options, although your
Office 2000 installation may show the shorter menus that reflect the options
you use most. You can force Office 2000 components to show the full set of
menu commands by selecting Tools, Customize, Options and unchecking the
option labeled Menus Show Recently Used Commands First.

The Office 2000 products are general purpose, meaning that you can customize the
applications to suit your needs. You can use Excel 2000 as your checkbook-balancing
program, for example, and as your company's interactive balance-sheet system.

You can integrate Office 2000 into your network system. This way, Office 2000 provides
useful features whether you are networked to an intranet, to the Internet, or to both. You
can share Office 2000 information with others across the network. Office 2000 continues
the trend that started with Office 97, the previous Office version, by integrating Internet
access throughout the Office 2000 suite.

> **STEP-UP**
>
> If you've mastered some of the advanced programming techniques in earlier versions of Office products, you will be glad to know that every program in the Office 2000 suite supports Visual Basic for Applications, which is often called Visual Basic, Microsoft's cross-program application programming language. Word 2000 does not support Word Basic (the programming language that Microsoft included with early versions of Word), however, because Word Basic is incompatible with other applications. Visual Basic for Applications (VBA) is fully compatible with Visual Basic 6, Microsoft's newest version of the programming language.

Introducing Word 2000

When you need to write a text-based document, look no further than Word. Word 2000 is a word processor that supports many features, including the following:

- Integrated grammar, spelling, and hyphenation tools (see Hour 6, "Managing Documents and Customizing Word 2000")

- Wizards and templates that create and format documents for you (see Hour 3, "Introducing Office 2000 Small Business Edition's Powerful Features")

- Automatic corrections for common mistakes as you type (see Hour 4, "Welcome to Word 2000"), using special automatic-correcting tools that watch the way you work and adapt to your needs

- Advanced formatting capabilities (see Hour 5, "Formatting with Word 2000")

- Numbering, bulleting, and shading tools (see Hour 5)

- Multiple document views so that you can see a rough draft of your document or the look of a final printed page as you write (see Hour 5)

- Drawing, border, and shading tools that enable you to emphasize headers, draw lines and shapes around your text, and work with imported art files (see Hour 18, "Office 2000's Synergy")

- Web-page development for Internet users so that they can turn their documents into Web pages (see Hour 20, "Creating Web Pages with Office 2000")

Figure 2.3 shows a Word 2000 editing session. The user is editing a business letter to send to a client.

FIGURE 2.3

Word 2000 helps you create, edit, and for-mat letters.

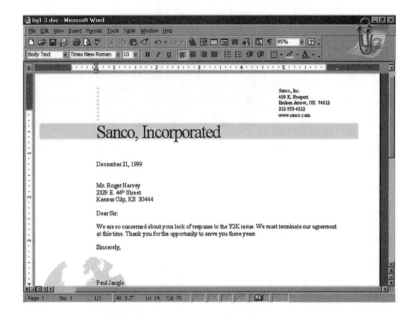

Introducing Excel 2000

Although Excel 2000 can be used for non-numeric worksheets, the primary goal of Excel 2000 is to help you organize and manage financial information such as income state-ments, balance sheets, and forecasts. Excel 2000 is an electronic worksheet program that supports many features, including the following:

- Automatic cell formatting (see Hour 8, "Excel 2000 Workbooks")
- Worksheet proofing tools, such as spell checking (see Hour 9, "Using Excel 2000")
- Automatic row and column completion of value ranges, with AutoFill (see Hour 9)
- Automatic worksheet formatting to turn your worksheets into professionally pro-duced reports (see Hour 12, "Formatting Worksheets to Look Great")
- Built-in functions, such as financial formulas, that automate common tasks (see Hours 10, "Editing Excel Worksheets" and 11, "Using Excel Formulas")
- Powerful maps, charts, and graphs that can analyze your numbers and turn them into simple trends (see Hour 12)
- Automatic worksheet computations that enable you to generate multiple what-if scenarios and decide between different courses of action (see Hour 8)

Figure 2.4 shows an Excel 2000 editing session. The user is getting ready to enter invoice information for a sale. As you can see, Excel 2000 can start with a predesigned form. If you have worked with other worksheet programs, you might be surprised at how fancy Excel 2000 can get. The wizards make creating advanced worksheets easy.

FIGURE 2.4

Excel 2000 helps you create, edit, and format numeric worksheets.

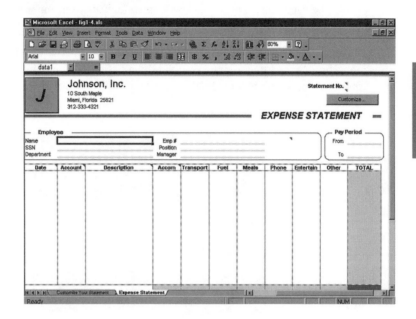

Introducing Outlook 2000

Outlook 2000 is a simple-to-use tool that manages your business and personal meetings, email, to-do lists, contacts, and appointments. Outlook 2000 provides many features, including the following:

- The capability to track your contact information, including multiple phone numbers and computerized email addresses (see Hour 14, "Communicating with Outlook 2000")

- The capability to track your computer activities in a journal (see Hour 14)

- Management of your email, phone calls, and to-do lists (see Hour 14)

- The capability to schedule appointments (see Hour 14)

- The capability to plan people and resources you need for meetings (see Hour 13, "Outlook 2000 Basics")

- The capability to sound an alarm before an important event (see Hour 13)

- The capability to set meetings and share calendar information with others (see Hour 15, "Power Calendaring")

- The capability to archive old data and transfer files between computers (see Hour 16, "Keeping House")

- The capability to check, delegate, and track all your important tasks (see Hour 17, "Getting Things Done")

Figure 2.5 shows an Outlook 2000 calendar screen. The user is getting ready to schedule a meeting on a particular day. As with all the Office 2000 programs, you can modify screen elements in Outlook 2000 so that they appear in the format most helpful to your needs.

FIGURE 2.5

Outlook 2000 tracks appointments and events.

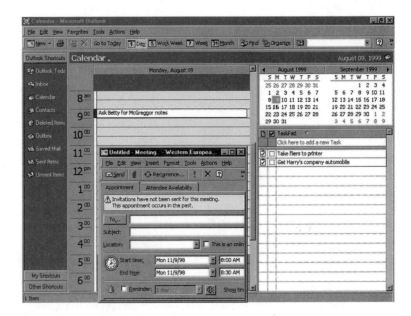

 Unlike previous versions of Office, Office 2000 includes no version of Bookshelf Basics.

Introducing Synergy and Sharing

Office 2000 programs are built to communicate with each other, making it easy for you to share your data between all Office 2000 applications. You can also share your data with the world by using the Internet—adding a new dimension to your hobbies or your business.

Under the hood, Office 2000 is one of the most tightly integrated application suites in existence for personal and business computing, and now that Microsoft has made it easy to publish your work on the Web, you'll experience a new level of overall integration, including the following:

- Learning how to control a drag-and-drop operation to produce a copy, a move, a link, or a shortcut in any Office 2000 application (see Hour 18"Office 2000's Synergy)

- Discovering how to access the Internet from within an Office 2000 product (see Hour 19, "Office 2000 and the Internet")

- Learning when to use the various Office 2000 wizards to generate Web pages (see Hour 20, "Creating Web Pages with Office 2000")

Figure 2.6 shows a personal Web page outline built by a Web Page Wizard.

FIGURE 2.6

This Web Page Wizard generates many varieties of Web page styles.

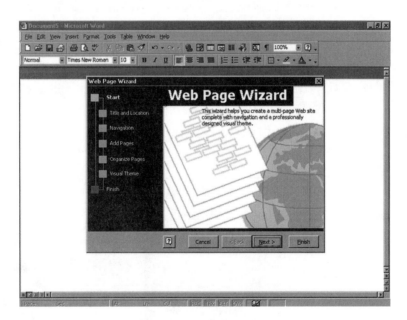

Introducing Publisher 2000

Although you can create professional documents and Web pages—including color pictures and artwork—from within Word 2000, nothing beats a *desktop publishing program* for high-quality publications that get your audience's attention. Today's color printers and copiers, scanners, and digital cameras give you a complete publishing house on your desktop.

NEW TERM A *desktop publishing program* enables you to efficiently combine text, charts, and graphics in various layout styles that can turn a drab document into an appealing publication.

Despite its power, Publisher 2000 is one of the easiest-to-use desktop publishing programs on the market and it sports many features, including these:

- Automatic wizards that guide you through the process of designing a number of publication types, including Web pages and resumes. You can also use Publisher 2000's wizard technology to make global changes to a publication after you've created it (see Hour 21, "Publisher 2000 Basics").

- A collection of lines, borders, buttons, fonts, and artwork that you can use to spruce up your publication (see Hour 22, "Designing Professional Publications").

- A postcard wizard that lets you design and create card-size publications, such as invitations, guest cards, and thank-you notes (see Hour 22).

- Management features that allow you to create lists of addresses or other information to be used in a mail merge (see Hour 23, "Creating and Printing Mass Mailings").

- Special tools you can call on to assist you when editing a Web page (see Hour 24, "Creating Web Pages with Publisher 2000").

Figure 2.7 shows a publication being created in Publisher 2000. Placing objects and creating columns of text is easy when you use the tools in Publisher 2000.

FIGURE 2.7

With Publisher 2000, your publications look great.

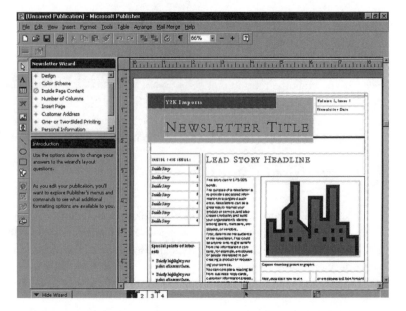

The Office 2000 Shortcut Bar

The Start menu is not the only way to start an Office 2000 product. In fact, you will probably forsake that menu and select from the Office 2000 *Shortcut Bar*. Figure 2.8 shows a typical Office 2000 Shortcut Bar, which automatically appears at the top of most Office 2000 user screens.

 The Office 2000 *Shortcut Bar* displays a toolbar from which you can quickly start Office 2000 programs and open Office 2000 documents at any time.

2

FIGURE 2.8

You can start Office 2000 programs quickly with the Office 2000 Shortcut Bar.

 Depending on your installed options, the Office Shortcut Bar shown in Figure 2.8 might look different from yours.

The Office 2000 Shortcut Bar offers pushbutton access to any Office 2000 product. You can open or create an Office 2000 document by clicking the appropriate button. The Office 2000 Shortcut Bar always stays *active* and appears on your screen, even if you work in non-Office 2000 programs. Therefore, you can access Office 2000 programs and documents from wherever you are.

 A window is *active* when its title bar is highlighted and its controls are available for you to use.

If you click the four-colored icon button on your Office 2000 Shortcut Bar (no ToolTip exists for this button), the Office 2000 Shortcut Bar displays a menu from which you can modify the Office 2000 Shortcut Bar's appearance or remove it from your screen. This icon is called the Shortcut Bar Control icon.

 If you use certain Office 2000 programs more often than others, you might want to select the Shortcut Bar's Customize option and add those specific program icons to the Office 2000 Shortcut Bar. If the Office 2000 Shortcut Bar contains buttons you rarely use, such as the New Journal Entry button, use Customize to remove any of the existing buttons.

To get rid of the Office 2000 Shortcut Bar, perform these steps:

1. Click the Office 2000 Shortcut Bar's Control icon to display the drop-down menu.
2. Click Exit. Windows displays the dialog box shown in Figure 2.9.
3. If you want to remove the Office 2000 Shortcut Bar just for this session, click Yes. If you want to keep the Office 2000 Shortcut Bar from appearing in subsequent Windows sessions, click No.

FIGURE 2.9

You can control when the Office 2000 Shortcut Bar appears.

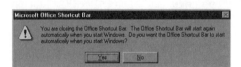

The Office 2000 Shortcut Bar appears automatically (unless you remove it) because Office 2000 installs the Office 2000 Shortcut Bar Startup command in your Start menu's Startup folder. If you click Yes to keep the Office 2000 Shortcut Bar from reappearing, Windows removes the command from your Startup folder.

You can add the Shortcut Bar Startup command to your Startup folder by selecting Start, Programs, Office Tools, Microsoft Office Shortcut Bar and clicking Yes when asked whether you want the Shortcut Bar to appear automatically when you start Windows.

You can move your Office Shortcut Bar to another location by dragging the bar to a different place on your Windows desktop.

Year 2000 Compliance

Whether you read this before or after January 1, 2000, you won't have to worry about Office 2000 mishandling dates. Microsoft carefully produced Office 2000 to comply with the Year 2000 Compliance standard, an internal 2000-compliance standard Microsoft developed to ensure that all Microsoft products stringently adhere to date-accurate information.

Microsoft has set up a year 2000 Web site that you can check for more information on the year 2000 problem and what tools Microsoft offers to help you manage dates that follow January 1, 2000. Check out the following Web address to access the Microsoft Year 2000 Resource Center: www.microsoft.com/technet/year2k

> **SUPPORT FOR THE EURO**
>
> Along the same lines as the year 2000 compliance, Europe is quickly moving toward a single economy, and Office 2000 provides support for the new Euro currency. Each individual country's former currency symbols still reside in Office 2000 as well.
>
> Enabling Office 2000 for a specific language is easier than ever before. To activate a specific language, select Start, Programs, Microsoft Office Tools, and then select the Microsoft Office Language Settings option. Select the language you want to enable from the Enabled Languages tab, and click OK to apply that language to the Office 2000 environment.

2

Getting Acquainted with Document Files

All Office 2000 products use a *document-centric* model. Whether you write a letter or a book (or create an Access 2000 database or an Excel 2000 worksheet), the text you write appears in a document. The term *document* is just an Office 2000 term for file.

NEW TERM *Document-centric* refers to the way that all Office 2000 products work with documents rather than traditional and distinct kinds of data files such as database files, worksheet files, and presentation files. The document-centric concept lets Office 2000 products work uniformly with each other's files. Although each Office 2000 product stores its documents in a different format from the other Office 2000 programs, document-centricity keeps terms uniform throughout the products.

After you create a document, name it the same way you label a file folder before you put it in a file cabinet. The document file's extension tells Office 2000 which application (such as Word 2000 or Excel 2000) was used to create that particular document. You can use either uppercase or lowercase letters for your document names. Although neither Windows nor Office 2000 considers Proposal.doc to be different from PROPOSAL.DOC, the document names are easier to read when you mix the case. If you let Office 2000 add the extension, as you should usually do when you name documents, Office 2000 adds a lowercase extension, such as .doc.

> One of the ways that Office 2000 integrates the Web more into its products is by offering a uniform file-saving format that is fully compatible with all Internet browsers. You will be able to view Word 2000 or Excel 2000 documents from Word 2000, Excel 2000, or any browser that supports the HTML format. You can elect to save specific documents in the HTML format or set up Office 2000 to save all documents in the HTML format.

Summary

This hour introduced the Office 2000 programs by showing you a little of what each program can accomplish. Before learning Office 2000 specifics, you need to get the big picture. This hour provided that big picture and introduced the Office 2000 tools that you will use.

All Office 2000 programs share a common interface. After you learn one Office 2000 program, the others are easy to master. Some users find that they can use Office 2000 for all their computer needs.

The next hour begins a tour of Office 2000's features so that you can begin to see what Office 2000 can really do.

Q&A

Q I've used Word and Excel. Do I need the other Office 2000 products?

A Only you can answer that question, because only you know whether you need a program to keep track of your appointments and contacts (Outlook 2000) or your Web site.

There are two other Microsoft Office 2000 applications you may find useful that do not come with the Small Business Edition: Access 2000 and PowerPoint 2000. If you need a powerful database or you want to do sleek business presentations beyond the capabilities of Publisher, you can upgrade through Microsoft.

If you need word processing and worksheet computing only, you may not need the other Office 2000 products—such as Outlook and Publisher—that come with the Small Business Edition. In this case, you need to install only those programs that you want to use. If you have truly mastered Word and Excel, however, you will be glad that Microsoft kept the same uniform interface throughout all the Office 2000 products because it enables you to use what you already know.

Q Why don't I see the Office Shortcut Bar?

A Your Office 2000 installer probably failed to install the Office Shortcut Bar. Just rerun the Office 2000 Setup program and install the Office Shortcut Bar. The Setup program acts like most other Windows-based installation programs, but if you feel uncomfortable running the Setup program, ask whoever installed Office 2000 for you to help. If you don't want to see the Office Shortcut Bar every time you start Windows, you can display the Office Shortcut Bar only when you want to see it by selecting Start, Programs, Office Tools, Microsoft Office Shortcut Bar and clicking No when asked whether you want the Shortcut Bar to appear automatically when you start Windows.

Q **Suppose that I want to keep track of names and addresses. Which Office 2000 product would I use?**

A This is actually a trick question. Word 2000, Excel 2000, and Outlook 2000 all track names and addresses! Word 2000 keeps track of names and addresses for mail merging (sending the same letter to many people); Excel 2000 includes a simple database feature that can track items such as names and addresses; and Outlook 2000 records all your name and address records. Generally, you should use Outlook 2000 for your names and addresses (all the other Office 2000 products can read Outlook 2000's data) and use the other Office 2000 products for their primary purposes.

Q **Is it true that all Office 2000 programs are simple after I learn one?**

A The Office 2000 programs share common interfaces, such as uniform menus and dialog boxes. After you learn how to use one Office 2000 program, you already understand the basic interface of the others. Therefore, you can concentrate on the specifics of each product instead of having to learn a new interface in each program.

2

Hour 3

Introducing Office 2000 Small Business Edition's Powerful Features

This hour previews the most impressive Office 2000 Small Business Edition features. If you are new to the Office environment, this hour will whet your appetite for Office 2000. After this hour, you'll be ready to study the specific Office 2000 programs and learn how they work.

Office 2000 attempts to move beyond the normal Windows-based help system. If you have used Windows programs in the past, you have probably read online documentation, clicked hypertext links to other related topics, and searched for keywords with which you need help. Office 2000 includes all these standard online help tools, but takes that help to a new level of functionality. Office 2000 provides some rather unusual help with the Office Assistant and its support for plain-language help queries. Every product in the suite of Office 2000 Small Business Edition programs includes these helpful guides. In a way, Office 2000 looks over your shoulder and offers advice about better ways of doing things.

In addition to improving the Windows online help system, Office 2000 helps disabled users by providing several accessibility options. These options magnify the screen's views and offer keyboard shortcuts that the user can define and control.

The highlights of this hour include the following:

- What Office Assistant is
- When Office Assistant offers help that you didn't even know you needed
- How to use group-related options that Office 2000 supports, such as revision marks
- Where to locate a huge assortment of drawings, photos, sounds, and videos that you can include in your documents
- How to work with templates and wizards

The Office Assistant

When you start any Office 2000 program, the first feature you will notice is the *Office Assistant*, an online cartoon character that hangs around as you work. Figure 3.1 shows the Office Assistant (named Clippit), who appears when you start an Office 2000 product.

FIGURE 3.1

Clippit, the helpful Assistant, remains faithful as you use Office 2000.

Clippit is here to help you.

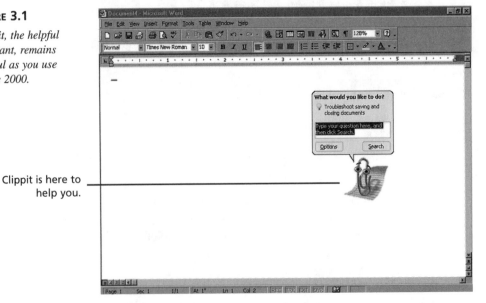

NEW TERM *Office Assistant*, an animated cartoon character, offers advice as you use Office 2000.

> You may see a different Office Assistant character. The next section, "Customizing Office Assistant," explains how to change the Office Assistant's animated character.

Keep your eyes on the Office Assistant as you work because you will be amused at the contortions it goes through as it provides advice. If you have your speakers turned on, you'll be able to hear the Office Assistant make noises.

You can move the Office Assistant to a different screen location by dragging the character. If the Office Assistant is about to cover an area in which you are typing, it automatically moves out of the way.

Suppose that you want help italicizing Word 2000 text. You can search through the online help system (via the Help menu), or you can click Office Assistant and type a question, such as **How do I italicize text?**, and press Enter. Office Assistant analyzes your question and displays a list of related topics (as shown in Figure 3.2). Click the topic that best fits your needs, and Office Assistant locates that help topic and displays the Help dialog box.

FIGURE 3.2

Office Assistant offers a lot of advice.

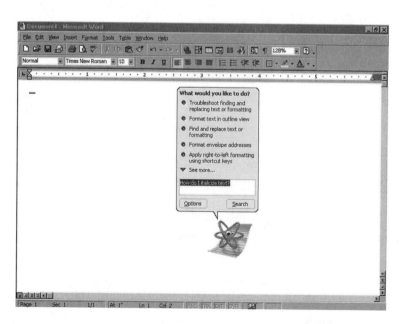

If you do something and Office Assistant can provide a better way to accomplish the same task, Office Assistant displays a yellow light bulb that you can click for shortcut information. If you begin to create a numbered list by using menus, for example, Office

Assistant displays the light bulb to let you know that you can create a numbered list by clicking a button on the toolbar.

Customizing Office Assistant

If you work on a slow computer, you might want to disable Office Assistant to keep things moving a little faster. When you right-click Office Assistant, a pop-up menu appears with these options:

- Hide—Gets rid of Office Assistant. You can display Office Assistant again by clicking the toolbar's Office Assistant button.

- Options—Displays the Office Assistant dialog box (shown in Figure 3.3), from which you can control the behavior of the Office Assistant (such as Office Assistant's response to pressing the F1 key).

- Choose Assistant—Enables you to change to a different animated Office Assistant character. As you work with Office 2000, check out all the Office Assistants (they are fun to see). You will learn how to change the Office Assistant character in the steps that follow.

- Animate!—Causes Office Assistant to dance around its window; Office Assistant likes to show off! Select Animate! a few times to see Office Assistant's contortions. As Office Assistant offers advice, it also moves through these animations. If you attempt to exit a program without saving your work, for example, Office Assistant gets your attention. (You will even hear Rocky, the canine assistant, barking!)

FIGURE 3.3

You can control the way that Office Assistant behaves.

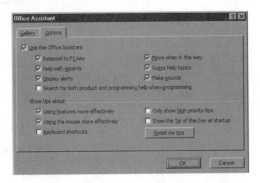

Office 2000 includes several Office Assistants to help you do your job. They differ in animation, but not in their advice. Suppose you get tired of Clippit and decide that you want to see a different Office Assistant. Try this:

1. Right-click Office Assistant.

2. Select Choose Assistant. Office Assistant displays an Office Assistant Gallery screen.

3. Click Back and Next to cycle through the Office Assistants. Each Office Assistant goes through a song and dance to convince you that it is the best.

4. When you come to an Office Assistant you like, click the OK button to begin using that Office Assistant.

This book's inside back cover lists all the Office Assistants from which you can choose.

The Office Assistant appears when you press F1, but you can return to the normal content-based help system if you prefer; simply right-click over the Assistant, select Options, and then click the option labeled Respond to the F1 key to disconnect the Assistant from the F1 keypress. Office 2000 uses a Web-like, HTML-based help system so that you can navigate the online help as you navigate Web pages. As Figure 3.4 shows, when you display non-Office Assistant help, Office 2000 displays two panes, with the help text in the left pane and a condensed Office 2000 program screen in the right pane. (You can drag the center bar left and right to adjust the width of the panes.) With the help shown in a second pane, you can keep working in the right pane while referring to helpful instructions in the left pane.

NEW TERM   **HTML** stands for *Hypertext Markup Language* and refers to a formatting language used to display Web pages.

FIGURE 3.4

Office 2000 products provide a two-pane Help view.

Help stays here...   ...while you work here.

Help topics   Help text

Using Office 2000 to Share Information with Others

Although many people use Office 2000 on single-user computers, Microsoft understands that today's office worker needs the ability to share information globally. Today's computers are often networked to other computers, either through a *network*, an Internet connection, or an *intranet* connection.

NEW TERM A *network* is a collection of two or more computers linked together to share programs and data.

NEW TERM An *intranet* is an internal network system that uses an Internet browser, such as Microsoft's Internet Explorer, to access information from other computers on the local area network.

As long as you use email programs such as Outlook Express, Outlook 2000, Microsoft Exchange, Windows Messaging, Microsoft Mail, or Netscape Messenger, you can create a Word 2000 document and send it to users on your mail system. When you send a document, the receivers can read the document and even make changes to the document by using Word 2000. Word 2000 keeps track of revisions, and each reviewer's notes appear separate from the others. Using Word 2000's Tools, Track Changes menu, you can accept or reject any of the reviewers' comments after the document gets back to you.

Office 2000 enables you to use all Office 2000 products together. Therefore, if you want to send a report with an Excel 2000 worksheet graph to someone over the network, embed that graph into the Word 2000 document (as explained in Hour 18, "Office 2000's Synergy") and send the Word 2000 document. The graph travels along with the document.

Office 2000 supports several document-routing options such as these:

- Send a document—Sends a copy of your document to your list of reviewers. Each reviewer can make changes to his or her copy, and then return the document to you.

- Route a document—Sends a single copy of your document to each reviewer in turn. Every subsequent reviewer can read the preceding reviewers' comments and add his or her own. The document finally gets back to you after the final reviewer makes revisions.

- Post a document—Sends a copy of your document to a public folder that everyone on your receiver list can read. Posting is useful when you have a company-wide policy or message that you want everyone to read. Posting requires that Microsoft Exchange Server, a separate program from those supplied with Office 2000, be run with a Public Folder shortcut. Your network administrator should be able to help set up a public folder.

Word 2000 keeps track of who made each revision. You can have the reviewers make changes to a copy or to the original document. To determine who made a revision, point to the edit and the editor's name appears over the edit, along with the date the edit was made.

> If the reviewers insert sound objects into the routed document, they can review the document with speech as well as with editing marks!

Figure 3.5 shows a screen from Word 2000 with revision marks. The revisions appear on your screen in color—a different color for each editor who made a revision—so that the revisions are easy to distinguish from the original text. Word 2000's Tools, Track Changes menu options for accepting and rejecting changes enable you to quickly incorporate or delete any and all revisions made by the editing team.

3

FIGURE 3.5

Revision marks enable a team of editors to revise the same document electronically.

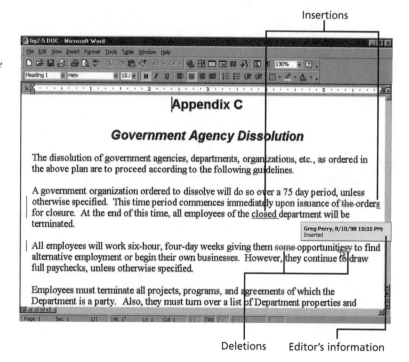

Both Word 2000 and Excel 2000 currently support revision marks. You can use the Tools, Track Changes menu options to see revision marks, hide revision marks (to see what the document will look like if you incorporate all revisions), and accept or reject revision marks.

> You can right-click a revision mark to get a pop-up menu that enables you to easily accept or reject the revision mark.

Working with Multiple Data Types

Office 2000 handles today's massive data needs. In the past, you worked primarily with text in word processors and with numbers in electronic worksheets. Today's multimedia computers require much more data support from programs. A database might hold text, numbers, pictures, sounds, and even Internet *hyperlink* connections, for example. Using OLE, COM, and ActiveX technologies (the advanced data-sharing and linking tools Office 2000 uses to track all kinds of data), your documents really come alive. You are no longer bound by outdated data limitations. You can elect to store all Office 2000 documents in a uniform, HTML format, or you can save each of the Office 2000 products' documents in their own specific formats. No matter how you save documents, all the Office 2000 programs can read each other's data.

NEW TERM A *hyperlink* is a word or phrase that you can click to display a different document or document section. Hyperlinks often describe Web page locations, but can also refer to other data and documents on your PC or on a network of computers.

Suppose that you are creating a Web page in Word 2000, and you want to insert a hyperlink to another Web site, as in Figure 3.6. The Insert menu enables you to do just that because a Web address's hyperlink is another kind of data—just as text and numbers are two kinds of data—that the Office 2000 Small Business Edition products support. Such multiple-data support frees you from the boundaries of yesterday's software and enables you to work from a global computing perspective.

FIGURE 3.6

The Office 2000 products recognize Web addresses and insert hyperlinks where you need them.

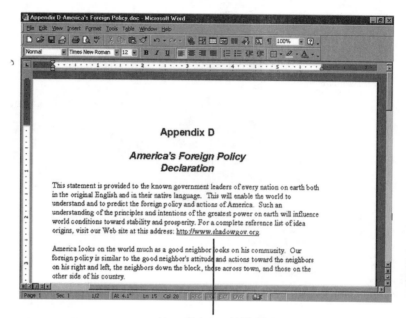

Hyperlink to a Web site

Office 2000 applications automatically turn Web addresses that you type into hyperlinks if the addresses begin with www or begin with http://. Therefore, you don't have to select from the Insert menu to embed hyperlinks to those sites (which you'll learn about next). You can turn off the automatic conversion of hyperlinks from the Tools, AutoCorrect dialog box. Throughout this 24-hour tutorial, you will learn more ways to work with the multiple data formats that Office 2000 supports.

When you want to insert a hyperlink into any Office 2000 document, you need only to select Insert, Hyperlink from the menu (Ctrl+K is the shortcut key). Office 2000 supports several kinds of hyperlinks, not just links to Web page addresses. When you select Insert, Hyperlink, the Insert Hyperlink dialog box appears, as shown in Figure 3.7.

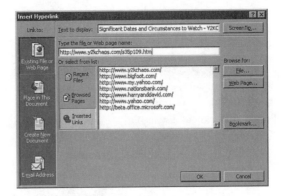

FIGURE 3.7

You can insert many different kinds of hyperlinks from the Insert Hyperlink dialog box.

The Insert Hyperlink dialog box enables you to insert many different kinds of hyperlinks, including the following:

- A Web page that appears when the user clicks the hyperlink
- A file on your own system or on another computer that is networked to your computer
- An email address that opens Outlook 2000 and creates a message to that email address when the user clicks the hyperlink
- Text that pops up, including a ScreenTip that appears when the user rests the mouse cursor over the hyperlink
- A bookmark inside the current document that the user can click to move to the bookmarked location

If you insert a hyperlink to a file, Office 2000 opens and displays that file when someone clicks on the hyperlink—even at another computer (that has Office 2000, of course).

One of the benefits of Office 2000's full support for HTML-based Internet Web pages is that any Office 2000 product can read your existing Web pages, and your created Web pages look consistent in any browser or Office 2000 program. In other words, you can open a Web page in Word 2000 and make edits directly to the page, even if you did not originally use Word 2000 to create the page.

Making Office 2000 Easier to Use

Several accessibility features make Office 2000 easier to use. You will become familiar with many of these features as you work with Office 2000. Following is a sample of some of these features:

- The Change Document option magnifies documents for easier viewing. Even the toolbar buttons are larger to make them easier to find.

- The Office 2000 programs contain many *AutoComplete* features with which you can begin typing items such as dates, times, days of the week or month, names, and any other AutoText entries you set up. Office 2000 completes the entry for you. If you begin typing a month name such as Nov, for example, Word 2000 displays a small box with November above your month abbreviation. If you press Enter, Word 2000 completes the month name for you! If you type a full month name, such as July, Word 2000 offers to complete your entry with the current date, such as July 7, 1999. You can accept the complete date by pressing Enter or ignore it by typing the rest of the sentence as you want it to appear.

NEW TERM   *AutoComplete* is an Office 2000 feature that completes text entries it recognizes as you type them.

3

- You can rearrange toolbar buttons and customize toolbars so that they contain only the buttons you use most frequently. As you learned in the previous lesson, Office 2000 analyzes how you use the menus and toolbars and begins to hide the options and buttons you use less frequently to reduce screen clutter. You can always see all menu options and toolbars when you want by displaying a menu for a couple seconds, until the hidden options appear. In addition, you can drag a toolbar left or right to see hidden options.

- You can assign shortcut keys to just about any task in any Office 2000 product. Suppose that you often need to color and boldface an Excel 2000 value. You can create a shortcut keystroke and press it whenever you want to pply the special formatting.

Clip Art

Not only can Office 2000 work with text, numbers, and even Web hyperlinks, but it can also work with sound, pictures, and moving video.

Office 2000 includes a huge collection of royalty-free *clip art* files for personal use that you can use when you want to embed a special data item—such as a picture or video—into a document, spreadsheet, or Web page. When you need a graphic to spice things up, or when you want to include an attention-getting sound file in an Outlook 2000 email message, select Insert, Picture, Clip Art to access the Office 2000 clip art collection called Microsoft Clip Art Gallery. The gallery includes several hundred sounds, pictures, and drawings arranged by category, as Figure 3.8 shows.

FIGURE 3.8

Office 2000 offers a wide array of clip art, including sounds, pictures, and drawings.

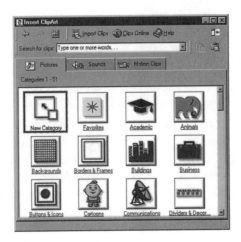

 Clip art is a data file that you can include in your own documents.

Perhaps one of the most impressive features from the Microsoft Clip Art Gallery is that you can click the Clips Online button to link to Microsoft's clip art Web site and search for even more files to use in your documents.

Templates

A *template* is a formatted outline of a document. Suppose that you follow a monthly budget, and you prepare monthly statements to follow. You like to include your savings account interest calculations, so you determine that Excel 2000 will function well as the creation tool for your statements.

 A *template* is an outline that holds the format of a document, worksheet, Web page, or other Office 2000 data file.

When you create your monthly statements, you have three options:

- Create each monthly budget from scratch.
- Modify a saved monthly budget to change the details for each subsequent statement.
- Create a monthly budget template and fill in the details for each statement.

Obviously, the first option requires the most work. Why create a new statement for each budget, adding the titles, date, time, details, summaries, creditors, and new investment information if many of those details remain the same from statement to statement?

The second option is not a bad idea if the statements are fairly uniform in design and require only slight formatting and detail changes. Some people feel more comfortable changing an existing statement's details than creating statements from scratch or using a template. New Office 2000 users might prefer to change an existing statement until they get accustomed to Office 2000's programs.

> Although templates are great for Office 2000 newcomers, you do not always want to start with them. Sometimes, it's easier to understand an Office 2000 program if you create your first few data files from scratch. For example, until you've created a Publisher 2000 document from scratch and until you've learned all the terminology related to it, the Publisher 2000 templates will not make much sense to you. After you master the fundamentals of the Office 2000 programs, you can leverage the power that templates provide.

When you get used to Office 2000, however, you'll discover that the template method makes the most sense for repetitive statement creation. The template provides a fill-in-the-blank statement; you don't have to format the same information from statement to statement, and you're guaranteed a uniform appearance.

Using Existing Templates

Office 2000 supplies several common templates, and each Office 2000 product contains templates of its own. For example, when you want to create a new Excel 2000 electronic worksheet, you can select from a blank worksheet or you can click the Spreadsheet Solutions tab to see four icons that represent templates. When you click a template icon, Office 2000 shows you a preview of that template (as shown in Figure 3.9).

FIGURE 3.9

Office 2000 provides several templates that you can preview.

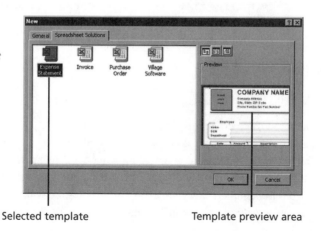

Selected template   Template preview area

After you select a template, the Office 2000 program opens it and presents the file. You can edit the template and save the details in a new file. The new file becomes your template file, which you can then use for subsequent documents.

> If you use the same template for the majority of your work, each Office 2000 program lets you specify a template that you want to be the basis for all new files you create. For example, if you create an Excel 2000 template, save the template under the name BOOK.XLT and store it in the XLSTART directory. Excel 2000 automatically loads that template every time you create a new worksheet.

Creating New Templates

Although Office 2000 supplies several predesigned templates, you won't find a template for everything, such as a monthly budget you may want to create. You may want specific titles, special formatting, and unusual expense items that don't often appear in routine monthly budgets.

Because your specific monthly budget template does not exist in Office 2000, you have to create your own. Generally, to create a template, follow these steps:

1. Create a properly formatted sample data file, such as a monthly budget, so that you know what design the template is supposed to produce.

2. Print the sample budget so that you can reference it later when designing the template from the sample.

3. Use File, New to create a new Office 2000 Excel 2000 worksheet.

4. Based on the document you created in step 1, add all titles, formatting, and footer information that do not change from statement to statement. Leave blank space for details.

5. Save the template. Select the Template option in the Save As Type text box to let Office 2000 know you're creating a template file and not a normal data file.

If you are new to Office 2000, creating the initial template may seem like a lot of work. (As you learn more about Office 2000, you'll see that creating a template document gets easier.) After spending the time to create the template, however, subsequent reports become extremely simple. Instead of creating a statement from scratch, you can create the reports from the template; all you need to do is enter the details. The template supplies the proper formatting and the information that doesn't change from report to report.

After you create the initial sample document in any Office 2000 product that you want to use as the basis for a template, you can save that file as a template by selecting File, Save As and then selecting Document Template as the document's type.

As you learn more about the Office 2000 products, you'll learn how to add specialized *fields* to the template to make the creation of your template-based statements even easier.

NEW TERM   A *field* is an area of a template designed to accept certain information, such as a name or phone number. The field contains all necessary formatting and spacing, so you need only be concerned with the data.

Wizards

One reason so many users have switched to Microsoft-based Office products is Microsoft's wizard technology. *Wizards* are step-by-step guides that walk you through the development of a document or through a complicated process, such as creating an Internet Web page from scratch. (You'll learn more about Office 2000's Internet integration later this hour and in Hour 19, "Office 2000 and the Internet.")

NEW TERM   A *wizard* is a step-by-step set of dialog boxes that guides you through the creation of a document or through a complicated selection process (such as a report's design).

Although each wizard has a different goal, all follow a similar pattern. Wizards display a series of dialog boxes, and each dialog box asks for a set of values. As you fill in the dialog boxes, you answer questions to help the program perform a specific job.

Generally, each dialog box within a wizard contains Next and Back buttons, which you can click to move back and forth through the wizard. If you change your mind after leaving one dialog box, you can back up to that dialog box and change its values.

Microsoft supplies you with several wizards you can use to create Office 2000 documents. For example, if you use Word 2000 to create a résumé, you can select the Résumé Wizard. Figure 3.10 shows the Résumé Wizard's opening dialog box.

3

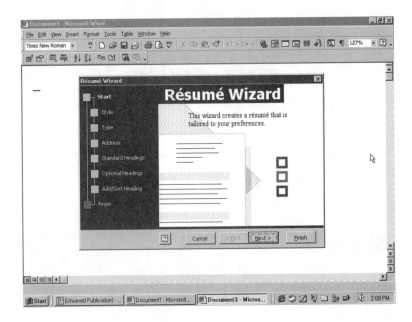

FIGURE 3.10

The opening Résumé Wizard dialog box.

When you select File, New, each Office 2000 product offers a list of template and wizard icons. You'll know the difference between them because the wizard icons include a waving magic wand.

Many wizards contain opening dialog boxes that display information about the wizard. Figure 3.10 informs you that you selected the Résumé Wizard. If you click the Next button, the wizard asks which of the following kinds of résumés you want to create:

- Entry-level résumé
- Chronological résumé
- Functional résumé
- Professional résumé

Clicking Next again displays a dialog box that requests your name and address information for the top of the résumé. Office 2000 is smart enough to automatically pull your name from the Office 2000 registration information, but you can change the name if you create résumés for other people. Often, wizard dialog boxes present you with a selection of styles, formats, graphic elements, and colors.

Every wizard's final dialog box includes a Finish button that you will click to complete the wizard and generate the document based on the wizard. Generally, wizards create shells of documents, such as Word 2000 template documents or a Publisher 2000 newsletter, that contain no data. It's your job to enter the details.

After a wizard designs a document, you are free to make whatever additional edits you need.

The first wizard appeared in Microsoft Publisher's first version. Publisher 2000 continues to set the standard for wizards by offering a huge catalog of publication wizards that are sorted by category.

Getting Ready for the Internet and Office 2000

Microsoft did not make Office 2000's Internet interface really stand out; instead, the Internet interface appears as just one of a long line of Office 2000 features so that you can access the Internet from within the Office 2000 environment. The seamless Web integration lets you get to Internet information much easier than with previous Office versions. The Internet interface between the various Office 2000 products differs a little, but the Internet interface is always underneath Office 2000, ready to handle the connection.

3

The Web Toolbar

All core Office 2000 programs contain a Web toolbar button that you can click to display the Office 2000 Web toolbar shown in Figure 3.12. The buttons give you Web access from within an Office 2000 program.

NEW TERM A *URL*, or *uniform resource locator*, uniquely identifies an Internet site.

If you're logged on to the Internet when you click a Web toolbar button, such as the Start Page button, Office 2000 takes you directly to your Start page, substituting your Web browser for the current Office 2000 program on your screen. If you're not logged on to the Internet before using the Web toolbar buttons, Office 2000 initiates your logon sequence for you.

> If you use Internet Explorer as your Web browser, type the name of any Office 2000 data file in the Web Address drop-down list, and Internet Explorer displays your properly formatted Office 2000 data file.

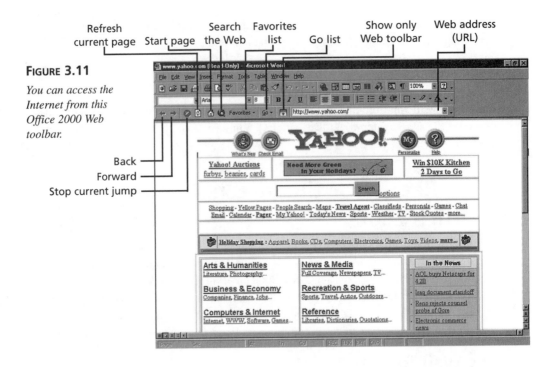

FIGURE 3.11

You can access the Internet from this Office 2000 Web toolbar.

An inserted hyperlink is just one way that you can connect an Office 2000 document to the outside, online world. The Office 2000 products enable you to create Web pages from data located inside your documents.

A Web site does not have to exist for you to insert a hyperlink to it. For example, you may be creating an in-house reference manual for your company's new Web site. You can insert a hyperlink to an address on your company site before the site actually appears on the Internet.

You can even use the Internet as your Office 2000 data repository. Not only can you access Internet Web pages from the Web toolbar, but you can also edit Web pages as if they were on your own PC. If you want to edit a document located on an FTP or HTTP site, just enter the document's URL when you open the document. You can also save to HTTP and FTP sites by using any of the Office 2000 Save commands. Keep in mind that you will be saving any edited Web pages to your local hard drive for your own use, however.

Summary

This hour introduced some of the fun features of Office 2000, including the Office Assistant, accessibility features, and clip art files. By routing documents to your coworkers over your network (or over the Internet, using Office 2000's built-in Internet support), you can all work on the same documents and track revisions as each of you reviews Office 2000 material.

This hour also explored three of the most powerful features in the suite of Office 2000 products: templates, wizards, and Office 2000's Internet interface.

Hour 4, "Welcome to Word 2000," introduces Word 2000. You'll soon see why Word 2000 is considered to be the most powerful word processor available.

Q&A

Q What if I want to use Office Assistant only when I need help?

A Right-click Office Assistant to display the pop-up menu and select Hide Assistant. The Office Assistant window disappears. When you want to use Office Assistant again, click the toolbar's Office Assistant button. You might want to display the Office Assistant's Options dialog box (right-click Office Assistant and select Options) to change the way Office Assistant responds to you. The Options dialog box enables you to modify the timing of Office Assistant's responses.

Q Why would I *route* a document instead of *send* a document if coworkers needed to make revisions?

A You should use the document routing option when you want to send the same document to multiple coworkers and let each coworker see the revisions made. When you send a document, Office 2000 sends a copy to each of the recipients, who then make revisions to that single copy and return it to you. Office 2000 users often route when they have more time to wait for revisions and when they want to send a document through a predetermined chain of organizational command.

Q Can I add my own collection of clip art files to the Microsoft Clip Art Gallery?

A Certainly. Not only can you add your own sound, video, graphic, and picture files to the Clip Art Gallery, but you also can add your own categories to organize the gallery in the way that works best for you. If you see a category or clip art image that you will probably never use, you can also remove that category or image from the gallery to make subsequent browsing through the gallery more efficient.

3

Q **What is the difference between a template and a wizard?**

A A *template* is a formatted shell, a design, or an empty data file. For example, an Excel 2000 accounts-receivable template would contain no data but would contain all the titles, fields, and formatting necessary for an accounts-receivable worksheet. After you load the template, you're able to add specific data easily, without having to format titles and totals.

A *wizard* is more than a formatted shell. A wizard is a step-by-step guide that presents a series of dialog boxes. As you fill in each dialog box, the wizard builds a data file for you. You can create complex documents, such as professional résumés, newsletters, and Web pages by answering a few simple questions within the series of dialog boxes.

PART II

Processing with Word 2000

Hour

HOUR 4

Welcome to Word 2000

This hour introduces you to Word 2000. You will soon see why Word is the most popular word processor on the market. With Word 2000, you can create documents of any kind with amazing ease. Word 2000 helps you painlessly create letters, proposals, Web pages, business plans, resumes, novels, and even graphics-based multicolumn publications, such as fliers and newsletters.

The highlights of this hour include the following:

- How to start Word 2000
- How to edit multiple documents at once
- When to use the Find and Replace text features
- How to modify Word 2000's automatic editing tools
- How to quit Word 2000 properly and why this is important

Starting Word 2000

You can start Word 2000 in several ways:

- Click the Office 2000 Shortcut Bar's New Office Document button and double-click the Blank Document icon to create a new document.

- Click the Office 2000 Shortcut Bar's New Office Document button and open a Word 2000 template or start a Word Wizard. Hour 3, "Introducing Office 2000 Small Business Edition's Powerful Features," explains how to use templates and wizards.
- Click the Office 2000 Shortcut Bar's Open Office Document button and select an existing document you want to edit.
- Use the Windows Start menu to start Word 2000 by selecting Microsoft Word from the Programs menu.
- Select a Word 2000 document from the Windows Start menu's Documents option. Windows recognizes that Word 2000 created the document, starts Word 2000, and loads the document automatically. (The Start menu's Documents option holds a list of your most recent work.)
- Click the Office 2000 Shortcut Bar's Word 2000 button to create a blank document.

Figure 4.1 shows the opening Word 2000 screen. (Your screen might differ slightly depending on the options that the installer set.)

If you forget what a toolbar button does, rest the mouse pointer over any button to learn the toolbar button's name.

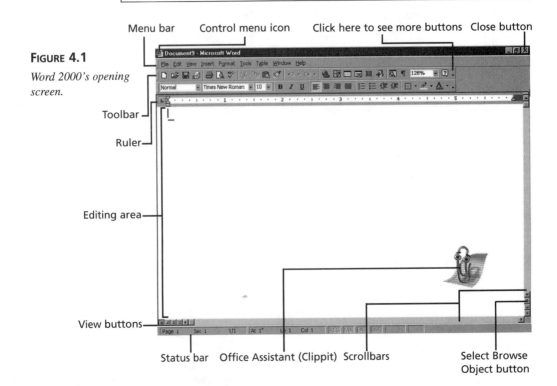

FIGURE 4.1

Word 2000's opening screen.

Menu bar   Control menu icon   Click here to see more buttons   Close button

Toolbar

Ruler

Editing area

View buttons

Status bar   Office Assistant (Clippit)   Scrollbars   Select Browse Object button

Editing with Word 2000

This section reviews fundamental Word 2000 editing skills and brings you up to speed if you are new to word processing. In this section, you learn how to do the following:

- Type text into a document
- Delete text
- Copy, cut, and paste text from one location to another
- Locate and replace text

Entering Text

When you start Word 2000, it displays a blank editing area in which you can type text to create a new document. You can also load an existing Word 2000 document and make changes to that document. If you have started Word 2000 through the Start menu's Documents option, Word 2000 starts with the open document you selected.

> If you want to work with an existing document, you must select File | Open and select that document. When finished, you save the document to long-term disk storage. You can close a document if you want to clear that document from the editing area; if you have not first saved changes, Office 2000 gives you a chance to save your work before closing the document.

4

The text you write appears in the editing area. The flashing vertical bar (called the *cursor* or *insertion point*) shows where the next character will appear. As you type, remember these basic editing points:

- Don't press Enter at the end of a line. As you type close to the right edge of the screen, Word 2000 automatically wraps the text to the next line for you.
- Press Enter at the end of each paragraph. Each subsequent press of the Enter key adds an extra blank line before the next paragraph.
- If you type a Web address in your document, Word 2000 automatically changes that Web address to a hyperlink that you can click to jump to that page if you (or someone who reads your document file) have Internet access.

NEW TERM   The flashing vertical bar that shows where your next typed character will appear is called the *cursor* or *insertion point*.

Insert mode is Word 2000's default startup mode. When in Insert mode, new typing appears at the text cursor, and new text pushes existing characters to the right (and down the page if needed). When in *Overtype mode*, new text replaces existing text.

NEW TERM Word 2000 uses *Overtype mode* when you want typed characters to replace existing characters.

NEW TERM Word 2000 uses *Insert mode* when you want to insert newly typed characters before existing characters.

The Word 2000 status bar indicates Word 2000's Insert mode. If the letters OVR are visible, Word 2000 is in Overtype mode. If OVR is grayed out, Word 2000 is in Insert mode. You can switch between the two modes by pressing Insert.

Not only can you insert text, but Word 2000 also enables you to insert blanks. Suppose you forget a space or want to insert three spaces before the start of a paragraph. Move the cursor to the place you want the blanks (to the left of text that you want to shift right) by pointing and clicking the mouse pointer to anchor the cursor in position. Press the Spacebar as many times as you need to shift the existing text to the right.

Word 2000 includes a new feature called *click and type* that enables you to double-click anywhere in the blank area of a document and begin typing where you click. If you double-click in the center of a blank line, Word 2000 automatically turns on centering for that line. If you double-click toward the right margin, Word 2000 right-justifies that margin. The next hour, "Formatting with Word 2000," explains more about margins.

NEW TERM *Click and type* enables you to double-click anywhere in a document and begin editing at that location.

 Remember that all menus and toolbars shown in this book's figures display all options but Office 2000 typically displays only the most common options when you display a menu or toolbar.

Navigating Word Documents

When you first type a document, you might enter the rough draft all at once and edit the text later, or you might be the kind of writer who likes to edit as you go. No matter how you write, you need to be able to move around a Word 2000 document quickly, locating text that you want to change or read. Much of the time you navigate through a Word 2000 document using these general practices:

- Use the four arrow keys to move the text cursor around the editing area.
- Click the scrollbars until you locate text you want.

- Click your mouse pointer anywhere inside the editing area to move the text cursor to that location.

- If you type more text than fits in the editing area, use the scrollbars, arrow keys, PageUp, PageDown, Ctrl+Home, and Ctrl+End keys to scroll to the portions of text that you want to see.

> If you open an existing document, press Shift+F5 to jump directly to the last typed letter or edited text that you made. Keep pressing Shift+F5 to jump to each of your previous edits.

To quickly navigate through a lot of text, press Ctrl+G (the shortcut for Edit, Go To) to display the Find and Replace dialog box (shown in Figure 4.2) with the Go To page selected. After you type a page number and press Enter, Word 2000 immediately takes you to that page.

FIGURE 4.2

Quickly jump to any page.

> The skills you learn here also apply to the other Office 2000 products. Excel 2000, for example, has a similar Find and Replace dialog box.

Selecting Text

Word 2000 is more of a document processor than a word processor; Word 2000 enables you to work with multiple words, paragraphs, pages, and complete documents. Earlier in this hour, you learned how to insert and delete individual characters; you now learn how to select entire sections of text you can move or delete.

When you or Word 2000 highlights (*selects*) text, you can perform tasks on that selection. You might want to select two sentences and underline them for emphasis, for example. Highlighted text that you want to work on as a single block is called a *selection* or *selected text*. Some people call a selected text section a block of text.

You can select text using your keyboard or mouse. Table 4.1 shows the mouse-selection operations.

TABLE 4.1   WORD 2000'S TEXT-SELECTION OPTIONS

To Select This	Do This
Any text	Click the mouse at the start of the text and drag the mouse to the end of the text. (Figure 4.3 shows a partial paragraph selection.)
Word	Double-click the word.
Sentence	Press Ctrl and click the sentence.
Line	Click to the left of the line.
Paragraph	Double-click to the left of the paragraph or triple-click anywhere inside the paragraph's text.
Entire document	Press Ctrl and click to the left of the document.

FIGURE 4.3

A partial text selection.

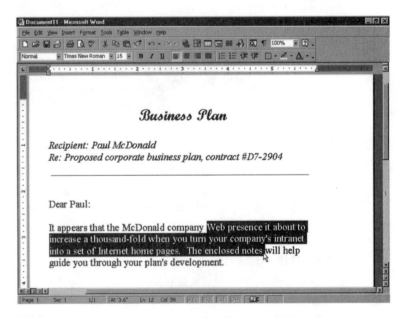

To select with your keyboard, move the text cursor to the beginning of the selection, press the Shift key, and move the text cursor (with the arrow keys or other cursor-movement keys you learned about in the section titled "Entering Text") to the final selection character. When you release the Shift key, the selected text appears.

Ctrl+A selects your entire document. When you want to apply global for-matting or Clipboard-related tasks (you will learn about the Clipboard in the next section) to the entire document, Ctrl+A makes quick work of selecting the entire document.

Deleting Text

No matter which mode you are in (Insert or Overtype), press Delete to delete any charac-ter at the text cursor's position. Delete also deletes selected text. Any characters to the right of the deleted character shift left to close the gap. Press the Backspace key to reverse the text cursor and erase the preceding character.

Here's a tip that even advanced Word 2000 gurus often forget: Ctrl+Backspace erases the word to the *left* of your text cursor, and Ctrl+Del erases the word to the *right* of your text cursor.

The section found earlier this hour titled "Selecting Text" illustrates how to select multi-ple characters. After selecting multiple characters, press Delete to delete the entire selec-tion.

Copying, Cutting, and Pasting

After you select text, you can *copy* or *cut* and move that text to a different location. One of the most beneficial features that propelled word processors into the spotlight in the 1980s was their capability to copy and move text. In the medieval days (before 1980), people had to use scissors and glue to cut and paste. Now, your hands stay clean.

NEW TERM To *copy* is to reproduce selected document text and send it to the *Clipboard*. You then can *paste* that copied text from the Clipboard into another document.

NEW TERM To *cut* is to send selected document text to the Clipboard and remove that text from the document. You then can paste that cut text from the Clipboard into another document.

Windows uses the Windows Clipboard during the copy, cut, and paste processes.

NEW TERM The *Clipboard* is an area of Windows where you temporarily store data that you can paste elsewhere.

4

To copy text from one place to another, select the text, copy the selected text to the Clipboard by selecting Edit, Copy (or by pressing Ctrl+C or clicking the Copy toolbar button), and paste (that's computer lingo for *insert from the Clipboard*) the Clipboard contents in their new location. To paste, select Edit, Paste, press Ctrl+V, or click the Paste toolbar button. You can paste the same text again and again wherever you want it to appear.

 NEW TERM   To *paste* is to send the Clipboard contents to a location inside your document.

When you cut text from your document (select Edit, Cut, click the Cut toolbar button, or press Ctrl+X), Word 2000 erases the text from your document and sends it to the Clipboard where you can paste the Clipboard contents elsewhere. In effect, cutting and pasting moves the text.

> You can also move and copy by using your mouse. Select the text you want to move, click the selection, and drag the text to its new location. To copy with your mouse, press Ctrl before you click and drag the selected text. Word 2000 indicates that you are copying by adding a small plus sign to the mouse cursor during the copy.

Beginning with Word 2000, you can paste up to 12 different selections of text on the Clipboard. The Windows Clipboard holds a maximum of one selection, but Office 2000 overrides the Windows Clipboard when you copy or cut more than one item to the Clipboard. You can copy or cut up to 12 items onto the Office Clipboard and paste one or more of those 12 items into an Office document such as a Word 2000 letter or Web page.

As you cut or copy more than one item to the Office Clipboard, you can display the Clipboard toolbar shown in Figure 4.4 that displays a new Windows document icon for each item on the Clipboard. The icon specifies which Office 2000 product you copied from. You can paste all the items into the document, paste one or more items, one at a time, into the document wherever you wish, or erase the entire Office Clipboard by clicking the Clear Clipboard button. To determine which icon represents certain copied text, rest your mouse over any document icon in the Clipboard window and Office 2000 displays a ToolTip that displays the first few characters of that Clipboard item.

FIGURE 4.4

The Office Clipboard can hold up to 12 items.

Finding and Replacing Text

Word 2000 locates text for you. When searching through extremely long documents, Word 2000's search capabilities come in handy. Suppose that you are writing a political letter, for example, and you want to correct a congressional district's seat name. Ask Word 2000 to find all occurrences of the word *district* by following these steps:

1. Select Edit, Find. Word 2000 displays the Find and Replace dialog box, as shown in Figure 4.5.

Some people prefer to use the Ctrl+F shortcut key; others click the Select Browse Object button on the vertical scrollbar (refer to Figure 4.1) and click the binoculars to display the Find and Replace dialog box. The Select Browse Object button has a round dot to distinguish it from the scrolling arrows. Use whatever method you can remember because you often search for (and replace) text in word processing sessions.

FIGURE 4.5

Enter text that you want Word 2000 to locate.

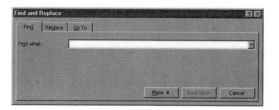

2. Type the word or phrase you want to find in the Find What text box. For example, type District to locate that word. By default, Word 2000 searches from the top of the document and does not worry about exactly matching your find text with its occurrences in the document.

3. When Word 2000 locates the first occurrence of the search word, Word 2000 highlights the word (as shown in Figure 4.6). (As you saw in the section titled "Selecting Text," this highlighted text is said to be *selected*.)

4. If the selected text is the text you wanted to find, click the Cancel button or press Escape to return to your document. Word 2000 keeps the selected text highlighted so that you can identify the found text. To remove the selection, press an arrow key or click anywhere in the editing area. If the selected text is not the text you want, click the Find Next button in the Find and Replace dialog box to search for the next occurrence of the text.

FIGURE 4.6

Word 2000 found a match.

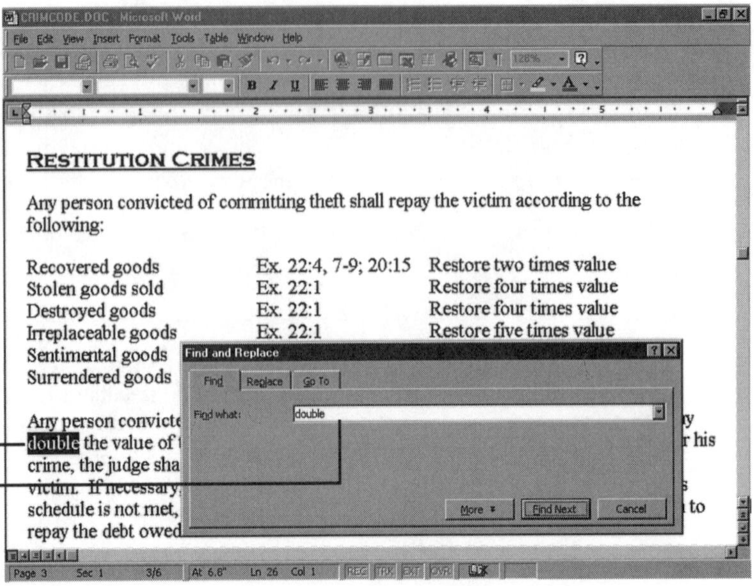

Selected text —
Search word —

As you probably can guess from the name of the Find and Replace dialog box, Word 2000 not only finds but also replaces text. Suppose that you wrote a lengthy business proposal to an associate you thought was named Paul McDonald. Luckily, before you sent the proposal over your corporate network (using Microsoft Outlook as shown in Hour 13, "Outlook 2000 Basics"), you realized that Paul's last name is spelled *Mac*Donald.

Tell Word 2000 to change all names of *McDonald* to *MacDonald* by following these steps:

1. Select Edit, Replace. Word 2000 displays the Find and Replace dialog box (shown in Figure 4.7) with the Replace tab displayed.

FIGURE 4.7

Make Word 2000 find and replace text for you.

2. Type McDonald in the Find What text box. Unless you change the default (you learn how to do this in the next section), you don't need to worry about distinguishing between uppercase and lowercase letters.

3. Press Tab to move the text cursor to the Replace with text box.

4. Type the replacement text (in this case, MacDonald). Use the correct case because Word 2000 replaces the find text with your exact replacement text.

5. If you want Word 2000 to replace all occurrences of the text, click the Replace All button. After Word 2000 finishes replacing all the occurrences, it indicates how many replacements were made.

   If you want to replace only one or a few of the occurrences (for example, there might be another person with the name McDonald in the business plan whose name is spelled that way), click the Find Next button, and Word 2000 locates the next occurrence of the text. Upon finding a match, Word 2000 selects the text and gives you a chance to replace it by clicking Replace. To skip an occurrence, click Find Next rather than Replace after a match is found that you want to ignore.

6. Press Esc or click Cancel when you are finished.

> If you want to delete all occurrences of a word or phrase, leave the Replace with text box blank when you click Replace All.

> Be careful when using Replace All because it could change more than you expect. To be safe, locate each replacement and click Replace individually so that you can see the context of the found text before you decide to replace it with something else. If you do use Replace All but then realize that Word 2000 replaced too much, use Word 2000's Undo feature to reverse the replacement.

Advanced Find and Replace

Both the Find and the Find and Replace dialog boxes (see the preceding section) contain More buttons. If you want more control over your text searches and replacements, click the More buttons when you want to find or replace text. The dialog box expands to show more options, as Figure 4.8 shows.

After you click the More button and the dialog box expands, the More button becomes a Less button that you can click to return to the simpler Find or Replace pages.

FIGURE 4.8

Advanced options enable you to control your find-and-replace operations.

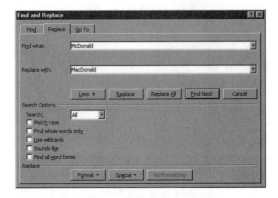

Table 4.2 describes each of the advanced find-and-replace options.

TABLE 4.2 THE ADVANCED FIND AND REPLACE DIALOG BOX OPTIONS

Option	Description
Search	Determines the scope of the find and replace. Select All to search the entire document starting from the beginning, Down to search the document from the text cursor's current position down in the document, and Up to search the document from the text cursor's current position up through the document.
Match Case	Finds text only when the text exactly matches the capitalization of your search text.
Find Whole Words Only	Matches only when complete text words match your search phrase. If this box is checked, Word 2000 does not consider McDonald a match for *McD*, for example. If unchecked, *McD* matches *McDonald*, *McDonald's*, and *McDonalds*.
Use Wildcards	Uses an asterisk (*) to indicate zero or more characters, or a question mark (?) to indicate a single character in your search. If you search for *Mc** and click this option, for example, Word 2000 matches on *Mc*, *McDonald*, and *McDonald's*. If you search for *M?cDonald*, Word 2000 considers *MacDonald* a match but not *McDonald*.
Sounds Like	Bases the match on words or phrases that phonetically match the search phrase but are not necessarily spelled the same way as the search phrase. Therefore, Word 2000 would consider both to and too matches for the search phrase too.
Find All Word Forms	Matches on similar parts of speech that match the search phrase. Therefore, Word 2000 would not consider the verb *color* to be a match for the noun color when you check this option.

Word 2000 cannot conduct a Word Form search if you have checked either the Use Wildcards or Sounds Like options.

AutoCorrecting and AutoFormatting

Word 2000 is smart. Often, Word 2000 fixes problems without you ever being aware of them, thanks to Word 2000's *AutoCorrect* feature. AutoCorrect uses a Microsoft-created technology called Intellisense to hunt constantly for errors. As you type, Word 2000 analyzes the errors and makes corrections or suggested improvements along the way. If you have selected Tools, AutoCorrect and selected `Replace text as you type` and `Automatically use suggestions from the spelling checker` options, Word 2000 makes spelling corrections as you type.

NEW TERM *AutoCorrect* is a Word 2000 feature that corrects your document as you type it.

The Office Assistant is always there to guide you, but AutoCorrect is integral to Word 2000 as well as to the other Office 2000 products. If AutoCorrect recognizes a typing mistake, it immediately corrects the mistake.

Following are just a few of the mistakes AutoCorrect recognizes and corrects as you type:

- AutoCorrect corrects two initial capital letters at the beginning of sentences. `LAtely, we have been gone` becomes `Lately, we have been gone`.
- AutoCorrect corrects sentences that don't begin with an uppercase letter by capitalizing the first letter for you.
- AutoCorrect capitalizes the names of days and months that you forget to capitalize.
- AutoCorrect corrects a sentence that you accidentally type in the Caps Lock key mode. For example, `lATELY, WE'VE BEEN GONE` becomes `Lately, we've been gone`.
- AutoCorrect replaces common symbols' predefined characters. When you type (c), for example, Word 2000 converts the characters to a single copyright symbol.
- AutoCorrect replaces common spelling transpositions, such as `teh` with `the`.

If AutoCorrect corrects something that you don't want corrected, press Alt+Backspace and AutoCorrect reverses itself.

All the AutoCorrections in this list are preset. You can add your own, as you will want to do when you run across common words and phrases that you often type. You will most

4

certainly want to add your initials to the AutoCorrect table, for example, so that you need only to type your initials when you want to enter your full name in a document.

To add your own AutoCorrect entries, perform these steps:

1. Select Tools, AutoCorrect. Word 2000 displays the AutoCorrect dialog box, as shown in Figure 4.9.

FIGURE 4.9

*Add your own
AutoCorrect entries.*

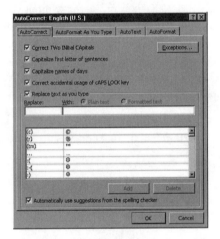

2. Type the AutoCorrect shortcut, such as an abbreviation, in the Replace text box.

3. Press Tab.

4. Type the AutoCorrect replacement text in the With text box.

5. Press Enter.

After you enter a new AutoCorrect entry, you can begin using the AutoCorrect feature immediately.

In addition to AutoCorrect entries, Word 2000 also automatically formats special character combinations within your document as you type. Word 2000 converts common typed fractions, such as 1/2, to their single character equivalent. You can control exactly which *AutoFormat* features Word 2000 uses by selecting Tools, AutoCorrect and clicking the AutoFormat As You Type tab. Figure 4.10 shows you what options you can control.

 AutoFormat is a feature within Word 2000 that changes the format of some text, such as fractions and dates, as you type.

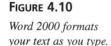

FIGURE 4.10

Word 2000 formats your text as you type.

Editing Multiple Documents

With Word 2000, you can work with multiple documents. You could be typing a letter to a friend and composing that memo to your out-of-state office before the mail runs, for example.

4

STEP-UP

Unlike previous versions of Word, Word 2000 tracks multiple documents in separate Word 2000 windows. Each window has its own taskbar button. Therefore, you can switch between documents by selecting from the Window menu, by pressing Ctrl+F6 to switch between the Word 2000 documents, or by pressing Alt+Tab or clicking a button on the Windows taskbar to activate the window that contains the document you want to see.

Instead of closing your letter, click the toolbar's New button to create a blank document. The new document appears on top of your letter. Switch between the letter and your memo by selecting the filename from the menu bar's Window option. In most instances, only one document is active (visible on the screen) at one time. When you issue a Close or Save command, Word 2000 closes or saves the active document.

Select Window I Arrange All to show both (or as many as you currently have open) documents simultaneously, as shown in Figure 4.11. (The documents must not be maximized before you select Arrange All.) When you display both documents, you can scroll each document individually, rearrange the window sizes to give more or less space to one of the documents, and copy and paste text between the documents. (The section that appeared earlier this hour titled "Copying, Cutting, and Pasting" explained how to copy, cut, and paste text within a document, between windows, and between applications.)

FIGURE 4.11

Word 2000 enables you to edit two or more documents simultaneously.

If you display multiple document windows, the window with the highlighted title bar and window buttons is the active window. It often helps to hide the ruler (select View, Ruler) to make more room to display your documents within multiple windows.

Word 2000 documents end with the .doc filename extension, as in Proposal.doc and Sales Notes.doc. (Filenames can have spaces in them.) You don't have to type the extension when opening or saving documents; Office 2000 automatically attaches the correct extension.

Correcting Mistakes

At any point you can *undo*, or reverse, your most recent edit or edits. Click the toolbar's Undo button. (This performs the same action as selecting Edit, Undo, and is easier to use in most cases.) If you delete a character or even an entire paragraph, for example, click Undo. Word 2000 puts the deleted text right back where it was originally!

NEW TERM An *undo* is the reversal of an edit.

> As you edit documents, Word 2000 changes its Edit | Undo menu option to reflect your last change; if you delete text, for example, the Edit menu's first option becomes Undo Clear, indicating that you can undo the clearing of text that you previously performed.

Word 2000 keeps track of multiple edits. Therefore, if you realize that the last three edits you made were wrong, click Undo three times and Word 2000 reverses those three edits no matter what the edits were. If you go too far, press the Redo toolbar button, and Word 2000 replaces the undo—in effect, undoing the undo! It gets confusing. If you click the arrows next to either the toolbar's Undo or Redo buttons, Word 2000 displays a list of up to 100 recent changes, which you can choose to ,undo or *redo as a group from that point forward.*

NEW TERM The reversal of an undo is a *redo*.

> Word 2000 can reverse any and all replacements you make with the Find and Replace dialog box.

In addition to undoing wrong edits, Word 2000 works in the background to keep your documents as safe as possible. Table 4.3 describes Word 2000's automatic file-saving features. (You can control these features through the Tools, Options dialog box.) Therefore, if you turn off your PC before saving your work, you still have the edits to the point of the most recently saved document.

4

TABLE 4.3 WORD 2000'S FILE-SAVING FEATURES

Feature	Description
Automatic backup	When you begin editing an existing document, Word 2000 saves a copy of the original document with the original name and the .bak extension (for *backup*). No matter how much you change (or mess up) your document, the original version is always safely stored until your next editing session on that document.
AutoRecovery	Automatically saves enough of your document to restore the complete document at that point. Subsequently, if your power goes out or your computer system crashes before you have a chance to save your document and exit Word 2000, and provided that you have turned on the AutoRecovery option, Word 2000 recovers the document the next time you start Word 2000. Ordinarily, you would lose your last edits and possibly your entire document. As long as you have turned on the AutoRecovery option, Word 2000 recovers the document the next time you start Word 2000. The more frequently you set AutoRecover's timer, the more likely you will be able to recover your most recent edits if a power failure or system crash occurs.

Quitting Word 2000

After you are finished with Word 2000, you can quit by performing any of the following:

- Select File, Exit.
- Press Alt+F4.
- Double-click the Control menu icon.
- Close the window.

Always quit Word 2000 and shut down Windows (by selecting Start I Shut Down I Shut Down) before turning off your computer; otherwise, you might lose your work.

Summary

This hour introduced Word 2000, Office 2000's word processing product. As you saw in this hour, Word 2000 makes entering text simple, and Word 2000 even corrects mistakes as you type.

One of Office 2000's many productivity factors is that the products in the Office 2000 suite often work in a similar manner. Therefore, many of the skills you learned in Word 2000 this hour carry over to the other products. If you have used Word in the past, you have already seen some of the improvements Microsoft made with Word 2000.

The next hour delves further into Word 2000 and shows you how to format your document's text. In addition, you see how the Word 2000 templates and wizards practically create your documents for you.

Q&A

Q What are the wavy lines I see beneath some of the that text I type?

A The red and green wavy lines indicate that Word 2000 found a spelling or grammatical error. Word 2000 is not perfect, just helpful, and sometimes Word 2000 incorrectly flags such errors when they are not really errors. You learn in Hour 6, "Managing Documents and Customizing Word 2000," how to handle the errors and teach Word 2000 what is correct.

Q Does it matter whether I press Tab or several spaces when I want to move text to the right?

A In some cases, pressing Tab and the Spacebar several times seem to produce the same visual results, but you should reserve Tab presses for those times when you want to indent or align several lines of text. You can more easily adjust tab spacing later if you want to change the indention.

Q I create special charts and tables with Word 2000, and I don't always want AutoCorrect to do its thing. How can I keep AutoCorrect from making certain corrections?

A Select the AutoCorrect corrections you need from the Tools, Options menu. If you want AutoCorrect to make a particular correction most but not all the time, you can always reverse a single AutoCorrect correction by pressing the toolbar's Undo button as soon as Word 2000 makes the AutoCorrect change.

4

HOUR 5

Formatting with Word 2000

This hour demonstrates Word 2000's formatting features, which add style and flair to your writing. Not only can Word 2000 help your writing read better, it can help your writing look better as well.

Word 2000 supports character, paragraph, and even document formatting. You can control every aspect of your document. If you don't want to take the time to format individual elements, Word 2000 can format your entire document automatically for you. When you begin learning Word 2000, type your text before formatting it so that you get your thoughts in the document while they are still fresh. After you type your document, you can format its text.

The highlights of this hour include the following:

- Which character formats Word 2000 supports
- What fonts are all about
- Why you should not get too fancy with most document formats

- How to apply paragraph formats
- When different views are helpful
- How to see a preview of your printed document

Simple Character Formatting

When you want to make a point, you can *format* your text. The three standard character formatting styles are underline, boldface, and italicized text. Figure 5.1 shows a document with boldfaced and italicized text on the top half and with underlined text on the bottom half.

FIGURE 5.1

Character formatting improves your documents.

Bold and italicized ——

Underlined

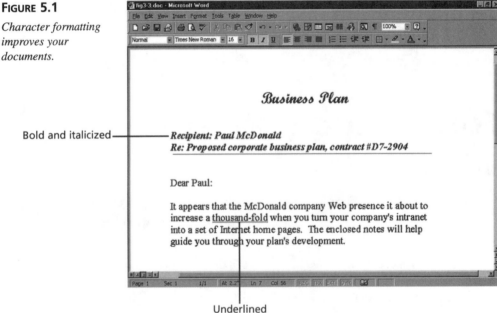

These special formatting styles are called *character formats* even though you can apply them to multiple characters, paragraphs, and complete documents as easily as you can apply them to single characters. The character formatting styles attach themselves to whatever text you select for the formatting.

NEW TERM   A *format* is the shape, size, and position that you can apply to selected text, margins, headers, footers, page numbers, and virtually any other element of a document.

Express but don't impress. You learn how to add a lot of fancy styles in this hour. Too many styles make your documents look busy and take away from your writing goals. Add only enough fanciness to add appeal to your writing.

To apply boldface, italic, or underlining, for example, select the text that you want to format and click the Bold, Italic, or Underline toolbar buttons. To apply formatting to a single word, first click within the word and then click the appropriate toolbar button.

The shortcut keys Ctrl+B (boldface), Ctrl+I (italic), and Ctrl+U (underlining) apply character formatting, and your hands don't have to leave your keyboard to click the mouse. Press one of the shortcuts before you type the text you want to format. When you want to stop formatting, press the same shortcut key to deactivate the formatting.

Applying Fonts

One of the most common formatting changes you can make is to change the *font* used in your document. A font determines the way your characters look, from their size to their curliness to their elegance. Fonts have different names, such as Courier New and Times New Roman.

New Term The *font* is a collection of letters, numbers, and special characters that contain the same typeface, thickness, and size. Consider *font* to be synonymous to *character*.

Think about your daily newspaper. The banner across the top of the page probably looks like old Gothic letters; the headlines are more standard type. Either might or might not be boldfaced, underlined, or italicized (although a newspaper rarely applies underlining styles). Throughout your paper, the articles might contain the same font as the headline, but the headline font may be larger and heavier than the articles' font.

The size of a font is measured in *points*. One point is 1/72nd of an inch. As a standard rule of thumb, a 10- or 12-point size is standard and readable for most word processed writing. As you type and move your text cursor throughout a document, Word 2000 displays the current font name and size on the formatting toolbar. To change any selected text's font name or size, click the drop-down arrow to the right of the Font Name box, or use the Font Size drop-down list to select a new value.

New Term A *point* is a font character measurement that equals 1/72nd of an inch.

5

Instead of using the toolbar to apply font and other format changes, you can set formats in the Font dialog box. When you select Format, Font, Word 2000 displays the Font dialog box, as shown in Figure 5.2. You can also display the Font dialog box by right-clicking selected text and choosing Font from the pop-up menu.

Not only can you set multiple character formats from one location (the Font dialog box), but Word 2000 displays a preview of the font in the dialog box's Preview area. Therefore, you can select various font names, sizes, and styles and see the results before actually closing the dialog box to apply those changes. When the previewed text looks the way you want, select OK and apply those changes to your selected text.

FIGURE 5.2

Set many character formats in the Font dialog box.

If you select the Hidden character format in the Font dialog box, the hidden text appears on your screen but does not print. Hidden text is great for notes to yourself and explanatory information that supports the surrounding text that you want to print. If you use hidden text, be sure to check the Hidden text option in the Tools, Options View page. Otherwise, the hidden text won't show up on your screen.

You can quickly see a list of font styles and select one by displaying the font drop-down list as shown in Figure 5.3. After selecting text, or before typing new text, you can select a new font style from this drop-down list. Unlike previous versions of Word, the Word 2000 font style drop-down list actually shows an example of each font next to its name.

Current font style

FIGURE 5.3

Examples of each font appear along with the font name.

Font style drop-down listbox

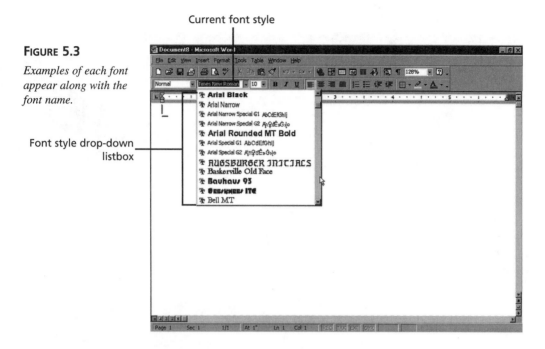

Applying Color

One special character format that you can apply almost as easily as the three from the preceding section is color. When you click the drop-down arrow next to the Font Color toolbar button, Word 2000 displays the small Font Color dialog box, as shown in Figure 5.4. Click a color, and Word 2000 changes your selected text to that color. In addition to text, you can apply color to the document's background by selecting Format, Background.

5

Remember that Office 2000 now easily links with the Internet and the Internet's fancy and colorful World Wide Web pages (see Hour 20, "Creating Web Pages with Office 2000"). When you use Word 2000 to create a colorful Web page, the Font Color button comes in handy.

The Highlight tool on the toolbar (available when you click the same More Buttons toolbar button you click to display the Font Color button) does outline text in color, but is not a color-formatting tool. Instead, the Highlight tool works great for marking important text that you want to reference later or make stand out to the next reader. When you select text and click the Highlight tool (click the Highlight tool's drop-down arrow to change the highlighting color), Word 2000 highlights the text as though you marked your screen with a yellow highlighter pen.

Click to display
the Font color table

FIGURE 5.4

*You can change the
color of text.*

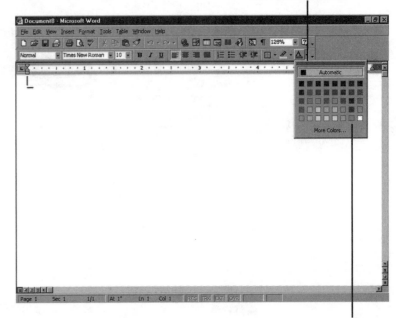

Font color table

Paragraph Formatting

Some formats work on characters; others are better suited for paragraphs. This section
describes the essentials for formatting your paragraphs so that your documents look the
way you want them to look.

> As with all the formatting commands, you can apply a paragraph format
> before typing to apply the formatting to all subsequent paragraphs that you
> type.

Justifying Text

Perhaps the most common paragraph formats are the justification formats. When you
justify text, you determine the text's alignment. Word 2000 supports these justification
options:

- Left-justification aligns (makes even) text with the left margin.
- Center-justification centers text between the left and right margins.
- Right-justification aligns text with the right margin.
- Full-justification aligns text with both the left and right margins.

To *justify* means to align the text flush with the left or right margin (or both as done in a newspaper column) so that it does not show a ragged edge.

The simplest way to justify text is to click anywhere inside the paragraph that you want to justify (or select multiple paragraphs if you want to justify several) and click the tool-bar's Align Left, Center, Align Right, or Justify (for full justification) buttons. As you learned in the preceding hour, the new click and type feature of Word 2000 enables you to click at the left, middle, or right of an empty line of text to justify the text that you then type there.

Although you can justify multiple paragraphs and even complete documents, a single paragraph (other than a word or sentence) is the smallest amount of text you can justify—hence, the term *paragraph format*.

 Newspaper, magazine, and newsletter columns are usually fully justified. The text evenly aligns with the left and right margins.

 Paragraph format refers to a format that you can apply to one or more selected paragraphs.

Setting Margins and More

The Page Setup dialog box (shown in Figure 5.5), displayed by selecting the File, Page Setup command or by double-clicking the top of the ruler, enables you to control your paragraph and page margins. Enter values for your top, bottom, left, and right margins so that your text does not print past the margin limits.

FIGURE 5.5

The Page Setup dialog box enables you to set margins, page size, and page layout.

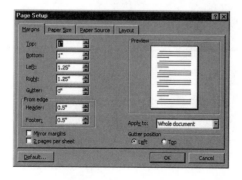

5

Many printers, especially laser printers, cannot print flush with the edge of
the paper. Generally, one-half inch is the minimum margin size these printers allow.

The *gutter* value, if you indicate one, shifts all other measurements away from the inside
margin of your page.

NEW TERM The *gutter* is an area of a page you reserve if you plan to bind your document.

The Header and Footer values determine how far from the top and bottom of your pages
the header and footer appear if you supply a header or a footer. (Hour 7, "Advanced
Word 2000," describes headers and footers.)

Using Tab Settings

Click the Tabs command button in the Format, Paragraph dialog box to display the Tabs
dialog box, as shown in Figure 5.6. A tab controls the horizontal spacing for certain
items in your text. The bottom line is that a tab keeps you from having to press your
Spacebar many times when you want to insert multiple spaces in your text. In addition,
a tab is more accurate when aligning text.

FIGURE 5.6

*The Tabs dialog box
enables you to specify
multiple tab settings.*

Table 5.1 describes each of the options in the Tabs dialog box. After you set tabs, press
your Tab key as you enter paragraph text to move the cursor to the next *tab stop*.

NEW TERM A *tab stop* is the location on a line where a Tab key press moves the cursor. You
set tab stops by adding them on the ruler or from within the Tabs dialog box.

TABLE 5.1 THE TABS DIALOG BOX OPTIONS

Option	Description
Tab stop position	Enables you to enter individual measurement values, such as .25" to represent one-fourth of an inch. After you type a value, press Set to add that value to the list of tab settings. To clear a tab stop, select the value and click Clear. Click Clear All to clear the entire tab list.
Alignment	
Left	Left-aligns text at the tab stop (the default).
Center	Centers text at the tab stop.
Right	Right-aligns text at the tab stop.
Decimal	Aligns lists of numbers so that their decimal points align with each other.
Bar	Inserts a vertical bar at the tab stop.
Leader	
None	Removes *leader* characters. A leader is a character that provides a path for the eye to follow across the page within a tab stop. By default, Word 2000 displays nothing (blanks only) for tab areas.
....	Displays a series of periods inside the tabs (often used for connecting goods to their corresponding prices in a price list).
----	Displays a series of hyphens inside the tabs.
_____	Displays a series of underlines inside the tabs.

NEW TERM A *leader* is a character that Word 2000 uses in a tab's blank area.

5

Later in this hour, the section titled "Making the Ruler Work for You" explains how to use the ruler to set and adjust tab settings.

Setting Indentation and Spacing

If you need to change *indentation* (the space between the page margin and where the text aligns) or *line spacing* (the amount of blank space between lines), select Format, Paragraph to display the Paragraph dialog box, as shown in Figure 5.7.

Indentation is the space between the page margin and where a line, lines, or paragraph of text aligns.

 Line spacing is the blank space between lines (sometimes called the leading).

FIGURE 5.7

The Paragraph dialog box holds indentation and spacing values.

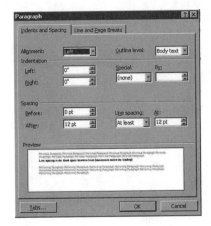

As you change the indentation, Word 2000 updates the Preview area at the bottom of the Paragraph dialog box to show your setting results. You can type a Left or Right indentation value or click the arrows to change the current values. A Left indention value indents not only the first line of a paragraph, but the entire paragraph's left margin. A Right indention value indents from the right. You can set off a particular paragraph from surrounding paragraphs, such as a quoted paragraph, by indenting the paragraph by specifying either a Left, Right, or Full (using both) indention value.

 Do not use the Spacebar to indent text on multiple lines because the text will not align properly. Use tab stops to ensure that text aligns down the page.

The drop-down Special values—(None), First Line, and *Hanging Indent*—determine how indentation applies itself to the paragraph. If you leave (None) selected, Word 2000 indents the complete paragraph by the Left and Right indentation values that you supply. If you select First Line, Word 2000 uses the value in the By field to indent only the first line of the selected paragraph.

 A *hanging indent* is an indentation of all lines of a paragraph except the first line.

If you indent the first line or apply a hanging indent, your Left and Right indentation values still apply to the entire paragraph. The first line and hanging indent values specify the *additional indenting* you want Word 2000 to perform on the first or subsequent paragraph lines.

The Spacing section enables you to specify exactly how many points you want Word 2000 to skip before or after each paragraph. You can also select multiple line spacing by selecting from the Line spacing field.

Increase or decrease a paragraph's indentation by clicking the Decrease Indent and Increase Indent buttons on the toolbar.

Making the Ruler Work for You

As you specify indentation and tab information, the ruler updates to indicate your settings. Not only does the ruler show settings, but you can also make indentation and tab changes directly on the ruler without using dialog boxes.

Figure 5.8 shows the ruler's various tab stops and indentation handles. Click anywhere on the ruler to add a tab stop after you select the appropriate tab from the tab selection area. To remove a tab, drag the tab stop down off the ruler. By dragging an indentation handle, you can change a paragraph's indentation on-the-fly.

Double-click the bottom of the ruler to display the Tabs dialog box, and double-click the top of the ruler to display the Page Setup dialog box.

5

Inserting Line and Page Breaks

Lines and pages do not always break the way you need them to. You may want to end a page early because you want to insert a chart at the top of the next page or start a new chapter, for example. Perhaps you want to put a sentence on a line by itself to make it stand out from the surrounding text. The Format, Paragraph dialog box's Line and Page Breaks tab enables you to control the way your document's lines and pages start and stop. When you click the Paragraph dialog box's Line and Page Breaks tab, Word 2000 displays Figure 5.9's settings.

FIGURE 5.8

Use the ruler to set and change tabs and indents.

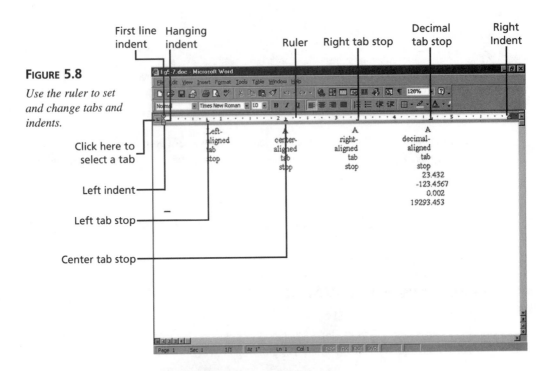

FIGURE 5.9

Control the way your paragraph lines break.

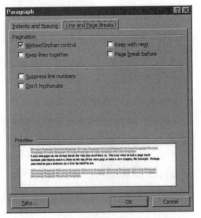

A *widow* is the last line of a paragraph that prints at the top of the next page, and an *orphan* is the first line of a paragraph that prints at the bottom of a page. Usually, widowed and orphaned lines look incomplete. If you click the Widow/Orphan control option, Word 2000 adjusts page breaks, if necessary, so that two or more paragraph lines always begin a page and so that two or more paragraph lines always end a page.

NEW TERM A *widow* is the last line of a paragraph that prints at the top of a page.

NEW TERM An *orphan* is the first line of a paragraph that prints at the bottom of a page.

The Keep Lines Together check box ensures that a page break never breaks the selected paragraph. The Keep with Next check box ensures that a page break never appears between the current paragraph and the next. The Page Break Before check box forces a page break before the selected paragraph even if a page break would not normally appear for several more lines.

By enabling the Suppress Line Numbers check box, law pleadings and other documents with line numbers will not print the lines on the selected paragraph lines. If you have set up automatic hyphenation (described later in this hour), the Don't Hyphenate option deactivates automatic hyphenation for the selected paragraph.

Viewing Your Document's Formatting

Try this: Type and format some text. Press Shift+F1. The mouse pointer changes to a question mark. When you click over text, Word 2000 displays all the information about that selected text, including the character and paragraph formatting applied. This is neat! (Figure 5.10 shows an example.) To get rid of the formatting description, press Shift+F1 again or the Esc key.

FIGURE 5.10

You can find out a lot about formats!

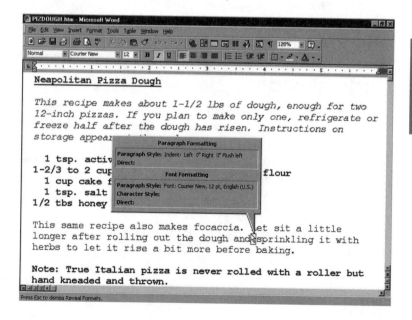

5

Formatting with Styles

A *style* is a collection of character and paragraph formats you can apply to your document. Each style has a name. Word 2000 comes with several styles, and you can also create your own.

 A *style* is a named collection of formatting styles applied regularly on specific kinds of text such as headings.

Click the drop-down arrow on the Style toolbar field (you may have to click the More Buttons button at the right of the toolbar to see the Style drop-down text box) to see the names of the styles. After you select a style, Word 2000 applies it to the current paragraph and subsequent paragraphs that you type. If you want to change a style's formatting or create a new style, select Format, Style to show the Style dialog box. If you want to modify the current style, click Modify; if you want to create a new style, click New.

Suppose that you routinely write résumés for other people, and you have created three separate sets of character and paragraph formats that work well, respectively, for the title of a résumé and an applicant's personal information and work history. Instead of defining each of these formats every time you create a résumé, format a paragraph with each style and store the styles under their own names (such as Résumé Title, Résumé Personal, and Résumé Work). The next time you write a résumé, you need only to click the Style toolbar button and select Résumé Title from the style list. When you then type the title, the title looks the way you want it to look without your having to designate any character or paragraph format.

Understanding Document Views

Now that you can format your document, you need to know how to display it onscreen to make the best use of the formatting during the editing process. Word 2000 supports several display views that present your document in different ways. Use the View menu to select a view, or click one of the view buttons on the horizontal scrollbar above the status bar (you must be displaying the scrollbars to see the view buttons).

The Normal View

For routine document creation and editing, the Normal view presents the cleanest screen approach and shows all character and paragraph formatting. If you choose to display special formatting characters such as italicized text, you will see those in the Normal view as well. All figures in this and the previous chapters show the Normal view.

The Web Layout View

When you want to view and edit Web pages in Word 2000, select the Web Layout view. The Web Layout view handles proper frame wrapping of text that Web pages require and displays graphics in their proper orientation for a Web page. Although you can display and edit a Web page in any Word 2000 view, the Web Layout view more accurately reflects the Web page as it will appear in a browser window.

> **STEP-UP**
> The Web Layout view replaces the Online Layout view of previous versions of Word.

The Print Layout

If you want to view your document exactly the way it will print, select the Print Layout view. The Print Layout view shows any details, such as headers and footers, and shows you where page breaks occur.

The Outline View

The Outline view gives you true expandable and collapsible views of your document in outline form. If you prefer to write from an outline, you can. Use the predefined heading styles to create your document's outline, and then expand on the outline when you are ready to add detail. (Figure 5.11 shows a document's Outline view.)

> Surprisingly, Word 2000 offers no way to print the Outline view.

5

The Outline view presents the structure of the document, and shows exactly as much detail as you want to see. By clicking the heading numbers (corresponding to the styles Heading 1, Heading 2, and so on) or the plus and minus signs on the Outlining toolbar, you can see more or less detail. All the detail stays with your document, but all the detail does not appear at one time.

Full Screen View

When you need to see as much of your document as possible, select View, Full Screen. Word 2000 hides the toolbars, status bars, and menus to give more screen real estate to your document. Click the Restore window or press Esc to return to the preceding viewing state.

FIGURE 5.11

*If you work with out-
lines, the Outline view
is for you.*

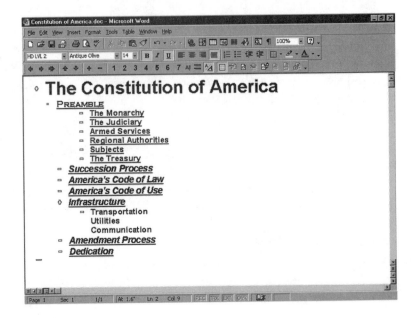

Print Preview

Print Preview shows how your document will look on paper. As Figure 5.12 shows, you can click Print Preview's Multiple Pages button to display several pages. You get a bird's-eye view of your printed document, which enables you to predict print format problems without wasting time or paper.

Click the Close button or press Esc to exit the preview.

If you want a closer view of your Print Preview, click the magnifying glass mouse pointer anywhere on the preview to see the preview in more detail.

If you select File, Web Page Preview, Word 2000 displays the document inside your browser's window to show you how the document will look as a Web page.

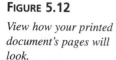

FIGURE 5.12

View how your printed document's pages will look.

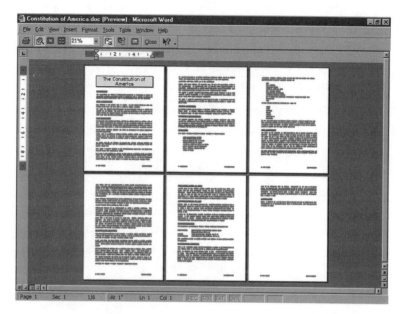

Determine Your Own View

The Zoom dialog box (shown in Figure 5.13), displayed by selecting View, Zoom, enables you to adjust the display size of your characters onscreen so that you can see more text on the screen. If your margins and font size make your document's text wider than your screen size but you want to see entire lines, shrink the percentage shown in the Zoom dialog box to squeeze more text on to your screen. You can enable Word 2000 to adjust the size to fill your entire screen by selecting the Page Width option.

5

FIGURE 5.13

Display as much of your text as you need to.

Inserting Numbers and Bullets

Word 2000 makes numbered and bulleted lists easy to produce. If you have set the proper AutoFormat options (see Hour 4, "Welcome to Word 2000"), follow these steps to create a properly formatted and indented numbered list:

1. Press Tab to start the first numbered item.

2. Type the number, such as 1. (follow the number with a period).

3. Press Tab.

4. Type the text that goes with the first numbered item.

5. Press Enter. The Office Assistant (if you have activated it) indicates that Word 2000 converted your previous text to a numbered list. You can change it back to regular text, deactivate the numbering, or click OK to continue the list.

6. Press Cancel if Office Assistant is present. Word 2000 automatically formats the first item and types the second number to prepare you for the next item.

7. Keep entering numbered items. When you finish, press Enter after a number, and Word 2000 converts that final numbered line to regular text.

In other words, to create a well-formatted numbered list, just start typing the list! Word 2000 formats and numbers your list after you enter the first item. If you want to convert a series of paragraphs or lines to a numbered list, select the text and click the Numbering toolbar button.

Here's another numbering trick: Before typing the numbered list, click the Numbering toolbar button. Word 2000 starts the list, types the first number for you, inserts a tab, and you only have to complete the numbered item. Word 2000 continues to add the numbers as you complete the list.

One of the best features of Word 2000 is that you can delete and insert numbered items from and to numbered lists, and Word 2000 automatically renumbers the other items!

If you want to create a bulleted list, type the items to be bulleted, select those lines, and click the Bullets button. Again, when you add and delete items, Word 2000 automatically adds or removes the bullets and formats new items.

Control the size of the bullets as well as the styles in your bulleted and numbered lists by selecting Format, Bullets and Numbering.

A Word About Word 2000's Wizards

This hour has discussed formatting your text and document as you type text or after you have entered the text. Word 2000's wizards, however, set up your document's format before you create your document. When you select File, New, Word 2000 displays a list of wizards and templates from which you can select.

Templates contain formatting that you can use, as well as automated buttons that you can click to format certain text elements. Wizards are more interactive and produce more customized documents than do templates.

For example, select File, New, click the Publications tab, and double-click the Brochure Wizard icon. Word 2000 walks you through a step-by-step procedure to create a brochure.

Summary

This hour explained the various format options available to Word 2000 users. Keep your audience in mind; don't overdo formats or your documents will look cluttered. Keep your documents readable and remember your presentation as you format.

You can apply the character formats to individual characters as well as to selected text and the entire document. Paragraph formats control the spacing and justification of paragraphs. The views enable you to see your document from various perspectives so that you can determine whether your formats work well together. Perhaps the best indicator of style is the Print Preview, which shows how your document will look when you print it.

The next hour moves into document management and Word 2000 customization. Depending on how you use Word 2000, you might want to change the way Word 2000 behaves in certain situations.

5

Q&A

Q How can I type an italicized paragraph?

A Before typing any text that you want formatted in any way, set up the formatting. If you want to italicize a word, phrase, or an entire document that you are about to type, press Ctrl+I (or click the toolbar's Italic button) before you type, and Word 2000 will italicize the text. If you have already typed a paragraph that you want to italicize, select the paragraph and press Ctrl+I or click the Italic toolbar button.

Q How can I see my entire page on the screen at once?

A If you have an extremely high-resolution monitor and graphics adapter card, you can probably see an entire document page when you select the full-screen view with View, Full Screen. If you want to see the toolbars, menu, and status bar, however, you probably have to adjust the zoom factor when you select View, Zoom. After you display the Zoom dialog box, click the Page Width option to enable Word 2000 to fit the text within your screen width, or you can control the width using the Percent option. The only other way to see an entire page is to select the Print Preview mode; in Preview mode, you can make simple margin adjustments but no text changes.

Q How can I make margin adjustments in Print Preview mode?

A You should adjust the margins only when displaying a single page. Therefore, if you see multiple page previews, click the One Page button to show a single page. Then click the View Ruler bar to add a ruler to the top of the page. Use your mouse to drag and adjust the left, right, top, and bottom margins. Although such margin adjustments are not as accurate as you can set from within the Page Setup dialog box, you can visually see the results as you make margin adjustments on-the-fly.

Hour 6

Managing Documents and Customizing Word 2000

This hour works more globally with your documents than the previous two hours. Instead of concentrating on specific editing skills, you learn how to manage document properties. Word 2000 can keep track of several document-related items, and that tracking really comes in handy if you work in a group environment.

The proofing tools in Word 2000 are powerful and work as you type. The spell checker acts as a mentor looking over your shoulder with a dictionary, supplying you with suggested spellings for mistyped words. Additionally, Word 2000 helps with grammar, hyphenation, and synonyms.

The highlights of this hour include the following:

- What document properties are
- Where to locate and change a document's properties

- How to request the spell and grammar checker
- Why you need to proof documents manually despite the proofing tools in Word 2000
- How to customize Word 2000 to behave the way you want

Understanding Document Properties

Each Word 2000 document (as well as the other Office 2000 documents) has properties. A *property* is information related to a particular document, such as the author's name and creation date. If you do not specify properties, Word 2000 adds its own to your document. You see the Properties dialog box (shown in Figure 6.1) when you select File, Properties.

NEW TERM Information related to a certain document, such as the number of paragraphs inside the document, the document name, or the document's author, is called a *property*. Other objects, such as icons, menu items, and toolbars also have properties of their own.

FIGURE 6.1

Track your document's properties.

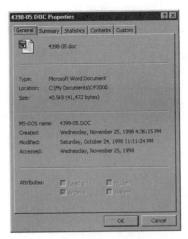

The tabs in the Properties dialog box provide the following information:

- *General*. Contains the document's file information, including the date and time you created, last modified, and last accessed the document.
- *Summary*. Tracks a document title, author (name to which software is registered by default), keywords, and comments you enter about the document.
- *Statistics*. Tracks the document's numeric statistics, such as character, word, page counts, and total editing time.

- *Contents*. Describes the parts of your document, such as the header, body, and footer.

- *Custom*. Keeps track of information you want in the order you specify. You can keep track of customized properties, such as the department responsible for creating or maintaining the document, a project group name that works on the document, and the person responsible for typing the document's information.

> As you add items to the Properties list box, indicate the item's data type (such as text or date) so that Word 2000 can properly format the property value that you want to track. The Custom tab is great for departments in which many people see and edit the same set of documents.

Some properties are available elsewhere in Word 2000. You can find a document's statistics, such as word and paragraph counts, for example, by selecting Tools, Word Count. Often, you can select from the menu option more quickly than displaying the document properties.

> If you create numerous documents and continually search through your disk files for particular ones, try adding search keywords to the Properties Summary page so that you can more quickly find that document using the Advanced Search option in the Open dialog box.

Using Word 2000's Advanced Proofreaders

Word 2000 offers these proofreading services for your writing:

- *Spell checker*. Checks your document's spelling either from beginning to end or as you enter it into the document.

- *Grammar checker*. Checks your document's grammar either from beginning to end or as you enter it into the document.

- *Thesaurus*. Provides synonyms when you need them.

NEW TERM A *thesaurus* is a list of synonyms.

- *Hyphenation*. Automatically hyphenates words at the end of lines, when appropriate, either from beginning to end or as you enter the text into the document.

6

STEP-UP

Previous versions of Word did not correct spelling errors as you typed your documents. You could request a manual spell check only after you typed the document. In addition, you could (and still can) right-click over a misspelled word underlined with a red wavy line and select the replacement. Only if you manually inserted an AutoCorrect entry would Word automatically correct spelling errors. Now when you type a misspelling, Word 2000 automatically substitutes the closest match in the spelling correction dictionary for the word so that you can keep typing.

Word 2000's built-in proofreading tools do not eliminate your proofing responsibilities! No matter how good Word 2000 is, Word 2000 cannot match human skills when deciphering the written language. Word 2000's spell check has no problem with this sentence, for example:

Wee road two the see too sea the waives.

The proofreading tools work only as guides to find those problems you might have missed during your own extensive proofing.

Perhaps the most important reason to learn the proofreading tools is that the other Office 2000 products use similar features. Therefore, after you learn how to use Word 2000's proofreading tools, you also know how to use the tools for an Excel 2000 worksheet, for example.

Using the Spell Checker

Word 2000 automatically checks your spelling and your grammar as you type your document. Any time you see red wavy underlines and green wavy underlines as you type, Word 2000 is letting you know about a possible spelling problem (the red line) or grammar problem (the green line).

Depending on the options you (or someone else) have set, your version of Word 2000 might not check both spelling and grammar as you type. Therefore, if you don't see any wavy lines, you should check your document's spelling and grammar after you have typed the document so that you don't miss anything. In addition, you may not see wavy lines if Word 2000 replaced all your misspellings with corrected entries.

To turn on and off the Check Spelling as You Type option, choose Tools, Options, and then click the Spelling & Grammar tab. On that tab, check the Check Spelling as You Type check box.

When you see a red wavy line, you can correct the problem in these ways:

- Edit the misspelling.
- Right-click the misspelling to display the pop-up menu shown in Figure 6.2. Word 2000 offers you the following options:
- Ignore all subsequent similar misspellings (in case you want to type foreign words or formal names, but you don't want to add those words to Word 2000's spelling dictionaries).
- Add the word to Word 2000's dictionary so that Word 2000 no longer flags the word as misspelled.
- Select AutoCorrect and choose a correct word to add the misspelling to the AutoCorrect entries so that Word 2000 subsequently corrects the word for you on-the-fly.
- Specify a different language dictionary to use.
- Display Word 2000's more comprehensive Spelling dialog box, as shown in Figure 6.3.

Word 2000 enables you to easily remove words that you accidentally add to your spelling dictionary. Select Tools, Options and click the Spelling & Grammar tab. Click the Dictionaries button. Select the dictionary from which you want to delete (most probably the Custom dictionary, which is the default unless you have created a new customized dictionary), and click the Edit button. Word 2000 displays the dictionary's words in a document so that you can delete the word or words you no longer want. (You can also edit any existing words or add new words.) Click the Save toolbar button. You must also turn on automatic spell checking by displaying the Spelling & Grammar page once again and checking the option labeled Check Spelling as You Type.

6

- Ignore the misspelling and leave the red wavy line.
- Ignore the misspelling, but check the entire document's spelling after you finish typing the document.

FIGURE **6.2**

Right-click to select your spell-correction choice when Word 2000 finds a misspelling.

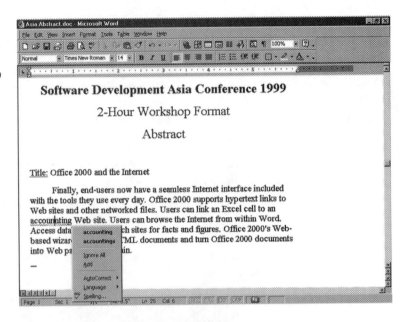

FIGURE **6.3**

The Spelling and Grammar dialog box offers more options than the pop-up menu.

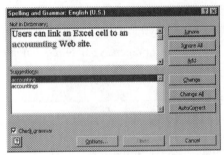

The Spelling and Grammar dialog box appears when you click the pop-up menu Spelling option for a misspelled word or when you select Spelling and Grammar from the Tools menu. Table 6.1 lists the options in the Spelling dialog box.

When you check the spelling of your document from Tools, Spelling and Grammar, Word 2000 checks from the cursor's current position down to the end of your document. If you want Word 2000 to check your entire document's spelling in one step (assuming you have turned off the automatic spell checking that occurs as you type), move your cursor to the top of your document (by pressing Ctrl+Home) before requesting the spell check.

TABLE 6.1 THE SPELLING DIALOG BOX OPTIONS PROVIDE SPELLING SERVICES

Option	Description
Ignore	Tells Word 2000 to ignore only this single occurrence of the misspelling.
Ignore All	Tells Word 2000 to ignore *all* occurrences of this misspelling in this document.
Add	Adds the word to Word 2000's spelling dictionary so that Word 2000 subsequently knows the word's spelling.
Change	Changes this single misspelling to the selected correction.
Change All	Changes all the document's misspellings of the current word to the selected correction.
AutoCorrect	Adds the misspelling and selected correction to your collection of AutoText entries.
Options	Displays the Spelling & Grammar options page (shown in Figure 6.4) on which you can modify the behavior of the spelling and grammar checker.
Undo	Undoes your most recent spell correction. The spell checker supports multiple undo levels so that you can undo more than one correction that you have made.

FIGURE 6.4

Change the Spelling & Grammar options dialog box.

6

Using the Grammar Checker

When you see a green wavy line beneath a word, Word 2000 is warning you about a possible grammar problem. Figure 6.5 shows the pop-up menu Word 2000 displays when you right-click a green wavy-lined word.

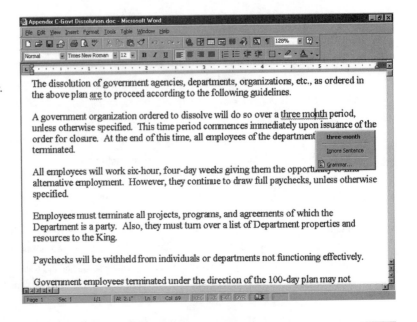

FIGURE 6.5

Word 2000 displays a pop-up menu when you right-click a word with a green wavy underline.

Wait until you finish your document before you check the grammar. The grammar-correction process takes a few minutes to complete. In most cases, you should turn off the automatic grammar checker to speed Word 2000's response time as you type your document (to do so, select Tools, Options, select the Spelling & Grammar tab, and then uncheck the Check Grammar as You Type check box). When you finish typing the document, select Tools, Spelling and Grammar button to start the process as well.

Keep Office Assistant turned on when you check grammar. Microsoft added a lot of plain-spoken, grammar-correcting advice to the Office Assistant's repertoire of helpful topics.

As with the spelling pop-up menu, you can replace the grammar problem with the suggested word or words, ignore the suspected problem (just because Word 2000 indicates a problem does not necessarily mean that one exists), or you can start the full grammar-checking system to correct that problem as well as the rest of the document.

When you check a document's grammar from the Tools, Spelling and Grammar option (to check the entire document) or by selecting the full grammar check from the pop-up menu, Word 2000 displays the same Spelling & Grammar dialog box you see when you check for spelling only. As Figure 6.6 shows, however, the Office Assistant chimes in with its advice as well. The Office Assistant advice often provides clear descriptions and examples of why your grammar might have a problem at the flagged location.

FIGURE 6.6

Select your grammar-correction choice when Word 2000 finds a problem.

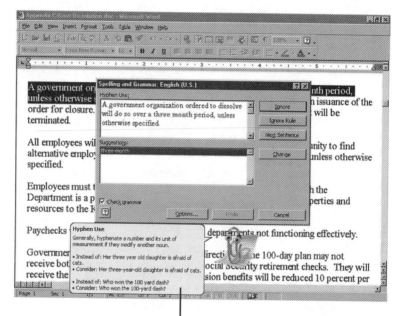

Office Assistant offers advice.

Using Automatic Hyphenation

Word 2000 can hyphenate your text as you type, or you can manually hyphenate your entire document. Word 2000 supports three kinds of hyphens:

- *Regular hyphens*. Break words at the end of lines (when needed) to maintain proper document formatting. You must turn on automatic hyphenation by selecting Tools, Language, Hyphenation and checking the Automatically Hyphenate Document option.

- *Optional hyphens*. Break special words (*AutoCorrect* becomes *Auto-Correct*, for example) only if those words appear at the end of lines (press Ctrl+- to indicate where you want the optional hyphen as you type the word).

NEW TERM   An *optional hyphen* breaks special terms and proper names only if those words appear at the end of a line.

- *Nonbreaking hyphens*. Keep certain hyphenated words together at all times; if the hyphenated name *Brian-Kent* appears at the end of a line and you want to prevent Word 2000 from breaking apart the names at the end of a line, for example, press Ctrl+Shift+- to add that word's hyphen when you type the word.

6

NEW TERM A *nonbreaking hyphen* keeps two hyphenated words together so that they never break at the end of a line.

You need to indicate optional and nonbreaking hyphens only when you type special words that Word 2000 would not typically recognize, such as company names and special terms.

You can adjust the amount of hyphenation that Word 2000 performs. Select Tools, Language, Hyphenation to display the Hyphenation dialog box, as shown in Figure 6.7. The Hyphenation Zone field enables you to determine the amount of space between the end of a line's last word and the right margin. (A higher value reduces the number of hyphens that Word 2000 adds.) If you want to keep the hyphenation to a minimum, consider limiting the number of consecutive lines that Word 2000 can hyphenate at one time by specifying a Limit consecutive hyphens to field value.

FIGURE 6.7

Specify automatic hyphenation.

To hyphenate your document manually after you have created it, select Tools, Language, Hyphenation and click Manual. Word 2000 prompts for your approval at each hyphen location.

If you want to stop Word 2000 from hyphenating particular paragraphs, select those paragraphs, select Format, Paragraph, click the Line and Page Breaks tab, and check the Don't Hyphenate option.

If you export your document text to another program or computer system (such as a desktop publishing or typesetting system) for publication, do not have Word 2000 hyphenate your document. The target system that produces the final output should control the hyphenation, if possible. If you have Word 2000 hyphenate your document, hyphens may appear in the middle of lines if the typesetter fails to eliminate all of Word 2000's hyphens.

Using the Thesaurus

When you just can't seem to think of a particular word, you can type a *synonym* (a different word whose meaning is similar) and solicit Word 2000's thesaurus for a suggestion. To see a list of synonyms, select a word (or click anywhere in the word) and select Tools,

Language, Thesaurus (or press Shift+F7). Word 2000 displays the Thesaurus dialog box, as shown in Figure 6.8.

 NEW TERM A *synonym* is a word whose meaning is similar to another.

FIGURE 6.8

Find synonyms fast.

From the Thesaurus dialog box, you can select a replacement word (Word 2000 then automatically replaces the original word with the replacement), or use the replacement word list to look up additional synonyms. If you cannot find a good synonym for dissolve but one of the replacement words for *dissolve* is *liquefy*, for example, look up synonyms for *liquefy* by selecting the *liquefy* entry in the Thesaurus dialog box and clicking Look Up. Through this link of related words, you might find the synonym for which you are looking.

 Use the Thesaurus dialog box when you want to see antonyms (words with meanings that are opposite to the selected word). Word 2000 supplies antonyms for some of the words as well. Click the Antonyms entry to see the *antonyms*.

NEW TERM *Antonyms* are words with opposite meanings.

Customizing Word 2000 to Work for You

6

If you don't like the way Word 2000 does something, you can usually customize Word 2000 to act the way you want. The Tools menu contains options that enable you to customize Word 2000:

- *Customize*. Enables you to change the layout of Word 2000's toolbars and menus.
- *Options*. Enables you to control the behavior of most of Word 2000's automatic and manual editing features.

Using the Tools, Customize Features

Figure 6.9 shows the dialog box that appears when you select Tools, Customize. (Your dialog box may show a different set of checked options.)

FIGURE 6.9

Customize toolbars and menus.

The Toolbars tab enables you to specify exactly which toolbars you want to see, if any, during your editing sessions. Although Word 2000 hides rarely used toolbar buttons, too many toolbars can clutter your screen and take away editing space, but different toolbars are useful at different times. Display the Tables and Borders toolbar, for example, any time you want to create or edit tables in your documents.

Most people modify the Commands tab when they want to add or remove an item from the menus in Word 2000. Select the menu from the Categories list, and Word 2000 displays that menu's items in the Commands list. You then can change a menu label or select one from the list that Word 2000 doesn't already display for that menu item. Additionally, if you start automating Word 2000 with *macros* (predefined keyboard shortcuts) or Visual Basic programs (which require some computer-programming skills), the Commands tab enables you to hook your own procedure commands to new menu items.

NEW TERM   *Macros* are predefined keyboard shortcuts.

The Options tab controls enable you to increase the size of the toolbar icons to read them more easily (at the expense of some editing area), to determine whether you want to see ToolTips, and to determine whether you want shortcut keys attached to those ToolTips.

Using the Tools, Options Features

Choosing Tools, Options opens up the Library of Congress of Word 2000 options. From this dialog box, you can modify the behavior of these Word 2000 features:

- *View*. Changes the way Word 2000 displays documents and windows.
- *General*. Determines colors, animation, behavior, and the measurement standard (such as inches or centimeters).
- *Edit*. Changes the way Word 2000 responds during your editing sessions.
- *Print*. Determines several printing options.
- *Save*. Specifies how you want Word 2000 to save document changes.
- *Spelling & Grammar*. Lists several spell-checking and grammar-checking settings that you can change. This is one place where you can turn these options on or off.
- *File Locations*. Enables you to set disk drive locations for common files.
- *Compatibility*. Lists a plethora of options you can change to make Word 2000 look and feel like other word processors, including previous versions of Word.
- *User Information*. Holds name, initials, and address of the registered party for use with document summaries and automatic return addresses.
- *Track Changes*. Determines the format Word 2000 uses when you make changes to documents in a group environment or when you want to track several revisions for the same document. (Word 2000 can keep track of multiple versions of a document.)

Summary

This hour explained how to manage your documents through the use of document properties. The document properties contain count statistics as well as other pertinent information that stays with your documents. If you work in an office environment, the properties help maintain order when many people edit the same document.

Part of managing your documents is proofing them to make them more readable and correct. The proofing tools in Word 2000 include a spell checker, grammar checker, hyphenation capabilities, and thesaurus. Although these tools don't replace human proofreading, they can help you locate problems.

You can customize almost any part of Word 2000. This hour gives you just a glimpse of the many modifications that can be made to Word 2000. Take the time to peruse the Tools, Options tabs. Even advanced Word 2000 users forget some of the options that can make their editing lives simpler. Check the options screens frequently as you learn Word 2000 and you will make Word 2000 work the way you want it to.

The next hour wraps up Word 2000 by teaching you its more advanced capabilities.

6

Q&A

Q Does Word 2000 update my document-property values for me?

A In some cases, Word 2000 updates your document's property values. As you type words into your document, for example, Word 2000 updates that document's word count. You must specify other user-specific properties, such as the document-search keywords and comments.

Q Why should I wait until after I create a document to proof it?

A Most Word 2000 users prefer to turn on the automatic spell checker but wait until their document is finished before hyphenating and checking the grammar. During the editing process, edits frequently change hyphenation locations; depending on your computer's speed, Word 2000 might slow down considerably to update changed hyphens when you change lines. Additionally, the grammar checker has to work constantly as you create your document, not only slowing down your edits but also indicating bad grammar in the places where you might be typing rough-draft material.

Q Should I modify Word 2000 settings if several people use the same computer?

A If you share a computer with others, you should not customize Word 2000 without telling the others what you have done. As a group, you might determine that certain Word 2000 options are better defined than others, but be sure to make customization changes only with the consent of others. Otherwise, the next person who uses Word 2000 might think Word 2000 no longer can check spelling, when in fact you have only turned off the spell checker temporarily.

HOUR 7

Advanced Word 2000

This hour wraps up our Word 2000 coverage by giving you an idea of Word 2000's uncommon features and advanced capabilities. Despite their advanced nature, Word 2000's advanced features are not difficult to use.

You will find a lot of tidbits throughout this chapter that you will use as you write. From inserting special characters to creating multiple-column newsletters, Word 2000 offers something for everybody's writing needs.

The highlights of this hour include the following:

- How to type special characters that don't appear on your keyboard
- How to insert the date, time, and page numbers in your documents
- When to add AutoText and when to add AutoCorrect entries
- How to prepare tables for your documents
- How to convert a single-column document into multiple columns
- What headers, footers, footnotes, and endnotes are all about

Using Special Characters

Symbols are special characters that don't appear on the standard keyboard. If you want to type special symbols, select Insert, Symbol to display the Symbol dialog box, shown in Figure 7.1.

 NEW TERM A *symbol* is a special character that doesn't appear on the standard keyboard (such as a copyright symbol).

FIGURE 7.1

Find a symbol you want to insert.

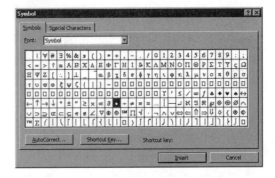

If you don't see the symbol you want to insert, select a different font from the Font dropdown list. Many fonts, such as *WingDings*, supply special symbols from which you can choose.

 If you find yourself inserting the same symbol over and over again, consider adding that symbol to your AutoCorrect table. Click the Insert, Symbol dialog box's AutoCorrect button to see the AutoCorrect dialog box (in which Word 2000 has already inserted the symbol); type the AutoCorrect entry that you will use to produce the special symbol, press Enter, and you have created the AutoCorrect entry for that symbol.

In addition to adding a symbol-based AutoCorrect entry, you can assign a shortcut key to any symbol. Click the dialog box's Shortcut Key button, type a shortcut keystroke (such as Alt+Shift+S), and press Enter. Word 2000 then assigns that shortcut keystroke to the special symbol. Subsequently, you won't have to display the Symbol dialog box to insert special symbols, but will only have to press the appropriate keystroke.

Many special characters already have AutoCorrect and shortcut-key entries. If you want to see these predefined symbols, click the Symbol dialog box's Special Characters tab to show the Special Characters page, as shown in Figure 7.2. Scroll through the list to see the predefined characters currently set.

FIGURE 7.2

Word 2000 comes pre-defined with many shortcuts for symbols.

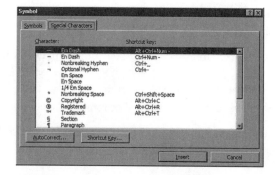

Inserting Dates, Page Numbers, and Comments

In addition to special characters, you can insert the date and time at the cursor's current position. Select Insert, Date and Time, and select the date and time format from Word 2000's selection list. If you click the Update Automatically option, Word 2000 constantly updates the date and time; if you leave the Update Automatically option unchecked, Word 2000 keeps the original date and time in the document.

Press Shift+Alt+D to insert the date at the text cursor's location.

If you want Word 2000 to insert page numbers at the top or bottom of the document's printed pages, select Insert, Page Numbers. Word 2000 displays the Page Numbers dialog box. Tell Word 2000 whether you want the page numbers to appear at the top or bottom of the document pages, as well as on which portion of the page they should appear (left, center, right, inside on facing pages, or outside on facing pages).

Word 2000 can format page numbers in several formats, such as 1, Page 1, -1-, Roman numerals, and even letters of the alphabet. Click Format to select from the various page number format options.

One of the most interesting items that you can insert in a Word 2000 document is a *comment*. A comment does not print, but shows up on your screen highlighted in yellow so that you are sure to see it.

7

NEW TERM A *comment* is a Word 2000 document message that you can see onscreen but that does not print.

Suppose that you want to remind yourself to do something later when you edit the document, such as format the title with information you will research at another time. Just write yourself a comment! The comment acts like a yellow sticky note. The comment stays attached to your text, but you can read or remove the comment whenever you want.

To insert a comment in your text, select Insert, Comment. Word 2000 displays the comment's annotation window, as shown in Figure 7.3.

FIGURE 7.3

Add comments to your writing.

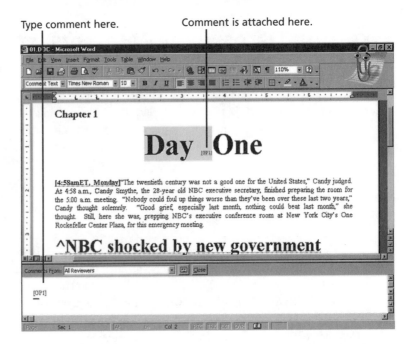

Word 2000 names each of your comments using your initials (found in the document property settings). After you type your comment and click Close, Word 2000 attaches the comment to your text and indicates the comment by highlighting the anchor text in bright yellow and inserting the comment name inside square brackets. Comments provide a convenient method for leaving messages for coworkers inside documents that you edit as a team.

Subsequently, when you edit your document, you see the yellow comments. If you right-click the comment, Word 2000's pop-up menu enables you to edit (or read) the comment, or delete the comment from the text.

Creating and Using AutoText Entries

Whereas AutoCorrect is great for quickly inserting formal names and common phrases, AutoText enables you to quickly insert completely formatted multilined text. AutoText is often called *boilerplate text*, which is a publishing term used for text that appears frequently.

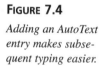 *Boilerplate text* is text that you often type, such as your company name and address.

Suppose, for example, that you often place your boldfaced, 16-point, name and address centered across the top of your personal letters. Instead of typing and formatting this text each time you need it, follow these steps to add the text as an AutoText entry:

1. Type and format the text you want to add to the AutoText entries. Make sure that it is exactly as you want it to be reproduced.

2. Select the text.

3. Select Insert, AutoText, AutoText. Word 2000 displays the AutoText page, which shows the AutoText entries currently in effect, as shown in Figure 7.4.

FIGURE 7.4

Adding an AutoText entry makes subsequent typing easier.

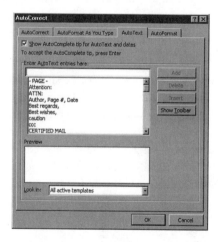

4. Type an abbreviation for the AutoText entry in the field labeled Enter AutoText Entries Here. You can either type this text to activate the AutoText entry or you can select from the available options listed.

5. Press Enter.

When you subsequently type the AutoText entry's abbreviation and press F3, Word 2000 replaces the abbreviation with your expanded formatted AutoText entry. AutoText entries require the F3 keystroke, whereas AutoCorrect entries automatically appear when you

7

type their abbreviations. Nevertheless, AutoText entries can be more complex and span multiple lines, whereas AutoCorrect entries are more limiting.

> **STEP-UP**
>
> Word 2000 contains an assortment of predefined AutoText entries. If you type **Created on** and press F3, for example, Word 2000 adds the current date and time to the end of the Created on text in your document. Select Tools, AutoCorrect and click the AutoText tab to see the AutoText entries defined.

> If you use the predefined AutoText entries often, consider adding better shortcuts. Add a second Created on AutoText entry called cron, for example, so that you don't have to type as much to enter the AutoText in your document. To add a cron entry that mimics that of Created on, type Created on and press F3 to display the current entry. Highlight the expanded words and select Insert, AutoText, AutoText. Type the new name, cron, and click Add to add the new entry.

Adding Tables to Your Documents

Word 2000's report-creation power shines when you see how easily you can create customized tables of information inside Word 2000. Tables are collections of information organized in rows and columns. Tables might contain numbers, text, graphics, or even combinations of any of these. Each row and column intersection is called a *cell*. When you use both Word 2000 and Excel 2000, you might want to embed part of an Excel 2000's worksheet into a Word 2000 table. Embedded worksheets enable you to report financial data from within Word 2000. (Hour 8, "Excel 2000 Workbooks," introduces Excel 2000.)

 A *table* is a collection of data organized in rows and columns.

 A *cell* is a single table entry.

Creating a New Table

To create a new table, perform these steps:

1. Select Table, Insert, Table. Word 2000 displays the Insert Table dialog box, as shown in Figure 7.5.

FIGURE 7.5

Use the Insert Table dialog box to prepare the new table.

2. Specify the number of columns and rows your table will need. You can change these values later if you need to. Estimate on the high end, however, because it is easier to delete additional rows and columns than to add them.

3. Enter a column width, or leave the Column Width field set to Auto if you want Word 2000 to guess the table's width. You can change a table's column width at any time (even after you enter data). You can request that Word 2000 automatically adjust each column's width to the widest data in the column by selecting the AutoFit to contents option. The Autofit to window option adjusts the column widths equally within the table's size if you resize the window that holds the table.

4. When creating your first table, press Enter. After you get used to creating tables, you can click the AutoFormat button to select from a list of predefined table formats, as shown in Figure 7.6.

FIGURE 7.6

Word 2000 can format your table automatically.

5. Click OK (or press Enter) to close the dialog box. Word 2000 creates your table and outlines the table's cells in a grid format.

7

 Word 2000 contains another tool that helps you build more customized tables. You can draw your tables by clicking the Insert Table toolbar button and dragging the resulting table of cells down and to the right until you have outlined the table size you prefer. In addition, you can draw tables freehand using the Word 2000 tools available as described in a later section titled "Drawing Tables Freehand."

Traversing the Table

One of the easiest ways to enter data in a table's cell is to click the cell (which moves the text cursor to the cell) and type. As you type past the cell's right margin, Word 2000 wraps the cell and increases the row height (if needed) to display the complete cell contents.

When you begin typing data, notice that Word 2000's automatic formatting might not match the table's data; perhaps one of the columns is too narrow or too wide. Use your mouse to adjust the size of a row or a column's width by clicking and dragging one of the table's four edges in or out. You can also expand or shrink individual columns and rows by dragging their edges.

When you move your cursor to a table's row or column edge, Word 2000 changes the mouse pointer to a table-adjuster cursor. When the mouse cursor changes, you can drag your mouse to resize the column or row.

Although you can click a cell with your mouse every time you want to enter or edit the contents of that cell, the table cursor-movement keystrokes come in more handy because you can traverse the table without ever removing your hands from the keyboard. Table 7.1 describes how to traverse a table's rows and columns.

TABLE 7.1 MOVING AROUND A TABLE

Press This...	To Move the Table's Cursor Here
Tab	The next cell
Shift+Tab	The preceding cell
Alt+PageUp	The column's top cell
Alt+PageDown	The column's bottom cell
Alt+Home	The current row's first cell
Alt+End	The current row's last cell

To highlight a row, click in the margin left of the row; Word 2000 highlights the entire row. Drag your mouse down or up to select multiple rows.

Inserting New Columns and Rows

Not creating enough rows or columns for your table is one of the first table problems you will encounter. To insert or delete rows or columns, select a row or column and right-click your mouse.

Suppose that you need to insert a column. Select the column that will appear after the new column by pointing above the column until the mouse pointer changes to a down arrow. Select multiple columns by dragging your mouse to the right after you have selected one column. Right-click your mouse to display a pop-up menu. The menu will differ, depending on whether you have selected a row or column first. Select Insert Columns, and Word 2000 inserts a new column before the selected column. The right-click menu also contains a Delete Columns command.

To highlight a row, point to the margin left of the row; Word 2000 highlights the entire row. Drag your mouse down or up to select multiple rows. When you right-click your mouse, the pop-up menu contains an Insert Rows and a Delete Rows command.

> After you create a simple table, click the table next to it and then select Table, Table AutoFormat to select a style, such as the shaded style in Figure 7.7. The table in Figure 7.7 is only a three-column table, but Word 2000 turned it into a professional-looking chiseled data storehouse.

FIGURE 7.7

Make sophisticated tables out of simple ones.

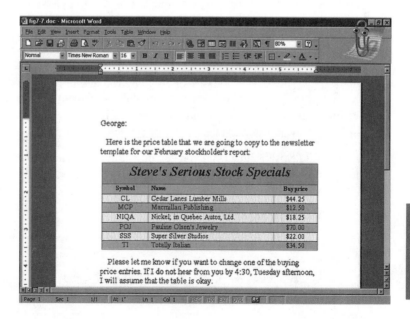

7

Drawing Tables Freehand

As you have seen, the Tables menu option gives you complete control over tables you create. Word 2000 goes one step further to help you create exactly the table you want. The toolbar's Tables and Borders tool enables you to draw tables freehand the way you might draw using a pencil and paper. The Tables and Borders tool enables you to quickly draw tables that don't necessarily have an equal number of columns for each row.

Follow these steps to use the Tables and Borders tool:

1. Click the location in your document where you want the new table.

2. Click the Tables and Borders tool. (You may have to click the More Buttons toolbar button first to locate the Tables and Borders button on your toolbar.) Your mouse cursor turns into a pencil shape, and the Tables and Borders toolbar appears.

3. Click and drag the pencil cursor diagonally down and across the page. A rectangular table outline appears. When you release the mouse, the outline becomes your table's outline.

4. Continue adding rows and columns by dragging the mouse. Notice that you can draw (by dragging) a partial row or partial column. If you draw a row or column you don't want, click the Tables and Borders Eraser tool and retrace the table lines you want to delete.

You can also change the table's line style by selecting a different style from the Tables and Borders toolbar and change the line's thickness by selecting from the Tables and Borders toolbar's Line Weight list box.

After you have drawn the table's basic outline, use the Border Color, Outside Border, and Shading Color tools to modify the table's colors. The remaining tools enable you to merge two or more cells into one, split long cells into multiple cells, change a cell's text alignment (as you might do with border columns), equally distribute columns or rows within an area, sort (alphabetically or numerically) cells within a selected row or column, and automatically sum a selected row or column.

Figure 7.8 helps to show what you can do with the freehand Tables and Borders tool. The top portion of the figure shows a table drawn freehand, and the bottom shows the results of entering the table's data and making a few simple edits using the Tables and Borders tools. Word 2000 makes tables as simple as drawing with a pencil and paper.

STEP-UP

Unlike previous versions of Word, Word 2000 enables you to draw multiple freehand tables next to each other as well as draw the table around existing text.

FIGURE 7.8

You can format your freehand tables into professional-looking tables.

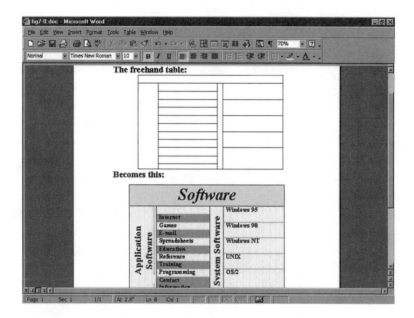

Creating Multiple Columns on a Page

When you want to create newspaper-style columns—such as those that appear in newsletters and brochures—configure Word 2000 to format your text with multiple columns. You can assign multiple columns to the entire document or to only a selected part of your document. Figure 7.9 shows a document with three columns and a single column at the top for the title area. Generally, you should type your document's text before breaking the document into multiple columns.

When you want to set multiple columns, follow these steps:

1. Select the text you want to convert to multiple columns. If you want to select your entire document, press Ctrl+A.

2. Select Format, Columns to display the Columns dialog box shown in Figure 7.10.

3. Click the preset column format and enter the number of columns you want to produce.

4. In the dialog box's Width and Spacing area, adjust the column width and spacing between columns if you want to adjust Word 2000's default. Generally, the default measurements work well. As you adjust the columns, Word 2000 updates the Preview area to give you an idea of the final result.

5. If you want a line between the columns, click the option labeled Line between.

6. When you click OK, Word 2000 formats your selected text into multiple columns.

7

FIGURE 7.9

You can use multiple columns for brochures and other pamphlets.

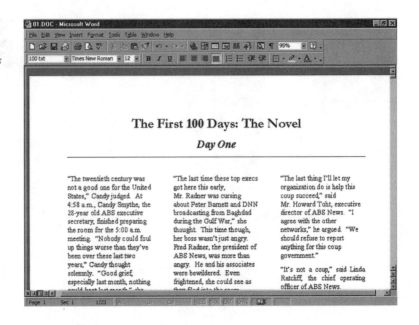

To add multiple columns quickly and let Word 2000 handle the spacing (which Word 2000 generally does well), select the text that you want to format into multiple columns and then click the toolbar button's Columns button. Drag your mouse to the left to select the number of columns (from one to four). When you release the mouse, Word 2000 formats the multiple columns.

FIGURE 7.10

Set up multiple columns with the Columns dialog box.

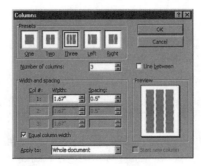

If you format your document into multiple columns that are right-justified, you will probably need to hyphenate the document. Thin, justified columns often contain a lot of extra spaces that Word 2000 inserts to maintain the right-justification. You may want to select File, Print Preview to see how your overall document looks with the narrow columns.

Creating Headers and Footers

A *header* is text that appears at the top of each page (or the pages you select, such as all even pages) in your document. A *footer* appears at the bottom of your pages. You don't have to add headers and footers to each page—Word 2000 enables you to type them just once, and it automatically adds them to each page.

 A *header* contains text that appears at the top of your document pages.

 A *footer* contains text that appears at the bottom of your document pages.

To add a header or footer, follow these steps:

1. Select View, Header and Footer to display the Header and Footer toolbar, as well as outline boxes where you can type the header and footer text. Figure 7.11 shows a document that displays this toolbar, as well as the Header entry box.

2. Type your header text. If you want to type footer text, click the toolbar's Switch Between Header and Footer button to display the footer text box and type your footer text. If you want to add page numbers, the date, or time to your header or footer text, click the appropriate toolbar buttons.

3. Click the Close button to anchor the header or footer in your document.

Word 2000 normally dims header and footer text so that you can easily distinguish between the header, footer, and the rest of your document text when editing your document within the Page Layout view. If you want to specify that the header (or footer) appear only on certain pages, select the File, Page Setup option and adjust the Headers and Footers values. You must be in the Page Layout view to see headers, footers, footnotes, and endnotes in their proper places on the page.

7

> If you want to edit a header or footer, double-click the dimmed header or footer text while editing your document. Word 2000 opens the Header and Footer toolbar and enables you to edit the header or footer text.

FIGURE 7.11

Use the Header and Footer toolbar to adjust your document's header and footer.

Header entry box

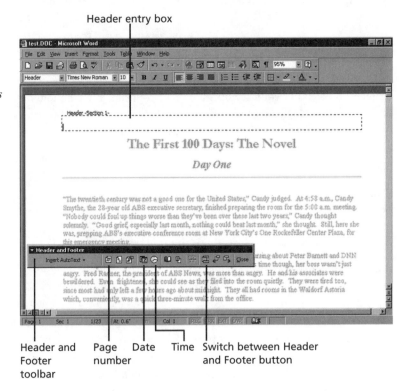

Header and Footer toolbar   Page number   Date   Time   Switch between Header and Footer button

Adding Footnotes and Endnotes

A *footnote* differs from a footer in that a footnote appears only at the bottom of the page on which you include it. Word 2000 inserts a footnote reference in the text where you choose to insert the footnote; if you later add text to the page so that the footnote reference moves to the next document page, Word 2000 automatically moves the footnote as well; therefore, the footnote always appears on the same page as its reference.

NEW TERM   *Footnotes* contain text that appears at the bottom of the page on which its corresponding footnote reference appears.

To insert a footnote, follow these steps:

1. Select Insert Footnote. Word 2000 displays the Footnote and Endnote dialog box shown in Figure 7.12. *Endnotes* are footnotes that appear at the end of your document rather than at the bottom of each page. Click the option you want to add, Footnote or Endnote.

FIGURE 7.12

Add footnotes and end-notes with this dialog box.

NEW TERM *Endnotes* are footnotes that appear at the end of your document, each with its own endnote reference number that appears in the document.

2. If you want Word 2000 to number the footnote (or endnote) sequentially starting with 1, click OK. If you want to use a different symbol for the number, click Custom mark and enter the reference you want to use.

3. Click OK. Word 2000 adds a separating line between your document and the note, adds the reference number to your document text where you inserted the footnote, and places the cursor at the bottom of the page next to the footnote reference number.

4. Type the footnote (or endnote) and click your mouse on the body of the document to resume editing.

Remember that you must display the Page Layout view to see headers, footers, foot-notes, and endnotes in their proper places on the page. If you display your document in Normal view, Word 2000 displays the supplemental notes in a separate window.

Summary

This hour wrapped up this book's discussion of Word 2000. You learned how to add the document extras that often turn simple writing into powerful cross-referenced published works.

If you need to display tabular information, let Word 2000 create and format your tables so that your data presentation looks clean. In addition, multiple columns work well for newsletters and brochures to keep the reader's attention.

7

To speed up your writing, use as many AutoCorrect and AutoText entries as you can. If you repeatedly type a phrase, sentence, or block of information, that text is a good candidate for AutoCorrect or AutoText.

Hour 8 introduces you to Excel 2000. As you will see, Excel 2000 enables you to present numeric data as professionally as Word 2000 presents your documents.

Q&A

Q Should I use AutoText or AutoCorrect?

A You must decide how much formatting and effort the boilerplate text requires. If you need to type the same text often but the text consists of only a word or two and requires no special formatting, use AutoCorrect (Tools, AutoCorrect). With AutoCorrect, Word 2000 makes changes for you as you type the AutoCorrect abbreviations. (Be careful not to create AutoCorrect entries from common words, or Word 2000 might replace text that you don't always want replaced.) If the text is lengthy or requires special formatting that spans multiple lines, however, add the text as an AutoText entry. After you type the AutoText abbreviation, press the F3 key to expand the abbreviation into the formatted full text.

Q Why can't I see my headers and footers while editing my document?

A Perhaps you are displaying your document in Normal view. Select View, Page Layout to see headers and footers in their correct positions on the page.

Q What is the difference between a table and a document formatted with multiple columns?

A Both tables and multicolumn documents have multiple columns. The multicolumn document, however, is useful when you want to create a newspaper-style document with flowing columns of text and graphics. A multicolumn document might contain a table in one of its columns.

Use tables when you want side-by-side columns of related information. Use multiple columns when you want your text to snake from the bottom of one column to the top of another.

PART III
Computing with Excel 2000

Hour

HOUR 8

Excel 2000 Workbooks

This hour introduces you to Excel 2000, Microsoft's spreadsheet program. Excel 2000 is to numbers what Word 2000 is to text; Excel 2000 has been called a *word processor for numbers*. With Excel 2000, you can create numerically based proposals, business plans, business forms, accounting worksheets, and virtually any other document that contains calculated numbers.

If you are new to electronic worksheets, you will probably have to take more time to learn Excel 2000's environment than you had to learn Word 2000's. Excel 2000 starts with a grid of cells in which you place information. This hour takes things slowly to acquaint you with Excel 2000 and explains the background necessary for understanding how an Excel 2000 working area operates.

The highlights of this hour include the following:

- How to start Excel 2000
- What workbooks and worksheets are
- How to enter various kinds of Excel 2000 data
- Which keys to use to navigate through Excel 2000 data
- How to quit Excel 2000

Starting Excel 2000

You start Excel 2000 when you perform one of these actions:

- Click the New Office Document button on the Office 2000 Shortcut Bar and double-click the Blank Workbook icon to create a new Excel 2000 document. (Click the General tab, if it is not already selected, to see the Blank Workbook icon.)

- Click the New Office Document button on the Office 2000 Shortcut Bar and click one of the Excel 2000-based tabs to open an Excel 2000 template or start a wizard. (Hour 3, "Introducing Office 2000 Small Business Edition's Powerful Features," discussed templates.)

- Click the Open Office Document button on the Office 2000 Shortcut Bar and select an existing Excel 2000 workbook that you want to edit. You may have to traverse directory folders to get to the workbook that you want to open.

- Use the Windows Start menu to start Excel 2000 by clicking Microsoft Excel on the Programs menu.

- Select an Excel 2000 document from the Documents option on the Windows Start menu. Windows recognizes that Excel 2000 created the document workbook and starts Excel 2000, loading the workbook automatically. (The Documents option on the Start menu contains a list of your most recent work.)

- Click the Excel 2000 button on the Office 2000 Shortcut Bar to create a blank workbook. (Depending on your Office 2000 Shortcut Bar's setup, you might not see the Excel 2000 button.)

Figure 8.1 shows the opening Excel 2000 screen. Your screen might differ slightly depending on the options you have set.

Understanding Workbooks and Worksheets

Excel 2000 enables you to create and edit *workbooks*. A workbook holds one or more *worksheets* (sometimes called *spreadsheets* or just *sheets*). A worksheet is a collection of rows and columns that holds text and numbers. Anytime you create, open, or save an Excel 2000 file, you are working with a workbook. The workbook approach keeps you from having multiple files that relate to the same project—instead, you can have all worksheets related to the same project in the same workbook (in one *.xls file). Your workbook name is the Excel 2000 name you assign when you save a file. You can save Excel 2000 worksheets and workbooks in HTML format if you want to maintain file-type consistency and if you ever want to embed your data in a Web page.

NEW TERM A *workbook* is a collection of worksheets stored in a single file. A workbook is useful for grouping a single project's worksheets together.

FIGURE 8.1

Familiarize yourself with Excel 2000's opening screen.

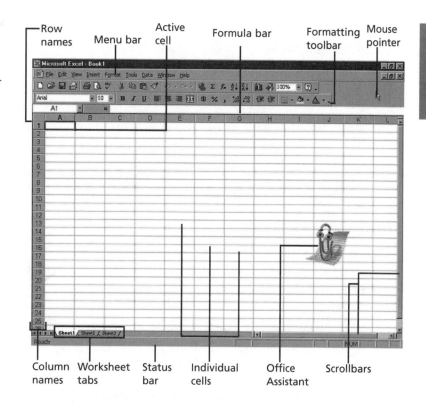

Row names — Menu bar — Active cell — Formula bar — Formatting toolbar — Mouse pointer

Column names — Worksheet tabs — Status bar — Individual cells — Office Assistant — Scrollbars

NEW TERM A *worksheet* is an Excel 2000 table-like document containing rows and columns that holds data and formulas.

A worksheet acts a lot like a Word 2000 table, except that Excel 2000 worksheets can do much more numeric processing than Word 2000 tables can.

> As with Word 2000 data, Excel 2000 often uses the term *document* to refer to a workbook file.

Blank Excel 2000 workbooks contain three worksheets named Sheet1, Sheet2, and Sheet3, as shown at the bottom of Figure 8.1. When you click a sheet's tab, Excel 2000 brings that sheet into view. If a workbook contains several worksheets, you might have to click one of the sheet-scrolling buttons to view additional worksheet tabs. Each column has a heading; heading names start with A, B, and so on. Each row has a heading, starting with 1, 2, and so on. The intersection of a row and column, called a *cell*, also has a name that comes from combining the row name and column number, such as C4 or A1. A1 is always the top-left cell on any worksheet. The gridlines help you to distinguish between cells, but you can turn off gridlines at any time from the Tools, Options, View page option labeled Gridlines.

 NEW TERM   A *cell* is the intersection of a row and column into which you enter text or numbers. A cell address is the column letter and row number location of the cell; B6 is the cell address for a cell located at column B and row 6.

> No matter how large your monitor is, you will see only a small amount of the worksheet area. Use the scrollbars to see or edit information in the off-screen cells, such as cell M17.

Every cell in your workbook contains a unique name or address to which you can refer when you are tabulating data. The cell address of the active cell (the cell that the cursor is in) appears at the left of the Formula bar. In Figure 8.1, the box reads A1 because the cursor is in cell A1.

When you move your mouse pointer across Excel 2000's screen, notice that the pointer becomes a cross when you point it to a cell area. The cross returns to its pointer shape when you point to another part of the Excel 2000 work area.

Inserting Worksheets in a Workbook

Just as Word 2000 enables you to edit multiple documents in memory at the same time, Excel 2000 enables you to edit multiple worksheets simultaneously (but those worksheets must all appear in the same workbook).

To insert a new worksheet into your workbook, right-click the worksheet tab that is to fall *after* the new worksheet. Select Insert from the pop-up menu. Excel 2000 displays the Insert dialog box, as shown in Figure 8.2, on which you can double-click the Worksheet icon and press OK. The Insert dialog box contains several kinds of items that you can add to a workbook, but worksheets are the most common items you add. The Insert, Worksheet command also inserts a new worksheet.

> If you don't like the default worksheet names (Sheet1, Sheet2, and so on), rename them by right-clicking the sheet name and selecting Rename. Type the new name. When you press Enter, the worksheet tab displays the new name.

FIGURE 8.2

Add a new worksheet to your workbook.

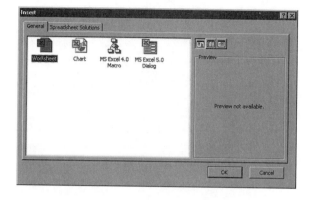

Deleting Worksheets from a Workbook

Situations arise when you only need a single worksheet in a workbook. You might want to track your monthly household budget, for example; such a budget rarely requires multiple worksheets. For your budget, the workbook is basically the same as the worksheet, but you should pare down excess worksheets instead of wasting memory on them. Excel 2000 makes it easy to delete excess sheets. Just right-click the tab of the sheet you want to delete and select Delete from the pop-up menu.

You can keep multiple workbooks open at once and move between them by pressing Ctrl+F6 (the same keystroke that moves between multiple Word 2000 documents in memory). Multiple workbooks are often difficult to keep track of until you become familiar with Excel 2000 and its worksheets. Display your Window menu to see a list of open workbooks if you want to review the ones you have opened.

Working with Multiple Worksheets

To specify the maximum number of worksheets that a workbook is to hold, select Tools, Options, click the General tab, and enter a number in the Sheets in New field labeled Sheets in New Workbook. When you create a new workbook, that workbook contains the number of sheets you requested. As you can see from Figure 8.3, Excel 2000's Options dialog box resembles Word 2000's. Many of the options are identical in both products, as well as throughout the Office 2000 suite.

One interesting workbook feature is the capability to rearrange worksheets within a workbook, and even to move worksheets between two or more workbooks.

FIGURE 8.3

The Options dialog box enables you to specify how many worksheets to include in your workbooks.

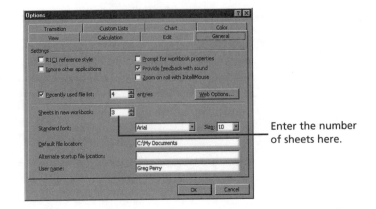

Enter the number of sheets here.

You can refer to a specific cell located within a workbook by prefacing the cell with its workbook name, followed by an exclamation point (!), to refer to a specific worksheet's cell. For example, Sheet3!G7 refers to the seventh row of column G inside the worksheet named Sheet3. Notice that you work from right-to-left when deciphering a reference such as Sheet3!G2.

If you don't like the current order of the worksheets in your workbook (the worksheet tabs indicate the worksheet ordering), click and drag a worksheet's tag (the mouse cursor changes to let you know you have grabbed the worksheet) to fall before another sheet's tab. If you work with two or three particular worksheets the majority of the time, move those worksheets together so that you can move between them easily.

Make a copy (instead of moving) of a worksheet by pressing Ctrl before you click and drag a worksheet from one location to another. Excel 2000 creates a new worksheet and uses the original worksheet for the new worksheet's data. Before you make extensive changes to a worksheet, you might want to copy it so that you can revert to the old version should anything go wrong.

Working with Multiple Workbooks

As your workbook fills up with worksheets, you need a way to manage those worksheets and move from one to another. When you then want to copy or move information from one to another worksheet, you can easily do so.

If you need to move a worksheet from one workbook to another, open both workbooks and select Window, Arrange, Tiled to display both worksheets, as shown in Figure 8.4. Drag one of the worksheet tabs to the other workbook to move the sheet. To copy instead of move, hold Ctrl while you drag the sheet name.

FIGURE 8.4

Display both workbooks if you want to move or copy worksheets or cells between them.

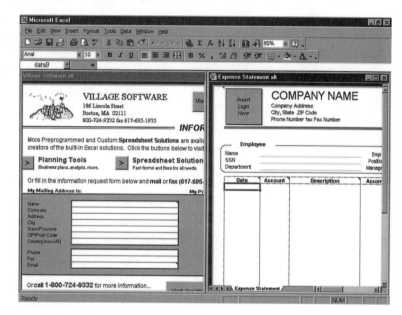

Entering Worksheet Data

Often, entering worksheet data requires nothing more than moving the cell pointer to the correct cell and typing the data. The various kinds of data behave differently when entered, however, so you should understand how Excel 2000 accepts assorted data.

Excel 2000 can work with the following kinds of data:

- *Labels*. Text values such as names and addresses
- *Numbers*. Numeric values such as 34, –291, 545.67874, and 0
- *Formulas*. Expressions that compute numeric results (some formulas work with text values as well)
- *Special formats*. Date and time values

As you will see in Part VI, "Combining the Office 2000 Products and the Internet," Excel 2000 works with data from other Office 2000 products. Additionally, you can *import* (transfer) data from other non-Microsoft products, such as Lotus 1-2-3.

NEW TERM   To *import* is to load data from another program into Excel 2000.

Entering Text

If you want to put text (such as a title or a name) in a cell, just place your cursor in the cell and type the text. Excel 2000 left-justifies the text in the cell. As you type, the text appears both in the cell and in the Formula bar. Remember that the Name box to the left of the Formula bar displays the name of the cell into which you are entering data. When you press Enter, Excel 2000 moves the cell pointer down one row.

> Press Tab to move the cell pointer to the right or the arrow keys to move the cell pointer in any direction after you enter data.

If you press Esc at any point during your text entry, Excel 2000 erases the text you typed in the cell and restores the original cell contents.

If your text is wider than the cell, Excel 2000 does one of two things depending on the contents of the adjacent cell to the right:

- If the adjacent cell is empty, Excel 2000 displays the entire contents of the wide cell.
- If the adjacent cell contains data, Excel 2000 *truncates* (cuts off) the wide cell to show only as much text as fits in the cell's width. Excel 2000 does not remove the unseen data from the cell; however, the adjacent cell, if that cell contains data, always displays instead.

Figure 8.5 shows two long *labels* (label is another name for text data) in cells C5 and C10. The same label, which is longer than standard cell width, appears in both cells. Because no data resides in D5, Excel 2000 displays all the contents of C5. The data in D10, however, overwrites the tail end of C10. C10 still contains the complete label, but only part of it is visible.

> You can increase and shrink the width and height of columns and rows by dragging the edge of the column name or row number. If you drag the right edge of column D to the right, for example, the entire column D (all rows in the column) widens.

NEW TERM   A *label* is text data inside an Excel 2000 cell.

There's no data in cell
D5 to overwrite C5.

Cell D10 contains data
that overwrites C10.

8

FIGURE 8.5

*Excel 2000 may or
may not display all of
a cell's contents.*

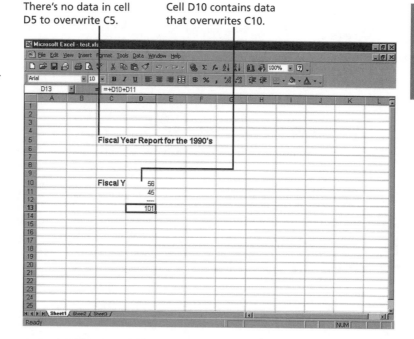

Some text data, such as price codes, telephone numbers, and Zip codes, fool Excel 2000. As you see in the next section, Excel 2000 treats numeric data differently from text data when you type the data into cells. If you want Excel 2000 to treat a number (such as a Zip code) as a text entry (calculations are not performed on the cell), precede the contents with a single apostrophe ('). For example, to type the Zip code 74137, type '74137; the apostrophe lets Excel 2000 know to format the value as text.

Entering Numbers

Excel 2000 accepts numeric values of all kinds. You can type positive numbers, negative numbers, numbers with decimal points, zero-leading numbers, numbers with dollar signs, percent signs, and even *scientific notation* (a shortcut for writing extremely large and small numbers).

NEW TERM *Scientific notation* refers to a format scientists, mathematicians, and engineers often use to write extremely large and extremely small numbers and is based on powers of 10 (such as 3.049 raised to the 1,016[th] power).

Excel 2000 right-justifies numbers inside cells. You can change the for a single cell or for the entire worksheet, as you see in Hour 9, "Using Excel 2000."

If you type a number but see something like 3.04959E+16 appear in the cell, Excel 2000 converted your number to scientific notation to let you know that the cell is not wide enough to display the entire number in its regular form. Excel 2000 does not extend long numbers into adjacent cells.

Entering Dates and Times

Excel 2000 supports almost every national and international date and time format. Excel 2000 uses its AutoFormat feature to convert any date or time value that you type to a special internal number that represents the number of days since midnight, January 1, 1900. As with all Office 2000 products, Excel 2000 is Y2K-compliant, meaning that Excel 2000 automatically displays all dates the user enters with four-digit year values by showing the full year. Excel 2000 should have little problem with the millennium change. Although this strange internal representation might not make sense now, you use these values a lot to compute time between two or more dates. You can easily determine how many days an account is past due, for example.

Excel 2000 uses a 24-hour clock to represent time values unless you specify a.m. or p.m. To convert p.m. times to 24-hour times, add 12 to all time values after 12:59 p.m. Thus, 7:54 p.m. is 19:54 on a 24-hour clock.

You can type any of the following date and time values to represent 6:15 p.m., July 4, 1976, or a combination of both 6:15 p.m. and July 4, 1976:

```
July 4, 1976
4-Jul-76 6:15 p.m.
6:15 p.m.
18:15
07/04/76 18:15
07-04-76 18:15
```

If you enter any of these date and time values, Excel 2000 converts them to a shortened format (such as 4/4/76 18:15). You can enter a date, a time value, or both. As with most Office 2000 formats, you can change this default format with the Format menu. The shorter format often helps worksheet columns align better.

Navigating in Excel 2000

8

Your mouse and arrow keys are the primary navigation keys used to move from cell to cell. Unlike Word 2000, which uses a text cursor, Excel 2000 uses a cell pointer to show you the currently *active* cell. The active cell accepts whatever data you enter next. As you press an arrow key, Excel 2000 moves the active cell pointer in the direction of the arrow.

 The *active* cell is the current highlighted cell that accepts data you type into it.

Table 8.1 lists the most commonly used navigational keystrokes used within a worksheet. Use your mouse to scroll with the scrollbars. To scroll long distances, press Shift while you scroll with the mouse.

TABLE 8.1 USING THE KEYBOARD TO NAVIGATE EXCEL 2000

This Key...	Moves to Here
Arrow keys	The direction of the arrow one cell at a time.
Ctrl+Up arrow, Ctrl+Down arrow	The topmost or bottommost row with data in the worksheet.
Ctrl+Left arrow, Ctrl+Right arrow	The leftmost or rightmost column with data in the worksheet.
PageUp, PageDown	The previous or next screen of the worksheet.
Ctrl+Home	The upper-left corner of the worksheet cell A1.
End, Arrow	The last blank cell in the arrow's direction.
Ctrl+PageUp, Ctrl+PageDown	Move to next or previous worksheet within current workbook.

Quitting Excel 2000

When you are finished with Excel 2000, quit by performing any of the following:

- Select File, Exit.
- Press Alt+F4.
- Double-click the Control icon.
- Click Excel 2000's Close button.

Always quit Excel 2000 and shut down Windows (by selecting Start I Shut Down) before turning off your computer so that you don't lose your work.

Summary

This hour introduced Excel 2000, and covered Excel 2000's screen and the concept of workbooks and worksheets. The workbook documents contain your worksheets, and your worksheets hold data, such as numbers and labels. As you see throughout this part of the book, Excel 2000 supports a tremendous number of formatting options so that you can turn your numeric data into eye-catching, appealing output.

Although Excel 2000 works best with numeric data, Excel 2000 accepts text (called labels), date, and time values as well. Excel 2000 is extremely lenient about how you type dates and times but immediately converts such values into a special internal number. This internal number enables you to calculate with dates when you need to determine the number of days between two dates or when you need to add a fixed number of days to a date to arrive at an ending date, such as a due date.

The next hour extends the concepts of this hour by showing you how to quickly add common data to an Excel 2000 worksheet. In addition, you learn how to edit the values that you type.

Q&A

Q I'm not good at math; can I use Excel 2000?

A If you were great at math, you wouldn't even need Excel 2000! Seriously, Excel 2000 does all the calculating. Your job is to place the numeric data on the worksheets so that Excel 2000 can do its thing. Many people use Excel 2000 for common household actions, such as tracking exercise routines and grocery lists. Excel 2000 is not just for accounting and mathematical applications. You learn, in Hour 10, "Editing Excel Worksheets," how to enter formulas.

Q Do I always enter the time along with the date?

A You can enter either a time value, a date value, or both when entering such information. Excel 2000 turns the information into an internal shortened format. (You can change the display format if you desire to make the data look better.) If you don't enter a date with a time value, Excel 2000 accepts the time value only and tracks just the time. If you enter a date, Excel 2000 tracks only the date.

HOUR 9

Using Excel 2000

This hour teaches you how to improve the accuracy of your worksheet data. You can easily edit cell contents with the tools Excel 2000 provides.

After you master worksheet editing skills, you then are ready to see how Excel 2000's AutoCorrect feature and the spell checker work to improve worksheets. Excel 2000 can also enter values for you. When you ask Excel 2000 to fill in a series of cell values, it uses some intuitive guesswork to complete any series that you begin. If you often enter a special series of numbers or labels, you can teach Excel 2000 that series to eliminate typing when you use the series again.

The highlights of this hour include the following:

- What you do to select multiple worksheet cells
- Why the spell checker and AutoCorrect are important to numeral-based worksheets
- How Excel 2000 fills in a series of values for you
- When you must teach Excel 2000 a new series
- How to find and replace worksheet data
- Why clearing a cell does not always equate to erasing the cell's contents
- How to use comments to describe a cell

Worksheet Editing

Some of the most important Excel 2000 skills you can learn are editing skills. Entering numeric data is error-prone at its best; the faster you edit cell values accurately, the faster you complete accurate worksheets. The following sections show you the primary editing tools Excel 2000 provides.

Selecting Cells

You can select a cell, a row of cells, or a column of cells just by clicking and dragging your mouse. As you drag your mouse, Excel 2000 selects a rectangular region. You notice as you drag your mouse that Excel 2000 displays the number of rows and columns you have selected. You see the message 10R X 4C appear in the toolbar's Name box as you select 10 rows and 4 columns, for example. When you release your mouse, Excel 2000 displays the selection's upper-left corner.

Not only can you select a rectangular region of cells, you can also select disjointed regions. Select the first area, and then press Ctrl while you click another cell and drag the mouse. The selection highlight appears in both places on your screen. Remove any selection by clicking your mouse on any cell or by pressing an arrow key.

Spell Checking

No worksheet program included a spell checker before Excel. After all, worksheets are for numbers, right? Of course, the primary purpose for worksheets is formatting, arranging, and calculating numbers. Numbers without titles, however, are worthless in most instances. You have to present your numeric data in such a way that the worksheet users understand the significance of your data. Given the amount of text you enter on your worksheets, a spell checker makes sense. You can only wonder why worksheet makers did not add spell checkers long before Microsoft added one to Excel.

You can check your worksheet's spelling as follows:

- Click the Spelling toolbar button
- Select Tools, Spelling from the menu
- Press F7, the spelling shortcut key

 Unlike Word 2000, Excel 2000 does not include a grammar checker or a synonym finder. Rarely do you include complete sentences on a worksheet, so the grammar checker would be wasted overhead in most cases.

The spell checker in Excel 2000 is the same one that Word 2000 uses (see Hour 6, "Managing Documents and Customizing Word 2000," for a quick review). The spell checker does not check every worksheet in your workbook, but only the current worksheet active on your screen. If Excel 2000 finds an error, you can choose to correct, ignore, or add the error so that the word no longer appears as an error (as might be the case for proper names).

AutoCorrect Worksheets

9

Use AutoCorrect as you type Excel 2000 entries just as you used AutoCorrect in Word 2000. When you type an abbreviation for an AutoCorrect entry, Excel 2000 converts that abbreviated form to the complete AutoCorrect entry for you when you press the Spacebar or leave the cell.

> Word 2000, Excel 2000, and all the other core Office 2000 products share the same AutoCorrect and spelling dictionaries. Therefore, when you make changes and additions in the AutoCorrect or spelling dictionaries of Word 2000 or Excel 2000, the other products recognize those changes.

To add AutoCorrect entries, perform the same steps that you do with Word 2000:

1. Select Tools, AutoCorrect.
2. Type your abbreviated AutoCorrect entry in the Replace field.
3. Press Tab.
4. Type the replacement text in the With field.
5. Click OK to return to the worksheet editing area.

Cell Editing

Much of your Excel 2000 editing requires that you correct numeric data entry. Of course, if you begin to type a number (or a formula, as you learn in the next hour) in a cell but realize you have made a mistake, press Backspace to erase your mistake or press the arrow keys to move the text cursor back over the entry to correct something.

If you have already moved to another cell when you recognize that you have entered an error, quickly correct the mistake like this:

1. Move the cell pointer to the cell you need to correct (click the cell to move the pointer there).

2. Press F2, which is the standard Windows editing shortcut key. (If you have still got your hand on the mouse, you can double-click the cell to edit the cell's contents.) You know Excel 2000 is ready for your edit when you see the text cursor appear in the cell.

3. Move the text cursor to the mistake.

4. Press the Insert key to change from Overtype mode to Insert mode or vice versa. As with Word 2000, Overtype mode enables you to write over existing characters, whereas Insert mode shifts all existing characters to the right as you type the correction.

5. Press Enter to anchor the correction in place.

If you want to undo an edit, click the Undo button. To redo an undo, click the Redo button. As you can see, after you have mastered one Office 2000 product (as you have Word 2000), you know a lot about the other products.

Finding and Replacing

Like Word 2000, Excel 2000 contains a powerful search-and-replace operation that can search your worksheet for values and replace those values if needed.

The find and replace feature in Excel 2000 works a little differently from that in Word 2000. The numeric nature of Excel 2000 requires a different type of find and replace. Therefore, read this section even if you have mastered the find and replace feature in Word 2000.

Figure 9.1 shows the Find dialog box in Excel 2000. You can request that Excel 2000 search by rows or columns. If your worksheet is generally longer than wide (as most are), select By Columns to speed your search. Indicate whether you want Excel 2000 to match your uppercase and lowercase search text exactly (not applicable for numeric searches), and select the proper Look In option of Formulas, Values, or Comments.

Use Formulas if you are searching for part of a formula (you learn all about formulas in Hour 11, "Using Excel Formulas"), use Values if you want Excel 2000 to search only the calculated cells (not within formulas), and use Comments if you want Excel 2000 to search through cell comments. Generally, you are searching through formulas, so Excel 2000 makes Formulas the default search target.

FIGURE 9.1

Excel 2000's Find dialog box looks for text or numbers.

The Find Entire Cells Only option indicates to Excel 2000 that a cell must contain your entire Find value and nothing else before a proper match will be made.

If you want Excel 2000 to replace the found value with another value, select the Edit, Replace command to display the Replace dialog box, as shown in Figure 9.2.

FIGURE 9.2

Let Excel 2000 replace values for you.

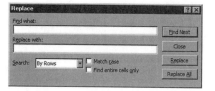

Click the Replace All button if you want Excel 2000 to replace all occurrences of the found text. (Be sure you want to replace all occurrences or you'll possibly overwrite data unexpectedly.) Otherwise, click Find Next to find the next matching value and, if that is a value you want to replace, click Replace. If it is not a value you want to replace, click Find Next to locate the next occurrence.

> If you want to find or replace within a limited worksheet range only, select the range before conducting the find or replace operation.

Reviewing Cut, Copy, and Paste in Excel 2000

If you have mastered the Copy, Cut, and Paste commands in Word 2000, those commands in Excel 2000 will be a breeze for you. As with Word 2000 and the other Office 2000 products, Excel 2000 uses the Windows Clipboard to hold data that you are copying, cutting, and pasting from within or between worksheets. If you open two workbooks at the same time and display both on your screen (by selecting Window, Arrange), you can easily copy, cut, and paste between the two workbooks.

To copy data from one location to another, select the cell or cells you want to copy and click the Copy toolbar button (or press Ctrl+C) to copy the worksheet contents to your Clipboard. Ctrl+A selects the entire worksheet to copy or cut. The contents stay in the original location because you elected to copy and not cut the cells. To paste the Clipboard contents to another location, select the first cell in the target location (which may reside in another workbook) and click the Paste toolbar button (or press Ctrl+V). Excel 2000 overwrites the target cells with the pasted contents, so be sure of the paste target when you paste Clipboard data.

STEP-UP

Office Assistant keeps a close eye on you at all times. If you attempt to paste data into a range that already has data, Office Assistant issues the warning shown in Figure 9.3. You can click OK to accept the overwrite or click Cancel to stop the paste.

FIGURE 9.3

Office Assistant warns you when you are about to paste over data.

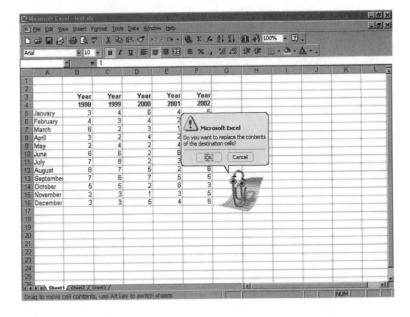

 As with all Office 2000 products, you can send up to 12 distinct items to the Clipboard and paste one or more of the copied items into your worksheet.

You can continue pasting the Clipboard to other worksheets as long as you keep selecting a target location and pressing Ctrl+V.

Excel 2000 supports drag-and-drop editing, so after you select the cells to copy, press Ctrl and drag the selection to its new location. You must drag the selection by pointing to one of the selection edges; if you attempt to drag from the center of a selected cell set, Excel 2000 changes the selection range. When you release your mouse button and the Ctrl key, Excel 2000 pastes the contents to the target location. Of course, drag-and-drop editing works only when you can see both the source and the target copy and paste locations.

To cut contents and place them elsewhere, just select the cells that you want to cut and press Ctrl+X (or click the Cut toolbar button). Excel 2000 removes the selection from its original location and places the selection on your Clipboard. You then can paste the Clipboard contents elsewhere. In effect, cutting and pasting performs a movement of the selected data. If you want to move the selection with your mouse, drag the selection without first pressing Ctrl as you did when copying the contents.

 If you want to drag and drop between two workbooks' worksheets but you only have one worksheet displayed, press the Alt key before dragging your selection. When you drag the selection over the target worksheet's name tab, Excel 2000 opens that worksheet, and you can drop the dragged contents to the open worksheet.

Clearing Data

Because of the nature of worksheets, erasing worksheet data differs from erasing word processed data. Other information on the worksheet can heavily depend on the erased data, as you see in the next hour's lesson. When you want to erase a cell's or selection's contents, first decide which of the following kinds of erasure you want to perform:

- Erase the selection and send the contents to the Clipboard (as you learned in the previous section).

- Clear only a portion of the selection, such as its formatting, comment, or data value.

- Completely erase the selection and all formatting and notes attached to the selection.

- Erase the selected cells and their position so that other cells in the row move left or cells below move up.

A worksheet's cell contains a lot more than just the numbers and text that you see on the worksheet screen. Not only can the cells also contain formulas and comments, but they often rely on other cells for information. Therefore, when you want to erase the selection, you must keep in mind how the selection affects other worksheet areas.

If you want to delete the selected cell's data, press Delete. Excel 2000 retains any formatting and comments that you had applied before you deleted the data.

If you want to more selectively erase a cell, select the Edit, Clear command and select from one of the five options listed here:

- The All option deletes the entire selection, including the contents, format, and attached comments (but not the actual cell).
- The Formats option erases only the selection's format; you can get rid of a cell's special formatting and revert to a general format without changing or erasing the contents of the cell.
- The Contents option deletes the cell contents but leaves the formatting and comments intact.
- The Comments option deletes any special comments that appear in the selected cells.
- The Hyperlinks option removes any Internet-based references within the cell.

Reverse an accidental deletion with Undo (Ctrl+Z).

Here's a quicker way to erase the values in cells: Select the cells and drag the fill handle up and to the left. As you drag the fill handle, Excel 2000 grays the cells that are erased when you release the mouse button.

To remove the selected cells as well as their contents and close the gap left by the deleted selection, select Edit, Delete to display the Delete dialog box, as shown in Figure 9.4. Select Shift Cells Left or Shift Cells Up so that Excel 2000 knows how to close the gap that the deletion leaves.

FIGURE 9.4

You can delete cells and move all other cells over those deleted cells.

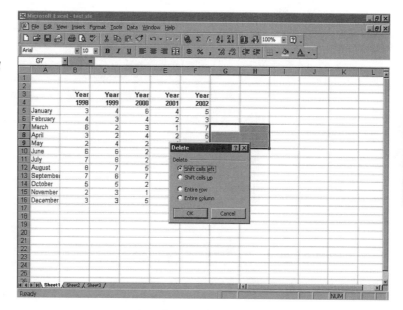

9

Speed Data Entry

Excel 2000 can often predict what data you want to enter into a worksheet. By spotting trends in your data, Excel 2000 uses educated guesses to fill in cell data for you. Excel 2000 uses *data fills* to copy and extend data from one cell to several additional cells.

NEW TERM *Data fill* refers to the capability of Excel 2000 to spot and continue trends in data that you have started, such as a series of numbers or dates.

One of the most common data fills you perform is to use Excel 2000's capability to copy one cell's data to several other cells. You might want to create a pro forma balance sheet for the previous five-year period, for example. You can insert a two-line label across the top of each year's data. The first line would contain five occurrences of the label Year, and the second line would hold the numbers 1998 through 2002. To use the data fill feature in Excel 2000 to create the five similar labels, perform these simple steps:

1. Click the B3 cell to move the cell cursor there.

2. Type Year. Don't press Enter or any cell-moving cursor keys after you type the label.

3. Locate the cell's *fill handle*. The fill handle is the small black box located in the lower-right corner of the active cell, as shown in Figure 9.5.

Fill handle

FIGURE 9.5

Excel 2000 filled in the four extra labels.

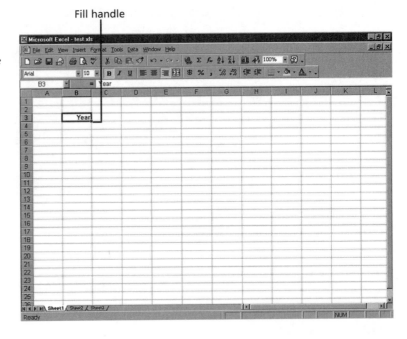

| NEW TERM | A *fill handle* is a cell pointer's box that you can drag to extend and copy the cell's contents. |

4. Drag the fill handle to the right across the next four columns. As you drag the fill handle, Excel 2000 displays the pop-up label Year indicating the value of the new cells.

5. Release the mouse button. Excel 2000 fills all five cells with the label.

If you drag the fill handle down, Excel 2000 copies the label down the column. Excel 2000 even fills a rectangular area if you drag the fill handle across and down the worksheet. Although the Edit, Fill command performs the same function as the fill handle, dragging the fill handle is much easier than selecting from the menu. Ctrl+D performs the same operation as Edit, Fill.

Smarter Fills with AutoFill

Even if the only fill Excel 2000 performed were the copying of data across rows and columns, the data fill would still be beneficial. Excel 2000 goes an extra step, however: It performs smart fills with a feature known as *AutoFill*. AutoFill is perhaps the single reason why Excel took over the spreadsheet market a few years ago and has been the leader ever since. When you use AutoFill, Excel 2000 examines and completes data you have entered.

NEW TERM *AutoFill* is the technique Excel 2000 uses to complete data from a cell or cell selection.

The five year *pro forma* period you were setting up in the preceding section included the years 1998 through 2002, for example. You can type 1998 under the first Year title and type 1999 under the second title. Select *both* cells using the same dragging technique you learned about in the Word 2000 section, and then drag the fill handle right three more cells. When you release the mouse button, you see that Excel 2000 properly fills in the remaining years, as shown in Figure 9.6).

FIGURE 9.6

Excel 2000's AutoFill feature knew which years to fill.

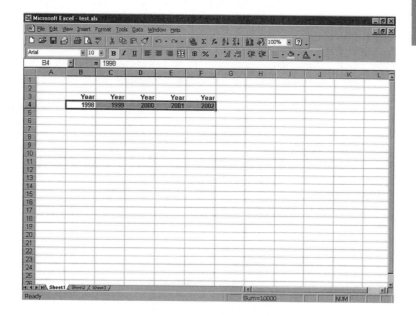

9

 If you had selected only one cell, Excel 2000 would have copied that cell's contents across the worksheet. Excel 2000 needed to see the two selected cells to notice the trend.

The years in Figure 9.6 don't exactly align under the first row, but in the next hour, "Editing Excel Worksheets," you learn how to format data to make your titles align.

Excel 2000 gets even better. If you want to use AutoFill to increment cells by a single number, as you are doing with the years, you don't really need to select two cells first. If you select any cell that contains a number, press Ctrl, and drag the fill handle, Excel 2000 adds a one to each cell to which you extend. Therefore, you could fill four years from 1999 through 2002 just by pressing Ctrl before you dragged the first year's fill handle to the right.

As you know, Excel 2000 works with text as well as with numeric values. AutoFill recognizes many common text trends, including the following:

- Days of the week names
- Days of the week abbreviations (such as Mon, Tue)
- Month names
- Month abbreviations (such as Jan, Feb)

Suppose that you want to list month names down the left of the pro forma sheet, starting in cell A5, because you need to report each month's totals for those five years. All you need to do is type January for the first month name, and drag that cell's fill handle to the twelfth cell below. Figure 9.7 shows the result.

FIGURE 9.7

Let Excel 2000 fill in the series of month names.

Excel entered these month names.

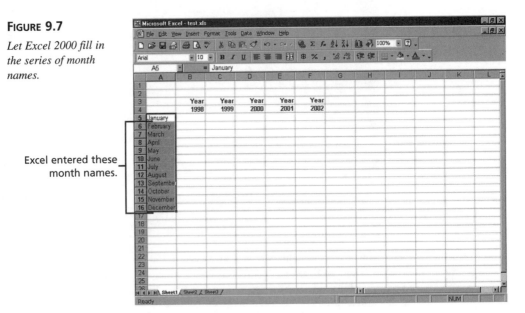

Design Your Own Fills

In addition to the month and weekday names and abbreviations, Excel 2000 can fill in any list of values. You can teach Excel 2000 a new list to use with AutoFill. After you have shown Excel 2000 the new list, anytime you type the first value and drag that cell's fill handle in any direction, Excel 2000 fills the remaining cells with your list.

To add your own AutoFill list to Excel 2000's repertoire of lists, perform these steps:

1. Select Tools, Options.

2. Click the Custom Lists tab to display the current AutoFill lists in effect.

3. Click the Add button.

4. Type your list of values for AutoFill. If you have six departments, you might enter something like Dept 1, Dept 2, Dept 3, Dept 4, Dept 5, and Dept 6. Press Enter between each value. Your screen should look like Figure 9.8.

5. Click OK to add your list to AutoFill's current list.

The next time you type the label Dept 1 in a cell and drag the fill handle to the right or down the worksheet, Excel 2000 fills in the remaining departments. If you fill only four cells, Excel 2000 uses the first four values. If you fill six or more cells, Excel 2000 fills all six departments and starts repeating the department names for any number over six.

FIGURE 9.8

Teach Excel 2000 new AutoFill entries.

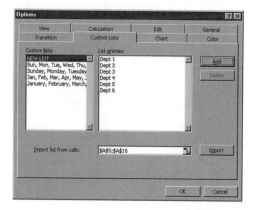

If you enter a series in a worksheet, and then decide that the series would make a great AutoFill list (in case you want to add the list to another worksheet), Excel 2000 doesn't make you re-enter the list. Just select the entire list by dragging the mouse pointer through the list. When you open the Custom Lists dialog box, click Import to add the selected range to the AutoFill entries.

AutoFill is fine for a typical range of titles and for a series of a dozen or fewer entries, but some data series consume numerous entries. When you want to enter a larger number of values in a series, perform these steps:

1. Type the first value of the series in the first cell.

2. Select the cell and all subsequent cells that will receive the rest of the series.

3. Select Edit, Fill, Series to display the Series dialog box.

4. Select Rows if you have selected cells from a row or Columns if you have selected cells from a column.

5. Select the type of series you are entering. Table 9.1 describes each of the four types from which you can choose.

6. Select the subtype. If the series is a series of months, for example, check Month.

7. Enter the Step value, which describes how each value in the series increases or decreases.

8. Enter the Stop value if necessary (you rarely need to enter one). If you want to enter a series that increases every three months, for example, you check the Month option, and type 3 for the Step value, Excel 2000 will know the final month and you won't need to enter it.

   Although you won't need to indicate to Excel 2000 where to stop in most instances, a Stop value is useful if you check the Trend option in the Series dialog box. Excel 2000 starts with your initial selected value (if numeric) and estimates the values between that starting value and the Stop value that you supply.

9. Click OK to create and enter the series of values.

TABLE 9.1   TYPES OF SERIES

Series Name	If You Type...	Excel 2000 Can Complete With
Linear	0	1, 2, 3, 4, 5
	−50, 0, 50, 100	150, 200, 250
Growth	2, 4	8, 16, 32, 64
	10, 100	1000, 10000
Date	1-Jan, 1-Apr	1-Jul, 1-Oct, 1-Jan
AutoFill	Acctg-101, Acctg-102	Acctg-103, Acctg-104
	Year '96	Year '97, Year '98

Adding Comments

As with Word 2000, you can insert *comments* in a cell. The comments act like yellow sticky notes onscreen, except that the notes in Excel 2000 aren't in the way when you don't want to see them. The comments don't appear in the cell; when you insert a comment, Excel 2000 indicates that the comment resides within the cell by flagging the cell's upper-right corner with a red triangle. When you point to the cell, Excel 2000 displays the attached comment.

NEW TERM A *comment* is a note attached to a cell that doesn't appear as part of the cell's data.

To attach a comment to a selected cell, select Insert, Comment. Excel 2000 opens the box shown in Figure 9.9. Type your comment here. Excel 2000 automatically places your name at the beginning of the comment. The name indicates who added the comment in case you work in a multiple-user environment. (You can erase the name if you don't want to see it.) You can leave coworkers notes if you edit worksheets as a team. You can also leave yourself a note to fill in data that you might get from an outside source later.

FIGURE 9.9

Add comments to cells.

Attached
comment flags

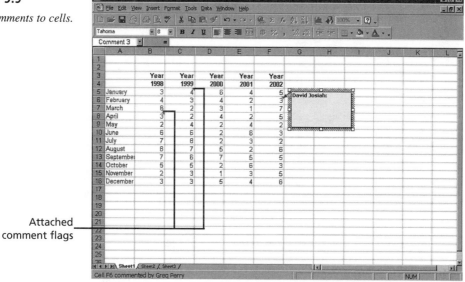

 If you select a group of cells and attach a comment, Excel 2000 attaches the comment only to the upper-left cell in the selection. Excel 2000 cannot attach a comment to an entire selection, only to individual cells.

The earlier section in this hour, "Clearing Data," tells you how to remove comments you no longer need.

Summary

Excel 2000's Copy, Cut, and Paste commands work much the same as the corresponding operations in Word 2000. This hour focused more on the differences than similarities between the products. Worksheet data differs from a word processor's, and you must handle certain kinds of Excel 2000 deletions differently from Word 2000 deletions.

This hour taught you how to speed up your data entry by using AutoFill and AutoCorrect. After you teach Excel 2000 your own special series, Excel 2000 fills in that series of values for you. Although accuracy is more important than speed, you will welcome the speedy data entry tools Excel 2000 provides.

The next hour shows how to work with ranges, formulas, rows, and columns. Now that you have covered the groundwork, you are ready to learn about Excel 2000's powerhouse tools for worksheets.

Q&A

Q How do I know whether Excel 2000 can fill a series I have started?

A Enter the first couple of values, select the cells, and drag the selection's fill handle to the right or down, depending on your desired fill direction. As you drag the fill handle, Excel 2000 shows, in a ToolTips-like pop-up box, which values will fill in the series. If Excel 2000 does not recognize the series, the pop-up values won't be correct. You then can teach Excel 2000 the new series as explained in this hour or enter the remaining values by hand. In many instances, you will be surprised at the power of Excel 2000; if the first two values in your series are 10 and 20, for example, Excel 2000 guesses that you want to extend the series by 10s.

Q Why does Excel 2000 sometimes select additional cells when all I want to do is extend a series?

A You are dragging the cell's contents, *not* the fill handle. Be sure that you drag the fill handle when you want Excel 2000 to complete the series. If you drag with one of the cell's straight edges rather than its fill handle, Excel 2000 attempts to move the cell contents from their original location to your dragging target; therefore, be careful that you have grabbed the fill handle when you are ready for the fill.

Q Why would I want to remove formatting, but not a cell's contents?

A You learn in the next hour how to apply a lot of formats to cells. You can apply a date format to a cell, for example, so that Excel 2000 displays a date based on the value and not a number. If you format a cell for a date and later—because of editing changes, that cell no longer holds a date but a value—you will want to remove the date format. Excel 2000 uses a general numeric format for all cells to which you don't specifically apply a different format.

HOUR 10

Editing Excel Worksheets

This hour teaches you additional Excel 2000 worksheet editing skills. You will be surprised how Excel 2000 helps you when you modify worksheets.

Understanding ranges is critical if you want to really master Excel 2000. Therefore, be sure that you master this hour. You will use range names and addresses frequently in Excel 2000 formulas and functions.

The highlights of this hour include the following:

- What Excel 2000 does when you insert or delete rows and columns
- How ranges differ from selections
- Why range names are important
- What the fundamental math operators do

Inserting and Deleting

As you saw in the preceding hour, the requirements for Excel 2000 are somewhat different from those for Word 2000, even though both programs perform tasks in a similar manner and with similar menu commands and dialog boxes. The nature of worksheets makes them behave differently from word-processed documents. The next few sections explain how to insert and delete information from your worksheets.

Inserting Entire Cells

Inserting cells, as opposed to inserting data inside a cell, requires that the existing worksheet cells move to the right and down to make room for the new cell. When you want to insert a cell, perform these steps:

1. Select the cell that should appear *after* the inserted cell.
2. Select Insert, Cells to display the Insert dialog box.
3. Click either the Shift Cells Right option or the Shift Cells Down option to determine the direction of the shift. The shift makes room for your new cell.
4. Click OK to begin the shift.

Some people prefer to use the mouse to shift cells right or down to make room for new data. Press Shift and drag the cell's fill handle (or the selection's fill handle if you have selected a group of cells) down or to the right. Excel 2000 grays out the areas that are left blank by the shifting. You may have to experiment with inserting cells a few times by inserting and then choosing Undo (Ctrl+Z) before you get the hang of it.

Inserting Rows and Columns

To insert a row or column (and thus move the other rows down or other columns to the right), perform these steps:

1. Select the row or column that appears *after* the inserted rows or columns by clicking its header to select the entire row or column. If you want to insert more than one row or column, select that many existing rows or columns by dragging the row or column selection.
2. Select Insert, Rows or Insert, Columns. Excel 2000 shifts the existing rows or columns to make room for the new empty row or column. Instead of selecting from the menu bar, you can point to the selected row or column and display the pop-up menu shown in Figure 10.1 by right-clicking the mouse and selecting Insert to insert the new row or column. (Excel 2000 inserts multiple rows or columns if you first selected more than one row or column.)

Deleting Entire Cells

When you deleted cells in the preceding hour, you learned how to remove selected cells completely from the worksheet and close the gap with the Delete dialog box. The Delete dialog box not only deletes cells, but also deletes entire rows and columns.

FIGURE 10.1

The pop-up menu offers insert, delete, and several other options.

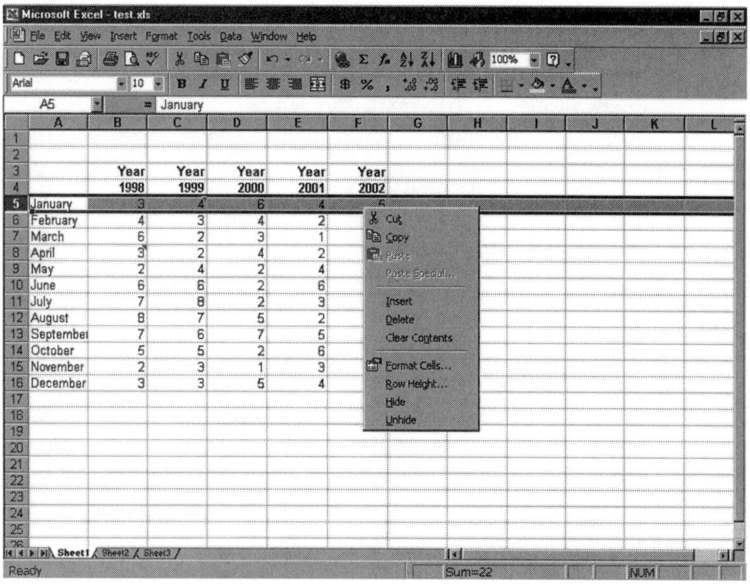

To delete a row or column, perform these steps:

1. Select a cell that resides in the row or column you want to delete.

2. Select Edit, Delete to display the Delete dialog box.

3. Select either the Entire Row or Entire Column option.

4. Click OK to perform the deletion. Excel 2000 shifts columns to the left or shifts rows up to fill in the missing gap.

> If you want to delete multiple rows or multiple columns, select cells from each column or row you want to delete before displaying the Delete dialog box.

Deleting Rows and Columns

Perform these steps when you want to delete a row or column (as opposed to erasing the contents of a row or column):

1. Select the row or column to delete.

2. Right-click the selected row or column to display the pop-up menu.

3. Select Delete. Excel 2000 shifts the remaining part of the worksheet to close the gap.

Working with Worksheet Ranges

A *range* is a group of cells. A selected group of cells comprises a range, but ranges don't always have to be selected. A range is always rectangular. A range might be a single cell, a row, a column, or several adjacent rows and columns. The cells in ranges are always contiguous. Even though you can select noncontiguous cells, ranges always form rectangular worksheet regions. You can perform various operations on ranges, such as moving and copying.

NEW TERM   A *range* is a rectangular collection of cells.

Figure 10.2 shows three ranges on a worksheet. You can describe a range by the address of the upper-left cell of the range (the anchor point) and the address of the lower-right cell of the range. As you can see from Figure 10.2, multiple-celled ranges are designated by listing the *anchor point*, followed by a colon (:), followed by the range's lower-right cell address. Therefore, the range that begins at B3 and ends at F4 has the range of B3:F4.

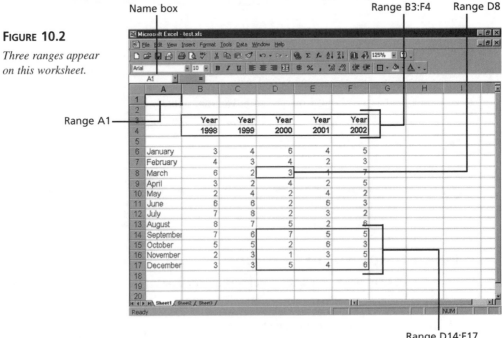

FIGURE 10.2

Three ranges appear on this worksheet.

NEW TERM   An *anchor point* is a range's upper-left cell address.

You will work quite a bit with ranges. One of the ways to make your worksheets more manageable is to name your ranges. You might assign the name Titles to your column titles, for example, Months to your column of month names, and so on.

To name a range, perform these steps:

1. Select the cells that you want to include in the named range.
2. Click the Name box at the left of the Formula bar (the text box that displays cell addresses).
3. Type the range name.
4. Press Enter. When you subsequently select the range, you will see that Excel 2000 displays the *range name* rather than the range address in the Name box.

10

NEW TERM   A *range name* is a name you assign to a range of cells. You can move a range to a new worksheet location and the range name stays the same.

Names are easier to remember than range addresses. If you create a payroll worksheet and assign the names GrossPay, NetPay, HoursWorked, TaxRate, and PayRate to the ranges that hold that data, for example, you never again have to type the range addresses. When you want to move or copy one of the ranges or use the range as a formula, just refer to the range name and let Excel 2000 figure out the correct addresses. You learn how to add ranges (including range names) to formulas in the section called "Using Formulas."

Here's an even better reason to name ranges: If you move a range, Excel 2000 moves the name with the cells! If you tracked range addresses and not names, you would constantly have to track down the latest addresses when you referred to the range. By naming ranges, you never have to worry about keeping track of addresses because the names won't change even if the addresses do.

Use meaningful names. Although AAA works as a name for a column of net sales figures, NetSales makes a lot more sense and is easier to remember. Your range names can include between 1 and 255 characters, and can contain alphabetic letters, numbers, periods, and underscores. Although you cannot include spaces, you can mix uppercase and lowercase letters and include underscores to help distinguish between words in a single name.

If you create a large worksheet and you need to return to a named range to make some changes, click the Name box and type the name. Excel 2000 instantly displays that range and selects the range for you.

Fight the urge to ignore range names when you create your worksheets. The tendency is to put off naming ranges until later, and later often does not come. By naming key ranges as you create your worksheet, you more rapidly create the worksheet and the worksheet contains fewer errors.

Using Formulas

Without *formulas*, Excel 2000 would be little more than a word processor for tables of information. When you use formulas, however, Excel 2000 becomes an extremely power-ful time-saving planning, budgeting, and general-purpose financial tool.

 A *formula* is a calculation that produces a result. Formulas can include math opera-tors, numbers, cell addresses, and range names.

 An *operator* is a symbol that requests a mathematical calculation such as a plus sign (+).

 Some people credit worksheet programs for the tremendous PC growth in the 1980s. Without formulas, worksheets would never have been able to create such a demand for personal computers.

On a calculator, you typically type a formula and then press the equal sign to see the result. All Excel 2000 formulas *begin* with an equal sign. For example, the following is a formula:

```
=4*2-3
```

The asterisk is an operator that denotes the times sign (*multiplication*). This formula requests that Excel 2000 compute the value of 4 multiplied by 2 minus 3 to get the *result*. When you type a formula and press Enter or move to another cell, Excel 2000 dis-plays the result, not the formula, on the worksheet.

As Figure 10.3 shows, the answer 5 appears on the worksheet, and you can see the cell's formula contents right on the Formula bar area. When entering a formula, as soon as you press the equal sign, Excel 2000 shows your formula on the Formula bar as well as in the active cell. If you click the Formula bar and then enter your formula, the formula appears in the Formula bar as well as in the active cell. By first clicking the Formula bar before entering the formula, however, you can press the left and right arrow keys to move the cursor left and right within the formula to edit it. When entering long formulas, this Formula bar's editing capability helps you correct mistakes that you might type.

FIGURE 10.3

Excel 2000 displays a formula's result on the worksheet.

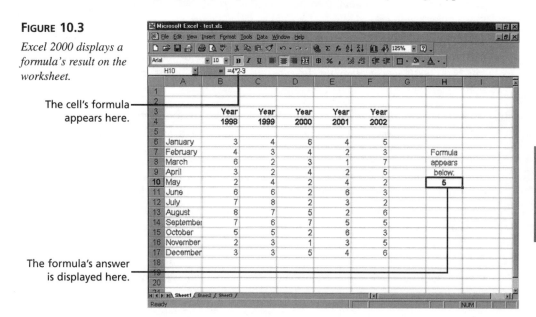

The cell's formula appears here.

The formula's answer is displayed here.

You can format a worksheet to show the actual formula rather than the answer, but you do something like that only when printing worksheet content listings that you want to study.

Excel's Primary Math Operators

Table 10.1 lists the primary math operators you can use in your worksheet formulas. Notice that all the example formulas begin with the equal sign.

TABLE 10.1 THE PRIMARY MATH OPERATORS SPECIFY MATH CALCULATIONS

Operator	Example	Description
^	=7 ^ 3	Raises 7 to the power of 3 (called *exponentiation*)
/	=4 / 2	Divides 4 by 2
*	=3 * 4 * 5	Multiplies 3 by 4 by 5
+	=5 + 5	Adds 5 and 5
-	=5 - 5	Subtracts 5 from 5

NEW TERM The *exponentiation* operator raises one number to a higher power.

You can combine any and all the operators in a formula. When combining operators, Excel 2000 follows the traditional computer (and algebraic) *operator hierarchy* model. Therefore, Excel 2000 first computes exponentiation if you raise any value to another power. Excel 2000 then calculates all multiplication and division in a left-to-right order (the first one to appear computes first) before addition and subtraction (also in left-to-right order).

NEW TERM The *operator hierarchy* dictates the order that operators compute in formulas: exponentiation, multiplication and division, and then addition and subtraction.

The following formula returns a result of 14 because Excel 2000 first calculates the exponentiation of 2 raised to the third power, and then Excel 2000 divides the answer (8) by 4, and then multiplies the result (2) by 2, and finally subtracts the result (4) from 18. Even though the subtraction appears first, the operator hierarchy forces the subtraction to wait until last to compute.

```
=18 - 2 ^ 3 / 4 * 2
```

If you want to override the operator hierarchy, put parentheses around the parts you want Excel 2000 to compute first. The following formula returns a different result from the previous one, for example, despite the same values and operators used:

```
=(18 - 2) ^ 3 / 4 * 2
```

Instead of 14, this formula returns 2,048! The subtraction produces 16, which is then raised to the third power (producing 4,096) before dividing by 4 and multiplying the result by 2 to get 2,048.

Using Range Names in Formulas

The true power of Excel 2000 shows when you use cell addresses and range names in formulas. All the following are valid formulas. Cell addresses or range names appear throughout the formulas.

```
=(SalesTotals)/NumOfSales
=C4 * 2 - (Rate * .08)
=7 + LE51 - (Gross - Net)
```

When you enter formulas that contain range addresses, you can either type the full address or point to the cell address. If you want to include a complete named range in a formula (formulas can work on complete ranges, as you see in the next hour, "Using Excel Formulas"), select the entire range and Excel 2000 inserts the range name in your formula. Often, finding and pointing to a value are easier than locating the address and entering the exact address.

If, for example, you are entering a formula for cells that are close to the formula's cell, when you get to the place in the formula that requires a close cell, don't type the cell address; instead, point to the cell. If you have entered a formula such as =7 + , instead of typing a cell address of LE51, you can point to that cell and Excel 2000 enters the cell's address for you. Immediately after typing the cell address for you, Excel 2000 returns your cursor to the formula (or to the Formula bar if you are entering the formula there) so that you can complete it.

After you assign a name to a cell, you don't have to remember that cell's address when you use that cell in formulas. Suppose that you are creating a large worksheet that spans many screens. If you assign names to cells when you create them, cells that you know you will refer to later during the worksheet's development, entering formulas that use that name is made easier. Instead of locating that cell to find its address, you need only type the name when entering a formula that uses that cell.

10

To assign a range name to a cell or to a range of cells, select the cell or range and click the Name box at the left of the Formula bar. Type the name and press Enter. Excel 2000 assigns the name to that cell or range.

Relative Versus Absolute Cell Addressing

When you copy formulas that contain cell addresses, Excel 2000 updates the cell addresses so that they reference *relative addresses*. For example, suppose that you enter this formula in cell A1:

```
=A2 + A3
```

NEW TERM A *relative address* is an address that references cells based on the current cell's location.

This formula contains two addresses. The addresses are relative because the addresses A2 and A3 change if you copy the formula elsewhere. If you copy the formula to cell B5, for example, B5 holds this:

```
=B6 + B7
```

The original relative addresses update to reflect the formula's copied location. Of course, A1 still holds its original contents, but the copied cell at B5 holds the same formula referencing B5 rather than A1.

An absolute address is an address that does not change if you copy the formula. A dollar sign ($) always precedes an absolute address. The address B5 is an absolute address. If you wanted to sum two columns of data (A1 with B1, A2 with B2, and so on) and then multiply each sum by some constant number, for example, the constant number could be a cell referred to as an absolute address. That formula might look like this:

=(A1 + B1) * J1

J1 is an *absolute address*, but A1 and B1 are relative. If you copied the formula down one row, the formula would change to this:

=(A2 + B2) * J1

 New Term An *absolute address* is an address that references cells using their specific addresses and does not change when you copy the cell holding the formula.

Notice that the first two cells changed because, when you originally entered them, they were relative cell addresses. You told Excel 2000, by placing dollar signs in front of the absolute cell address's row and column references, not to change that reference when you copy the formula elsewhere.

$B5 is a partial absolute address. If you copy a formula with $B5 inside the computation, the $B keeps the B column intact, but the fifth row updates to the row location of the target cell. If you type the following formula in cell A1:

=2 * $B5

and then copy the formula to cell F6, cell F6 holds this formula:

=2 * $B10

You copied the formula to a cell five rows and five columns over in the worksheet. Excel 2000 did not update the column name, B, because you told Excel 2000 to keep that column name absolute (it is always B no matter where you copy the formula). Excel 2000 added 5 to the row number, however, because the row number was relative and open to change whenever you copied the formula.

The dollar sign keeps the row B absolute no matter where you copy the formula, but the relative row number can change as you copy the formula.

The bottom line is this: Most of the time, you use relative addressing. If you insert or delete rows, columns, or cells, your formulas remain accurate because the cells that they reference change as your worksheet changes.

Copying Formulas

Excel 2000 offers several shortcut tools;copying that make copying cells from one location to another simple. Consider the worksheet in Figure 10.4. The bottom row needs to hold formulas that total each of the projected year's 12-month values.

FIGURE 10.4

A total row is needed for the project's yearly values.

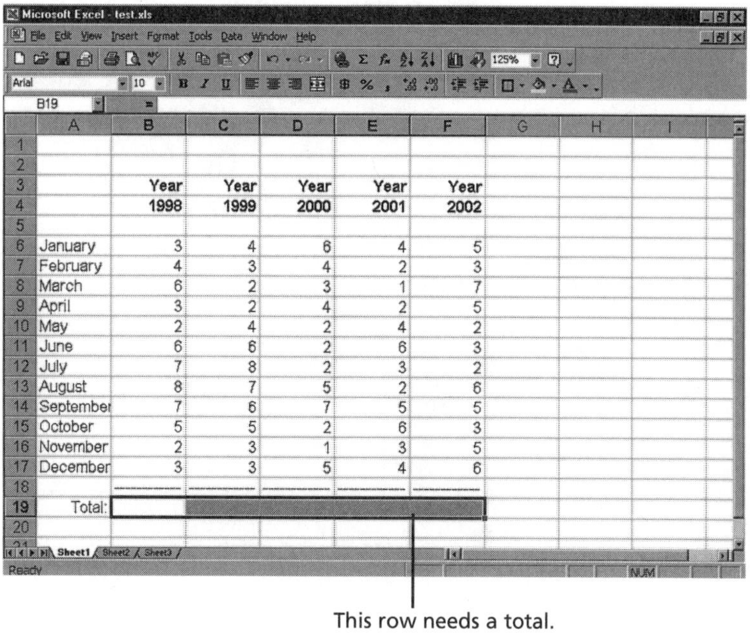

	A	B	C	D	E	F	G	H	I
1									
2									
3		Year	Year	Year	Year	Year			
4		1998	1999	2000	2001	2002			
5									
6	January	3	4	6	4	5			
7	February	4	3	4	2	3			
8	March	6	2	3	1	7			
9	April	3	2	4	2	5			
10	May	2	4	2	4	2			
11	June	6	6	2	6	3			
12	July	7	8	2	3	2			
13	August	8	7	5	2	6			
14	September	7	6	7	5	5			
15	October	5	5	2	6	3			
16	November	2	3	1	3	5			
17	December	3	3	5	4	6			
18									
19	Total:								
20									

10

This row needs a total.

How would you enter the total row? You could type the following formula in cell B19:

```
=B6+B7+B8+B9+B10+B11+B12+B13+B14+B15+B16+B17
```

After you have typed the formula in B19, you then *could* type the following formula in cell C19:

```
=C6+C7+C8+C9+C10+C11+C12+C13+C14+C15+C16+C17
```

You then could type the values in the remaining total cells. Instead of doing all that typing, however, copy cell B19 to cell C19. Hold Ctrl while you drag the cell edge of B19 to C19. When you release the mouse, cell C19 properly totals column C! Press Ctrl and copy C19 to D19 through F19 to place the totals in all the total cells. ;copyingThe totals are accurate, as Figure 10.5 shows.

If cell B19 contained absolute addresses, cells C19 through F19 would all total column B!

FIGURE 10.5

Relative references make totaling these columns simple.

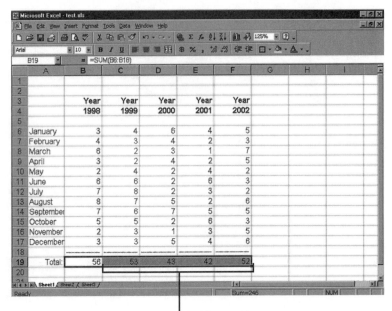

These were copied from B19.

Summary

This hour extended your worksheet knowledge by giving you more editing tools with which to insert and delete columns, rows, and cells. After you name important worksheet ranges, you won't have to track specific addresses in your worksheet; the name is easier to remember, and Excel 2000 changes the range if you insert data in or delete it from the range.

The next hour will teach you more about the use and effectiveness of formulas in Excel and how to format cells to add appeal to your worksheet.

Q&A

Q What is the difference between a selection and a range?

A Selections cannot be named, and can be comprised of several disjointed areas of your worksheet. A range, on the other hand, can be named, and can be any contiguous rectangular collection of cells, including a single cell or your entire worksheet data area. Often, you select an entire range, but all selections are not ranges.

Q Why would I ever use absolute addressing?

A Relative addressing seems to make the most sense for most worksheets. If you have to rearrange your worksheet, all your relative addresses update as well.

Absolute addresses are great when a formula references a single cell, such as an age or pay value, that rarely changes. You could use dollar signs to anchor the single cell in the formula that uses that cell, but keep the other addresses relative in case you need to copy the formula around the worksheet.

10

HOUR 11

Using Excel Formulas

After you set up formulas, your job is done; Excel 2000's job has just begun, however. If you change any value in the worksheet, Excel 2000 recalculates all formulas automatically!

This hour shows you how to use range names and addresses in Excel 2000 formulas and functions to quickly and effectively manipulate your data.

In addition, you also learn how to format worksheets to make them look better. This hour teaches the formatting essentials, so you will be ready for the fancy stuff in the next hour.

The highlights of this hour include the following:

- How to organize formulas so that they compute in the order you want them to
- Which functions save you time and prevent errors
- How to format cells to add eye-catching appeal to your worksheet

Recalculating Worksheets

Excel 2000 keeps your worksheet fresh and accurate as you modify values. You can use the same worksheet each month and change only the monthly data. If you leave the formulas intact, Excel 2000 computes and displays the correct answers.

You can turn off the automatic recalculation and manually recalculate when ready if you use a slow computer and want to save time when editing a large worksheet. Select Tools, Options and click the Calculation tab. Click the Manual option to force manual recalculation. If you now change the data, Excel 2000 does not recalculate your worksheet until you press F9 (the Calculate Now shortcut key).

Working with Functions

The last hour explained how to enter a formula once, using relative addresses, and copy that formula to other cells. Although you only have to type the formula one time, this kind of totaling formula is tedious to type and introduces greater chance for error:

```
=B6+B7+B8+B9+B10+B11+B12+B13+B14+B15+B16+B17
```

Fortunately, Microsoft includes several built-in *functions* that perform many common mathematical calculations. Instead of writing a formula to sum a row or column of values, for example, use the Sum() function.

NEW TERM   *Functions* are built-in calculations and data manipulations that perform the work of formulas to return values.

Function names always end with parentheses, such as Average(). A function accepts zero or more *arguments*. The arguments, if any, go inside the parentheses. Always separate function arguments with commas. If a function contains only a single argument, you do not use a comma inside the parentheses. Functions generally manipulate data (numbers or text), and the argument list inside the parentheses supplies the data to the function. The Average() function, for example, computes an average of whatever list of values you pass in the argument list in Average(). Therefore, all the following compute an average from the argument list:

```
=Average(18, 65, 299, $R$5, 10, -2, 102)
=Average(SalesTotals)
=Average(D4:D14)
```

NEW TERM   An *argument* is a value on which a function operates (most often indicated by cell addresses). Arguments appear inside the parentheses of a function.

As with many functions, Average() accepts as many arguments as needed to do its job. The first Average() function computes the average of seven values, one of which is an absolute cell address. The second Average() function computes the average of a range named SalesTotals. No matter how many cells comprise the range SalesTotals, Average() computes the average. The last Average() function computes the average of the values in the range D4 through D14 (a columnar list).

The Sum() function is perhaps the most common function because you so often total table columns and rows. In the preceding section, you entered a long formula to add the values in a column. Instead of adding each cell to total the range B6:B17, you could more easily enter the following function:

```
=Sum(B6:B17)
```

If you copy this Sum() function to the other cells at the bottom of the yearly projections, you achieve the same results as the added values, but the worksheet is easier to maintain if you need to make modifications later.

Suppose that you want to track 24 biweekly totals rather than 12 monthly ones. Insert 12 additional blank rows, change the row titles (to something like JanWk12, JanWk34, FebWk12, and so on), and enter the biweekly values. You won't have to change the total calculations! When you insert rows within the Sum() range, Excel 2000 updates the range inside the Sum() function to contain the 12 new values.

Use AutoSum for Speed

Before looking at a table of common functions, Excel 2000 helps you with summing functions by analyzing your selected range and automatically inserting a Sum() function if needed. Here's how to do that:

1. Select the range that you want to sum. If you want to sum the months over the projected years for this hour's sample worksheets, for example, select the row with the January label, as shown in Figure 11.1.

2. Click the AutoSum toolbar button. Excel 2000 guesses that you want to sum the selected row and inserts the Sum() function in the cell to the right of the row.

3. Make any edits to the summed value if Excel 2000 included too many or not enough cells. You can click the cell and press F2 to edit the sum. Usually, no edits are required.

FIGURE 11.1

Getting ready to request a sum.

AutoSum button —

Excel 2000 places the Sum( ) function here.

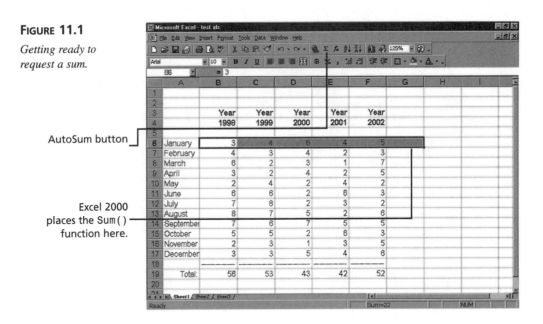

After Excel 2000 generates the Sum() function, you can copy the cell down the rest of the column to add the monthly totals. However, can you see another way to perform the same monthly totals with one selection? Select the entire set of monthly values with one extra blank column at the right (the range B6:G17). Excel 2000 sees the blank column and fills it in with each row's sum when you click AutoSum. You now can select the new column of totals and let AutoSum compute them. Figure 11.2 shows the result of the new sums after you add underlines and a title.

Common Functions

Functions improve your accuracy. If you want to average three cell values, for example, you might type something like this:

```
=C2 + C4 + C6 / 3
```

This formula does not compute an average! Remember that the operator hierarchy forces the division calculation first. If you use the Average() function, as shown next, you don't have to worry as much about the calculation's hierarchy.

```
=Average(C2, C4, C6)
```

FIGURE 11.2

AutoSum in action.

◻ Microsoft Excel - test.xls									_|◻|×
🗎 File Edit View Insert Format Tools Data Window Help									_|◻|×

	A	B	C	D	E	F	G	H	I
							G19		=SUM(B19:F19)
1									
2									
3		Year	Year	Year	Year	Year			
4		1998	1999	2000	2001	2002			
5									
6	January	3	4	6	4	5	22		
7	February	4	3	4	2	3	16		
8	March	6	2	3	1	7	19		
9	April	3	2	4	2	5	16		
10	May	2	4	2	4	2	14		
11	June	6	6	2	6	3	23		
12	July	7	8	2	3	2	22		
13	August	8	7	5	2	6	28		
14	September	7	6	7	5	5	30		
15	October	5	5	2	6	3	21		
16	November	2	3	1	3	5	14		
17	December	3	3	5	4	6	21		
18									
19	Total:	56	53	43	42	52	246		
20									

AutoSum summed the entire column.

11

Another advantage of using functions is that you can modify them more easily than you can long calculations. If you want to throw another cell value into the previous average, for example, you only need to add the extra cell to Average(); if you use a formula, you must remember to change the 3 to 4.

Table 11.1 describes common Excel 2000 built-in functions that you find a lot of uses for as you create worksheets. Remember to start every formula with an equal sign and to add your cell addresses to the parentheses, and you are set!

TABLE 11.1 COMMON EXCEL 2000 FUNCTIONS

Function Name	Description
Abs()	Computes the absolute value of its cell argument. (Good for distance- and age-difference calculations.)
Average()	Computes the average of its arguments.

continues

TABLE 11.1 CONTINUED

Function Name	Description
Count()	Returns the number of numerical arguments in the argument list. (Useful if you use a range name for the argument list.)
Counta()	Returns the number of all arguments in the argument list. (Useful if you use a range name for the argument list.)
CountBlank()	Returns the number of blank cells, if any exist, in the argument range. (Useful if you use a range name for the argument list.)
Max()	Returns the highest (maximum) value in the argument list. (Useful if you use a range name for the argument list and you need to pick out the highest value.)
Min()	Returns the lowest (minimum) value in the argument list. (Useful if you use a range name for the argument list and you need to pick out the lowest value.)
Pi()	Computes the value of mathematical pi (requires no arguments) for use in math calculations.
Product()	Computes the product (multiplicative result) of the argument range.
Roman()	Converts its cell value to a Roman numeral.
Sqrt()	Computes the square root of the cell argument.
Stddev()	Computes the argument list's standard deviation.
Sum()	Computes the sum of its arguments.
Today()	Returns today's date (requires no arguments).
Var()	Computes a list's sample variance.

> Excel 2000 supports many more functions than Table 11.1 lists. Excel 2000 even supports complex mathematical, date, time, financial, and engineering functions. As you learn more about Excel 2000 and create more complex worksheets, you will run across these functions as you read through the online help.

Advanced Functions

Some of the functions require more arguments than a simple cell or range. Excel 2000 contains many financial functions, for example, that compute loan values and investment rates of return. If you want to use one of the more advanced functions, click on an empty cell and then click the Paste Function toolbar button to display the Paste Function dialog box, as shown in Figure 11.3.

FIGURE 11.3

Let Excel 2000's Paste Function dialog box type complex functions for you.

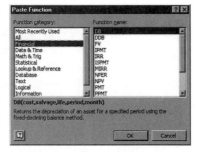

When you select the category in the left column, the Paste Function dialog box displays a list of functions within that category. When you click one of the functions, the Paste Function dialog box gives you a helpful mini-description. When you find the function you need, double-click it; Excel 2000 displays an additional dialog box that requests each of the function arguments, such as the one shown in Figure 11.4. As you continue with the Paste Function dialog box, Excel 2000 builds the function in the cell for you. As you get more proficient, you no longer need the help of the Paste Function dialog box.

FIGURE 11.4

The Paste Function produces this dialog box that walks you through each function argument.

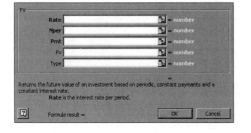

The Office Assistant offers more help with defining the function that you create from the Paste Function dialog box.

Introduction to Worksheet Formatting

Until now, you have seen no fancy worksheets. I kept the fancy stuff out of the way so that you could concentrate on the work at hand. It is now time to show you how to pretty things up. This hour is about to come to a close, but you still have time to learn some cell-formatting basics and you can continue with Excel 2000's more advanced formatting features in the next hour's session.

Justification

Excel 2000 right-justifies numbers (and formulas that result in numbers) and left-justifies text labels. You don't have to accept Excel 2000's default justification, however. To left-, center-, or right-justify the contents of any cell (or range), select the cell (or range) and click the Align Left, Center, or Align Right toolbar buttons. Center titles above columns and adjust your numbers to look just right.

> Excel 2000 offers a trick that even some Excel 2000 gurus forget: If you want to center a title above several columns of data, type the title in a cell above the data. If you cannot center the title over the values by clicking the Center toolbar button, select all the cells around the title so that you have selected as many columns as there is data. Click the Merge and Center toolbar button. Excel 2000 centers the title, even though the title resides in a single cell, across the entire column selection.

Row and Column Height and Width

As you learn more formatting tricks, you will need to adjust certain row and column widths and heights to hold the newly formatted values. To adjust a row's height, point to the line that separates the row number from previous or subsequent rows. When the mouse pointer changes to a double-pointing arrow, drag the row's top or bottom edge up or down. Excel 2000 adjusts the entire row height as you drag your mouse. Sometimes large titles need the larger row heights. When you release the mouse, Excel 2000 anchors the new row height where you left it.

In the same manner, to change the width of a column, point to the column name's left or right edge and drag your mouse left or right. Excel 2000 adjusts the column width to follow your mouse movement. When you release the mouse, Excel 2000 anchors the new column width where you left it.

> If you shrink a column width so that the column can no longer display all the data, Excel 2000 displays pound signs (#####) to warn you that you need to widen the column. Your data is still stored in the cell—it just cannot be displayed.

To adjust the column width so that the column (or range of columns) is exactly large enough to hold the largest data value in the column, select the column (or columns) and double-click the right edge of the column name. Excel 2000 adjusts the column to hold the widest data value in the column.

Font Changes

Feel free to change the worksheet's font to add appeal. Simple font changes, such as boldfacing, italicizing, and underlining, greatly improve the look of titles. The Bold, Italic, and Underline toolbar buttons add the proper formatting to your selected cell or range. If you select Format, Cells and click the Font tab, Excel 2000 displays the Font dialog box (virtually identical to that of Word 2000), in which you can select a new font name and size. As Figure 11.5 shows, simple font changes can make a big improvement on otherwise dull worksheets.

FIGURE 11.5

Already this worksheet looks better.

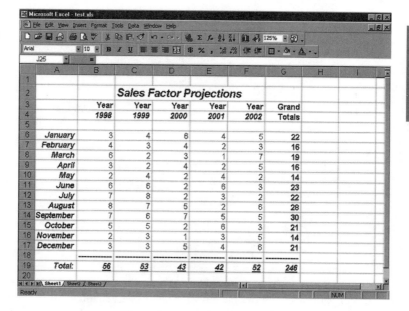

11

If you format a row with a font that's larger than the current row size, Excel 2000 adjusts the row height to make room for the new font.

Of course, you can use the Font and Font Size toolbar buttons to change a font name or size without displaying the Font dialog box.

Making Format Changes

Now that you have mastered Excel 2000 basics, it is time to learn the general format categories Excel 2000 uses for worksheet data. Table 11.2 describes each of the format categories. Unless you change the default, Excel 2000 uses the General format for data of all kinds.

TABLE 11.2   EXCEL 2000'S FUNDAMENTAL FORMATS

Format Name	Description
General	The numeric data has no special formatting and generally appears exactly the way you enter the data.
Number	You can set the number of decimal places Excel 2000 displays for all numeric values.
Currency	Displays a dollar sign and two decimal places for dollar amounts.
Accounting	Aligns currency and decimal points in a column.
Date	Displays date and time values as values whose formats you can change.
Time	Displays only the time portion of a date and time value.
Percentage	Displays a percent sign. If you type 50 into the cell, Excel 2000 changes your value to 50%.
Fraction	Displays numbers as fractions (great for stock quotes).
Scientific	Uses scientific notation for all numeric values.
Text	Formats *all* data as text. Great for Zip codes that are all numbers but that you never use for calculations.
Special	Formats Zip codes, phone numbers, and Social Security numbers.
Custom	Lets you define your own cell format. You can decide whether you want to see the plus or minus sign, and you can control the number of decimal places.

Format a selection by selecting Format, Cells and clicking the Number tab to display a scrolling list of formats, as shown in Table 11.2. If you select the Time format from that list, you must select one of the Time format display variations so that Excel 2000 knows how you want the time displayed.

You can also right-click the selection and select the Format Cells command from the pop-up menu. When you do, you see a dialog box that enables you to assign the formats directly to your data.

You can also use Excel's autoformatting capabilities to easily add style to your worksheet. (The next hour covers AutoFormats.)

Several formatting toolbar buttons exist that enable quick formatting of cells using the most common format styles. If you select a cell or a range of cells, you can change the selection's format more quickly with a toolbar button than with the Format, Cells dialog box. Not all Excel's formats are available through the toolbar, but these are: Currency Style, Percent Style, Comma Style, Increase Decimal (to increase the number of decimal places), and Decrease Decimal (to decrease the number of decimal places).

Summary

One of the most powerful aspects of worksheets is their recalculation capability. If you change data or a formula, Excel 2000 recalculates the entire worksheet as soon as you make the change. You are always looking at the computed worksheet with up-to-date formulas, no matter what kind of data changes you make. When you add formulas to cell calculations, you not only improve your worksheet accuracy, but you finish your worksheets faster.

The next hour picks up where this one leaves off, going into formatting in more detail. Additionally, you see that graphics spruce up your worksheet and are easy to produce.

Q&A

Q Can I share formulas between two worksheets?

A Yes, you can link a formula in one worksheet to another worksheet simply by denoting the name of your "donor" worksheet, along with an exclamation point (!) in the formula bar of the "receiving" worksheet. For example, on a new worksheet, the PMT worksheet function below would calculate interest for the range D5:D15 on another worksheet named "Receipts" in the same workbook.

```
=PMT(Receipts!D5:D15)
```

Q What's the difference between the formatting you get by clicking the Center toolbar button and the formatting you get by clicking the Merge and Center button?

A If you need to center the contents of one cell, both centering formats perform the same task. If want to center data (such as a title) above a range of cell columns, however, select the range the centered cell is to go over and click Merge and Center; Excel 2000 completes the centering across the multiple columns.

11

HOUR 12

Formatting Worksheets to Look Great

This hour concludes your Excel 2000 tutorial by explaining how to format your worksheet with professional styles. The AutoFormat feature in Excel 2000 quickly formats your worksheet within the boundaries you select. If you want to format your worksheet by hand, the formatting commands you learn in this hour enable you to pinpoint important data and highlight that data so that others who look at and use your worksheets find your highlighted information.

After you create and format your worksheets, use the Chart Wizard in Excel 2000 to produce colorful graphs. Often, a worksheet's trends and comparisons get lost in the numeric details. The graphs that the Chart Wizard generates look great, and Excel 2000 does all the drawing work for you.

The highlights of this hour include the following:

- What AutoFormat can do with your worksheets
- How to apply custom formats to selected cells

- When special orientation and wrapped text improve your worksheet appearance
- How to use the Chart Wizard to produce graphs that show data trends and comparisons
- How to modify your charts so that they look the way you want them to

AutoFormatting Worksheets

Before diving into additional formatting commands, you should know that the AutoFormat feature in Excel 2000 converts an otherwise dull worksheet into a nice-looking professional one. A worksheet's presentation is almost as important as the data within the worksheet. If your worksheet needs sprucing up, try AutoFormat after you have formatted individual cells because AutoFormat gives a good-looking, consistent dimension to your entire worksheet. After AutoFormat finishes, you can add finishing touches to the worksheet by adding more specific formats to highlight important cell information, such as special totals that you want to make stand out.

To use AutoFormat, press Ctrl+A to select the entire worksheet. Select Format, AutoFormat to display the AutoFormat dialog box, as shown in Figure 12.1.

FIGURE 12.1

Let AutoFormat improve your worksheet.

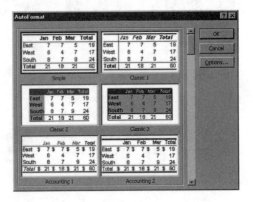

Scroll through the AutoFormat samples and choose any format. When you click OK, Excel 2000 applies the format to your selected worksheet cells. Figure 12.2 shows that AutoFormat knows to highlight totals and also knows to separate headings from the data detail.

To omit certain AutoFormat format styles, click the Options button in AutoFormat to check or uncheck styles. You can keep AutoFormat from changing your worksheet's font, for example, by unchecking the Font option that appears.

FIGURE 12.2

*AutoFormat improved
the appearance of this
worksheet.*

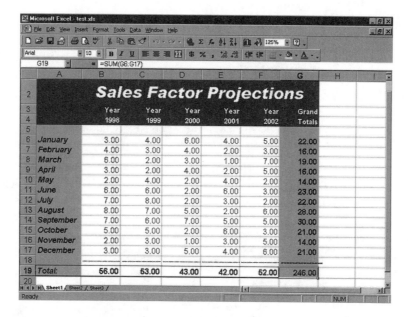

Making Your Own Default Format

Suppose that you often print worksheets to fax to others, and your fax requires boldfaced
worksheets so that the recipients can read the numbers. Instead of changing your worksheet text to boldface before faxing the worksheet, you can make bold face the default
font style. Excel 2000 enables you to change several of the font defaults, so if you find
yourself applying the same font style over and over, consider making that style part of
Excel 2000's default style.

To modify the default style, follow these steps:

  1. Select Format, Style to display the Style dialog box, as shown in Figure 12.3.

FIGURE 12.3

*You can change any
named style.*

12

2. Select the default style, Normal, from the Style Name drop-down list box. (The *Normal style* is probably already the style you see when you open the dialog box.) Like Word 2000, Excel 2000 enables you to modify styles and even create customized styles of your own. When you apply the style changes you added by selecting Format, Style, Excel 2000 applies the style set by the Style dialog box to the selected cells.

 Normal style is the default style Excel 2000 normally uses for all your worksheet cells.

3. To change the Normal style, click the Modify button. Excel 2000 displays the Format Cells dialog box, as shown in Figure 12.4, from which you can modify the named style.

FIGURE 12.4

The Format Cells dialog box modifies any format currently set.

4. Click OK to close the Format Cells dialog box.

5. Click OK to close the Style dialog box. Excel 2000 applies your style to the selected cells. If you made changes to the Normal style, Excel 2000 automatically uses that format on future worksheets unless you modify the format or style.

 If you plan to create additional worksheets that are similar to the one you just created, consider saving the worksheet as a template with File | Save As and then selecting the template type. When you are ready to create the next similar worksheet, load the template; your formats will already be in place.

Additional Formatting Options

Many of Excel 2000's formatting features are identical to Word 2000's, such as bold face, italics, underline, font color, and fill color (the cell's background color). In addition, you now know how to change a selection's alignment. Excel 2000 supports several special formats that go further to improve the look of your worksheets. AutoFormat uses some of these special formats, and you can create your own styles that use these formats as well.

The following sections briefly introduce you to these Excel 2000 formatting options, which provide you with additional ways to add impact to your worksheets. You can change any of these formats from the Format Cells dialog box. Open the Format Cells dialog box by selecting Format, Cells, by changing one of the stored styles as you learned in the preceding section, or by right-clicking a selection and choosing Format Cells.

Special Alignment

Not only can you left-justify, center-justify, and right-justify, as well as justify across selected cells, you can also orient text vertically or to whatever slant you prefer. When you click the Format, Cells Alignment tab, Excel 2000 displays the Alignment dialog box, shown in Figure 12.5, in which you can adjust text orientation.

FIGURE 12.5

Align text with the Format Cells dialog box Alignment page.

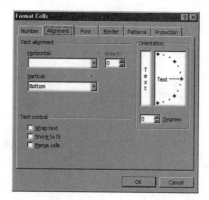

12

STEP-UP

The vertical text orientation in Excel 2000 is easier to adjust than in previous versions because Excel 2000 draws a line to show the text rotation angle as you change the angle.

When you click the Alignment dialog box's first orientation text box (the text box with the word Text dropping down the screen), Excel 2000 changes all selected cells to vertical orientation. If you want to slant text, such as titles, select a different Degree value or click the rotating text pointer to the slant you desire. When you click OK, Excel 2000 rotates the selected text to your chosen angle. Figure 12.6 shows an example of slanted titles produced by selecting a negative 45-degree angle in the Alignment dialog box. The text prints at an angle as well.

FIGURE 12.6

You can change the vertical alignment of selected text.

Slanted text alignment ——

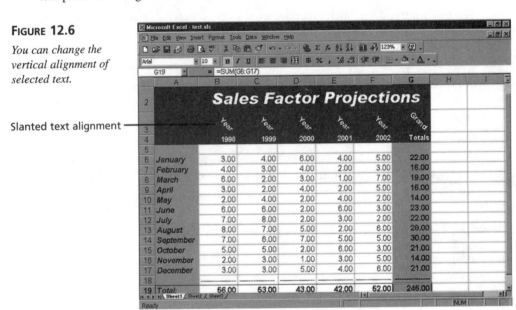

If you need to include a lot of text in one or more cells, you already know (from Hour 8, "Excel 2000 Workbooks") that Excel 2000 either truncates the cell or pours the cell's contents into the next cell to the right. Excel 2000 offers several other options, as well. When a cell requires a lot of text, select the Wrap Text option from the Alignment dialog box. Excel 2000 wraps the text within the cell's width, increasing the cell (and, therefore, row) height to display all the wrapped text. If you click the Shrink to Fit option, Excel 2000 decreases the cell's font size (as much as feasible) to display the entire cell contents within the cell's current width and height. If you click Merge Cells, Excel 2000 combines adjacent cells into a single wide cell.

Special Cell Borders

With the Format, Cells Border dialog box, shown in Figure 12.7, you can apply an outline, or *border*, around selected cells.

FIGURE 12.7

Add borders around cells to highlight key data.

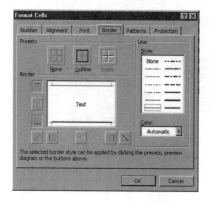

 NEW TERM A *border* is a cell outline that you can apply to enclose selected cells.

The Border dialog box enables you to add a border to any side of the selected cells as well as diagonal lines inside the cells so that you can show a cell x'd out or otherwise cross off a cell's contents for a printed report. As you select among the Outline and Inside options, the preview area shows what the resulting border looks like.

> The Borders toolbar button is quicker to use than the Border dialog box, but you cannot control as many border details.

12

Select Line Style options from the Border dialog box to change the pattern of the border that you choose. If you want to remove any selected cell's border, click None.

Special Cell Shades

The Format, Cells Patterns dialog box enables you to add color or a shading pattern to selected cells. Although the Fill Color toolbar button colors cell backgrounds more quickly than the Patterns dialog box, the Patterns dialog box enables you to add a shading pattern to the background.

When you click the Patterns drop-down box from the Patterns dialog box, Excel 2000 displays pattern options, as shown in Figure 12.8.

FIGURE 12.8

Choose a pattern for the selected cell.

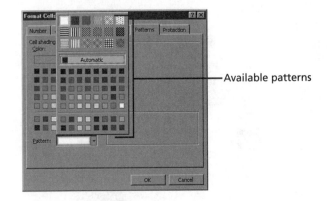

—Available patterns

Locked and Hidden Cells

When you create worksheets for others, you want to lock titles and formulas so that users can enter and change the data areas without harming the worksheet's format. A hidden cell is useful when you want to block a cell's value from showing temporarily.

> The *locked* and *hidden* cell status activates only when you activate worksheet protection by selecting Tools | Protection and selecting one of the protection options.

 A *locked cell* is one whose contents you cannot change if the worksheet is protected.

 A *hidden cell* is one whose contents you cannot see if the worksheet is protected.

The Format, Cells Protection dialog box controls the locked and hidden status of selected cells. You can enable and disable locking as well as control the hidden status by clicking the appropriate Protection dialog box options. Excel 2000 does not ensure that your users won't deactivate the protection and modify the worksheet. The protection helps protect the worksheet from accidental damage, but anyone can modify the protection status and change locked cells.

Cell locking is great when you want to keep accidental worksheet changes from occurring. If the protection needs to go further than simple safety, add a password when you protect the selection. Only someone with the worksheet's (or workbook's) password can unlock locked cells or show hidden cells. To add a password, select Tools, Protection. You can add a password to the worksheet or to the entire workbook.

Creating Custom Graphs

A picture is worth a thousand words and numbers, and Excel 2000 produces professional-looking graphs from your worksheet data. You don't need to know a lot about graphing and charting unless you want to create extremely sophisticated Excel 2000 graphs. You can use Excel 2000's *Chart Wizard* in most cases to produce great-looking graphs quickly and easily. When you click the Chart Wizard toolbar button, Excel 2000 displays the opening screen of the Chart Wizard dialog box, as shown in Figure 12.9.

 The *Chart Wizard* is an Excel 2000 wizard that displays your worksheet data as a colorful graph.

FIGURE 12.9

Excel 2000's Chart Wizard creates graphs for you.

12

Choosing the Chart Type

Table 12.1 describes each of the chart types that Excel 2000 creates. You can select an appropriate chart type from the Chart Wizard's opening screen. To preview your worksheet when formatted with any chart, select a chart type, and then a chart subtype, and click the button labeled Press and Hold to View Sample. Excel 2000 analyzes your worksheet data and displays a small sketch of the chart you selected.

TABLE 12.1   EXCEL 2000 CHART OPTIONS

Chart type	Description
Column	Shows changes over time and compares values.
Bar	Compares data items.
Line	Shows trends and projections.
Pie	Illustrates the proportional size of items in the same series.
XY (scatter)	Shows relationships of several values in a series.
Area	Emphasizes the magnitude of changes over time.
Doughnut	Illustrates the proportional size of items in multiple series.
Radar	Each category contains an *axis* that radiates from the center of the graph (useful for finding the data series with the most penetration, as needed in market research statistical studies).
Surface	Locates optimum combinations between two data series.
Bubble	Shows relationships between several series values, but also (with circles, or bubbles of varying sizes) shows the magnitude of data intersections.
Stock	Illustrates a stock's (or other investment's) high, low, and closing prices.
Cone, Cylinder, Pyramid	Indicates trends and comparisons with special 3D cone, cylinder, and pyramid symbols.

NEW TERM   An *axis* is a graph edge that bisects the chart at right angles and indicates the data values in the chart, such as time or dollar amounts.

> If you are new to graphing, you may not know which graph works best for a particular worksheet. Try one! If you see that a bar graph does not show a trend that you want to demonstrate, generate a line graph. Excel 2000 makes it easy to select from among several graphs to find the best graph for your needs.

Selecting Data for Your Graph

A *data series* is a single group of data that you might select from a column or row to graph. Unlike a range, a data series must be contiguous in the row or column with no cells in between. Often, a series is comprised of a time period, such as a week, month, or year. One person's weekly sales totals (from a group of several salespersons' weekly totals) would also form a series. Some graphs, such as pie charts, graph only a single series, whereas other graphs show comparisons between two or more data series.

NEW TERM A *data series* is a single column, row, or set of cell values that you group together, such as a given region's sales for a week, month, year, or a single salesperson.

As you look through the graph samples, if one of the series looks extremely large in comparison to the others, Excel 2000 is probably including a total column or row in the graph results. Generally, you want to graph a single series (such as monthly costs) or several series, but not the totals—the totals throw off the data comparisons. Therefore, if you see extreme ranges at the beginning or end of your graph, select only the data areas (not the total cells) from the Chart Wizard's second dialog box, shown in Figure 12.10.

You need to tell the Chart Wizard which direction the data series flow by clicking either Rows or Columns from the Chart Wizard's second dialog box.

FIGURE 12.10

Be sure to select only data areas for your graph.

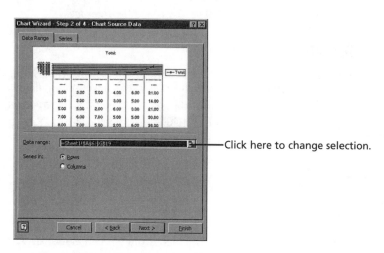

Click here to change selection.

When you click the Next button to see the third Chart Wizard dialog box, shown in Figure 12.11, Excel 2000 enables you to enter a chart title that appears at the top of the resulting chart as well as axis titles that appear on each edge of your chart.

FIGURE 12.11

Enter titles that you want to see on the chart.

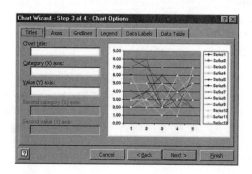

12

You find other tabs in the Chart Wizard's third dialog box that enable you to control the placement of the *legend* and a *data table*.

 A *legend* describes how the chart's patterns and colors represent the information in the graph.

 A *data table* is a miniature summarized worksheet that appears beneath the graph. The table shows numerically what the graph represents graphically.

Click Next to see the final Chart Wizard dialog box, in which you determine exactly where and how to place the generated graph. Excel 2000 can create a new worksheet for the graph or embed the graph inside the current worksheet as an embedded object. You can, in turn, embed the object in other Office 2000 products, as you learn in Part VI, "Combining the Office 2000 Products and the Internet."

Modifying the Graph

Click the Finish button to see your resulting graph. If you have chosen to embed the graph inside your current worksheet, you may have to drag the graph's *sizing handles* to expand or shrink the graph. In addition, you can drag the graph anywhere you want it to appear on your worksheet. Excel 2000 displays the floating Graph toolbar right below the graph in case you want to change it.

 Sizing handles are eight black handles that appear around certain objects, such as graphs, with which you can resize the object by dragging.

If your graph does not display data the way you prefer, you can click the Graph toolbar buttons to change the graph's properties. You can even change the graph type (from a line chart to a bar graph, for instance) from the Graph toolbar without rerunning the Chart Wizard. The Graph toolbar ensures that all data selections and titles remain in place when you change your graph. If you need to make more extensive graph changes, rerun the Chart Wizard.

In addition to using the Graph toolbar, you can often change specific parts of your graph by right-clicking the graph. If you point to your chart's title and right-click your mouse, for example, Excel 2000 displays a pop-up menu from which you can choose the title's pattern, font, and alignment.

When you single-click a graph's element, such as the legend or a charted data series, Excel 2000 displays sizing handles so that you can resize the element. If you double-click an element, Excel 2000 displays a dialog box with the element's properties, such as color and shape, so that you can modify the way the element appears on the graph.

Summary

This hour completed your Excel 2000 tutorial! You can now format your worksheets to look any way you want. If you want to let Excel 2000 give formatting a try, select your worksheet data and start Excel 2000's AutoFormat feature. Add color, patterns, shading, and borders to your worksheets.

The Excel 2000 Chart Wizard turns your data into great-looking graphical charts. By working through the Chart Wizard's dialog boxes, you give Excel 2000 all the information needed to generate custom graphs. Graphs can be used to analyze data, compare values, and often show trends faster than the worksheet's details can show.

Now that you have learned how to create great looking worksheets, you may need to share those worksheets with someone (like your employees—or your boss!). Why not use Outlook 2000? The next hour introduces Outlook 2000, Office 2000 Small Business Edition's powerful calendaring, scheduling and email application.

Q&A

Q When would I want to create a style?

A If you find yourself applying the same kinds of format commands on cells quite often, consider giving that set of format commands a style name by using the Format, Style dialog box. After you create a style, you can apply that style by selecting it from the Style dialog box's list.

Q How can I change a locked cell?

A If you lock a cell, your intent is to not allow changes. Locked cells are especially useful when you create worksheets for others to use. By locking the titles and formulas, you ensure that the user can only change data areas. Nevertheless, if you need to edit a locked cell, deactivate the worksheet's protected status. After you edit the cell, activate the protection so that the worksheet is safe from inadvertent changes.

Q I get confused with all the graph terms; how do I know which chart works best for my worksheet?

A Often the best way to find the right chart type is to try a few. Excel 2000's Chart Wizard is so simple and fast that you can generate several chart types before you find just the right one. As you produce more and more charts, you begin to judge better which graphs work best for certain kinds of worksheets.

12

PART IV

Organizing with Outlook 2000

Hour

Hour 13

Outlook 2000 Basics

This hour introduces Outlook 2000, a program that could change the way you organize your life! For several years, software developers have attempted to produce an all-in-one organizing and planning program; however, these programs were separate from other programs. If you used your word processor and needed an address, you had to open a separate organization program, look up the address, and type it into the word processor. Outlook 2000 integrates with the other Office 2000 products, however, and shares a menu interface with Word and Excel.

Outlook 2000 can be addictive because it handles the details of your life so well. Not only is Outlook 2000 a truly interactive planning and scheduling program, but it is also fun to use.

The highlights of this hour include the following:

- What Outlook 2000 is all about
- How Outlook 2000 differs from Outlook Express
- What screen elements Outlook 2000 has
- How to navigate through the Calendar views

- How to schedule meetings and events
- Which tools help you manage tasks
- How to keep notes

An Outlook 2000 Overview

You can use Outlook 2000 to do the following:

- Organize your Calendar
- Schedule meetings
- Keep an appointment book
- Track a prioritized to-do task list
- Record your business and personal contacts
- Keep a journal
- Write notes to yourself that act like yellow sticky notes when you view them (similar to the Excel 2000 comments you learned about during Hour 9, "Using Excel 2000")
- Send and receive all your email and network documents from one location

---

STEP-UP

Microsoft first introduced Outlook in Office 97. For its first version, Outlook 97 contained a rich feature set but had some problems common in many first software versions, such as its slow startup and long program-termination speed. With the improved Office 2000, you will be happy to find that the program is more efficient, contains more features, and improves the way they work.

 Do not confuse Outlook 2000 with Outlook Express. Outlook Express is an add-on program that comes with Internet Explorer 4, Internet Explorer 5, and Windows 98. If you have upgraded to Internet Explorer 4 or 5, you also have Outlook Express. Outlook Express is a slimmed-down version of Outlook 2000. Outlook Express supports only email, a more limited contact *database* called the Windows Address Book, and a handful of other Internet-related features. Outlook Express does not replace Outlook 2000, so feel free to use Outlook 2000 rather than Outlook Express for your contact information.

A *database* is a collection of related information, such as the name and address information that you can store in Outlook 2000.

Starting Outlook 2000

Start Outlook 2000 by performing one of the following tasks:

- Click one of several Outlook 2000-related buttons on the Office 2000 Shortcut bar. The New Message button sends email, the New Appointment button creates a new appointment, the New Task button enters a new task in the scheduled task area, the New Contact button creates a new contact in your contact database, and the New Note button opens a new note to which you can add text.

- Use the Windows Start menu to start Outlook 2000 by selecting Microsoft Outlook 2000 from the Programs menu.

- Click the Windows taskbar's Outlook button. (Depending on your desktop settings, you may not see the Outlook button located in the Quick Launch toolbar.)

- Click the Office 2000 Shortcut bar's Microsoft Outlook button to start Outlook 2000. (Depending on your Office 2000 Shortcut bar's setup, you may not see the Outlook button.)

Figure 13.1 shows the opening Outlook 2000 screen. Your screen might differ slightly depending on the options that you chose during installation. The opening Outlook 2000 screen shows the Outlook Today view, an overview of messages, to-do tasks, and appointments for the current time period.

FIGURE 13.1

Outlook 2000's Outlook Today opening screen summarizes your current activities and messages.

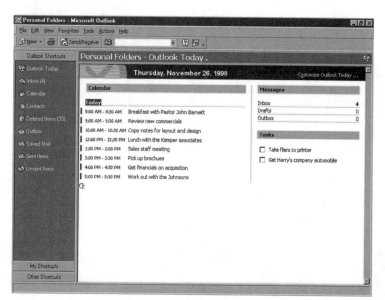

13

STEP-UP

Outlook 97 did not offer the Today view, the all-in-one summary screen. To locate your appointments, read email messages, and check to-do tasks, you had to navigate to different parts of the program.

Depending on your Outlook 2000 configuration, Outlook 2000 may open to a different screen, such as the Calendar view shown in Figure 13.2. Outlook 2000's program areas appear in different window formats. The formats correspond to folders in Outlook 2000 that appear in the left-hand Shortcut bar. Here are the folders that you can set to appear upon startup:

- *Outlook Today*. The at-a-glance overview of your current activities, as shown in Figure 13.1.
- *Inbox*. A collection of your email messages, organized in topic folders that you set up, or contained in the default Inbox folder.
- *Calendar*. The scheduling screen where you can track appointments, as shown in Figure 13.2.
- *Contacts*. A card catalog of contact name and address information.
- *Tasks*. Items you have to prioritize and complete.
- *Journal*. A log of activities you perform on the computer.
- *Notes*. Notes on any topic that you want to organize.

All of Outlook 2000's data falls within one of these folder-based formats. As you progress through the rest of this and the next hour's lesson, you will master the use of these folders and their contents.

FIGURE 13.2

Outlook 2000 might open in the Calendar folder, showing you the contents of your Calendar folder.

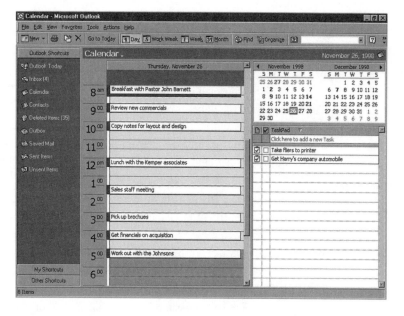

 You can change the first folder that appears by selecting Tools, Options, clicking the Other tab, and then clicking the Advanced Options button. The Startup in This Folder drop-down box determines the folder that appears when you first start Outlook 2000.

 Not only can you specify folders to view, but you can also specify views that are different configurations of screens with Outlook 2000 data. You can customize views so that your Outlook 2000 screens look any way you want them to look.

13

The Outlook 2000 screen's format differs quite a bit from that of other Office 2000 products. You won't see the typical toolbars. The following screen descriptions appear on Outlook 2000's Inbox folder view (see Figure 13.3) and elsewhere throughout Outlook 2000's screens:

- *Outlook Bar*. Contains shortcuts to some of the Outlook 2000 features. You can rearrange the Outlook Bar contents and resize its icons. The Outlook Bar enables you to access all of Outlook 2000's most frequently used areas, called *groups*. Click the group names, such as My Shortcuts, to view additional groups.

NEW TERM A *group* is an area on the Outlook Bar that separates one set of related folders from others.

- *Folder list.* Displays your Outlook 2000 data in folders, such as those described earlier in this section. Many folders exist, in addition to those described earlier, and you can create your own new folders to organize data as well. As you use Outlook 2000, you subdivide your work into the folders. Your Inbox and Outbox mail appears in folders within their respective folders in the Folder list, for example. If a number appears in parentheses after a folder name, the number represents the number of unread items in that folder. If you receive three new email messages, for example, (3) appears after the Inbox folder name.

- *Information viewer.* Displays items from the selected folder. As you work with items, both the Information viewer's format and content changes. When you look over your daily incoming mail, for example, the Information viewer displays summaries of your mail. When you want to read something specific, you can display the entire item in the Information viewer and hide the summaries. The Information viewer contains the Preview pane when you view the contents of your Inbox folder.

- *Preview pane.* Shows the selected item's contents, assuming you've displayed the Preview pane from the View menu.

- *Items.* Contains the folder contents such as contacts, appointments, and email messages.

If you don't see the Folder list, select View, Folder List. You can select the option once again to hide the Folder list if you decide you want more room for the items within the Information viewer window.

Toolbar   Items

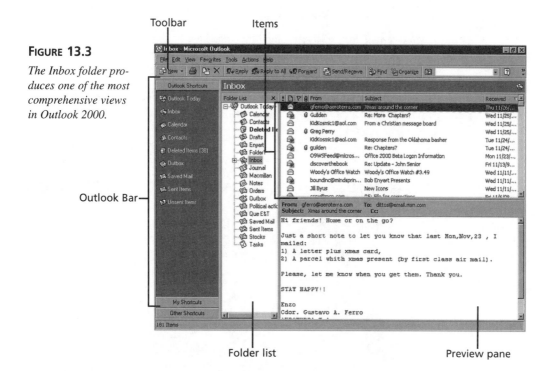

FIGURE 13.3

The Inbox folder pro-duces one of the most comprehensive views in Outlook 2000.

Outlook Bar

Folder list   Preview pane

Using the Calendar in Outlook 2000

Outlook 2000 includes a Calendar that not only enables you to organize and track dates, but also enables you to track birthdays and anniversaries (and gives you automatic time-for-gift reminders), find open dates, keep a task list, and schedule meetings. It can also remind you of appointments. The following sections show you how to use the Outlook 2000 Calendar to organize your life.

Not only does Outlook 2000 remind you of specific appointments with an audible and visible reminder, but Outlook 2000 easily sets up recurring appointments, such as weekly sales meetings or birthday reminders.

13

When you are ready to work with Outlook 2000's Calendar, display the Calendar by clicking the Calendar icon on the Outlook Bar at the left of the screen, selecting Calendar from the Folder list, or by selecting Go, Calendar. To display more of your Calendar, you can decrease the amount of screen space devoted to the Outlook Bar and Folder list by dragging their edges toward the left side of the screen.

You can adjust the screen columns to show more of any Outlook 2000 feature. Most Outlook 2000 users prefer to hide the Folder list, displaying it only when needed by selecting View, Folder List. Figure 13.4 shows the Outlook 2000 screen with the Calendar activated once again. Notice the Folder list is hidden to give more room to the appointments in the Calendar.

Schedule pane   Monthly Date
                                 navigator pane

FIGURE 13.4

Working with the Calendar.

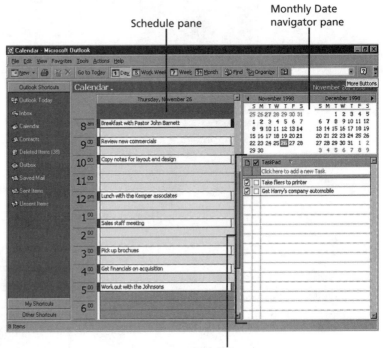

Task list pane

Navigating Times and Dates

Notice that the Calendar appears with these major sections:

- Monthly calendar pane (also called the Date navigator)
- Schedule pane
- Task list pane

When you first open Calendar, the monthly calendar (also called the Date navigator) always highlights the current date (getting its information from the computer's internal clock and calendar). The current date is highlighted and the current day's appointments display if you have entered any. The Calendar might show two months or just one, depending on your screen settings. You can navigate the Calendar through days and months by following these simple guidelines:

- Change days by pressing the left- or right-arrow keys or by clicking a date with your mouse.
- Change months by clicking to the left or right of the Calendar's month name or by clicking the Calendar's month name and selecting from the pop-up month list that appears.

Click through the Calendar's days and notice that the daily time planner changes days accordingly. Although you may not have any appointments set yet, you quickly see how you can look at any day's appointments by clicking that day's date. The weekend day appointment pages are darkened to remind you that you are looking at Saturday or Sunday. In addition, Outlook 2000 darkens all weekday times before 8:00 a.m. and after 5:00 p.m. The darkened areas are typical nonbusiness hours. Of course, you can enter new appointments into the darkened areas. The darkened highlight is just Outlook 2000's way of letting you know the times are not normal business hours.

You can change the hours that Outlook 2000 designates as business hours by selecting Tools, Options and clicking the Calendar Options button. The Start Time and End Time list boxes hold the business hours that Outlook 2000 maintains. In addition, you can select other days to appear as workweek days in case you normally work on Saturday or Sunday. If you want Outlook 2000 to use a color that differs from the default yellow highlight, you can also select another color.

13

The Calendar also provides a month-at-a-glance format when you click any of the seven day abbreviations above the Calendar's day numbers. (Figure 13.5 shows the month-at-a-glance calendar that appears when you select the entire month.) When you click any of the month's weekday abbreviations in the Date navigator area, Outlook 2000 displays the schedule for the entire month. If you highlight a week in the Date navigator calendar, Outlook 2000 displays the schedule for that week.

Entire month
selected

FIGURE 13.5

*The month-at-a-glance
calendar provides a
long-range overview
of your schedule.*

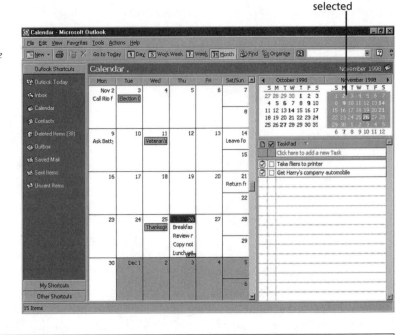

 If you select two or more days, Outlook 2000 displays your selection's at-a-
glance planning calendar.

As you acquaint yourself with Outlook 2000's Calendar, select from the View menu to
customize the screen for your particular needs. In addition, you can drag any bar separating the window panes to provide more or less room to any portion of the Outlook 2000
screen that you need.

Setting Appointments

To schedule an *appointment*, perform these steps:

1. In Day view, select the day on which you want to schedule the appointment by
   clicking it.

2. Select the appointment time. You might have to click the time planner's scrollbar or
   use your up- and down-arrow keys to see the time you want.

3. Double-click the appointment time to display the Appointment dialog box, shown
   in Figure 13.6.

Figure 13.6

*Scheduling an appoint-
ment is easy.*

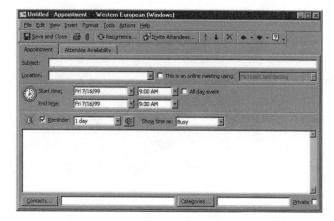

4. Enter the appointment's subject and location. Outlook 2000 keeps track of your locations as you add them, so you don't have to retype them for subsequent appointments. (You need only to select them from the drop-down list.)

5. Set the start and stop times (use Tools, Options and click the Calendar options button to change the default of 30-minute appointments if you often have different appointment lengths) or click the All Day Event option if you want to schedule an all-day appointment.

6. Set your reminder time if you want a reminder. Outlook 2000 audibly and visibly reminds you of the appointment at the time you request.

7. Click the Recurrence toolbar button if the appointment occurs regularly. Outlook 2000 displays the Appointment Recurrence dialog box, shown in Figure 13.7. Set the recurrence options to enable Outlook 2000 to schedule your recurring appointment.

> You could select Actions, New Recurring Appointment to go directly to the Appointment Recurrence dialog box when you set up recurring appointments

13

8. Click OK to close the Appointment Recurrence dialog box.

9. Click the Save and Close button. Outlook 2000 displays your appointment in the time planner.

New Term An *appointment* is an activity for which you reserve time but which does not require other people or resources.

FIGURE 13.7

*Calendar easily
accommodates
appointments that
occur regularly.*

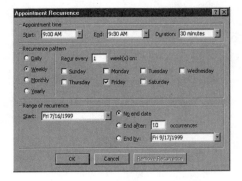

If you don't run Outlook 2000 at all times in the background, it cannot
remind you of pending appointments. Therefore, you should add Outlook
2000 to the Windows Startup folder so that Outlook 2000 starts automatically every time you start up your computer.

If you need to change a set appointment, double-click the appointment to display the
Appointment dialog box, in which you can change the appointment details. Drag
the appointment's top or bottom edges from the time planner to increase or decrease the
appointment's duration. Drag the appointment's side edges to change the appointment's
start time.

Click the New Appointment button on the toolbar to schedule a new
appointment without first selecting the appointment's date and time.

You can remove an appointment at any time by right-clicking over the appointment to
display a pop-up menu and then selecting Delete.

Instead of using the Appointment dialog box to schedule an appointment, you can enter
an appointment quickly by clicking the appointment time once to highlight it and entering the text for the appointment directly on the daily planner. When you press Enter,
Outlook 2000 adds the appointment to the daily planner.

Outlook 2000 reminds you of the appointment with an audible alarm 15 minutes before the appointment. If you want to adjust the alarm lead time or make the alarm recurring, double-click the appointment entry to display the Appointment dialog box.

> You may not want an audible alarm on all appointments. If you use your laptop in meetings and do not want audible alarms interrupting conversations, for example, you can remove any appointment's audible alarm by right-clicking the appointment and selecting Reminder from the pop-up menu. You can select Reminder again from that same menu to set the audible alarm once again.

Scheduling Meetings

In Outlook 2000 terminology, a *meeting* differs somewhat from an appointment. An appointment is for you; it does not involve other resources (such as people and equipment). A meeting, however, requires that you schedule more people than yourself, and perhaps requires that you reserve other resources (such as audio-visual equipment and a room in which to hold the meeting). If you work in a networked environment, Outlook 2000 can scan other people's computer schedules to help you plan meetings that others can attend.

New Term A *meeting* is an appointment that involves other people and resources.

Follow these steps to schedule a meeting:

1. Create an appointment for the meeting's day and time.
2. Click the Attendee Availability tab in the Appointment dialog box. (Figure 13.8 shows the dialog box that appears.)
3. Click the Invite Others button and type (or select from the name list) the names of those attending. The list might include people or resources, such as podiums. Outlook 2000 gets the names from your Contacts folder, but you can enter new names as needed.
4. Use the scrollbars to view the free and busy times for the people you invite. You must also select the meeting time. Outlook 2000 shows you the attendees' available free time when you click AutoPick, or you can use your mouse to schedule the attendees even if their free times all conflict. (Outlook 2000 adjusts for time zones if you invite someone from another time zone.)

13

FIGURE 13.8

You can schedule meetings, invite people, and reserve resources.

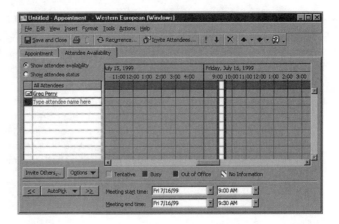

Obviously, you must be organized and know the attendees quite well to have access to their schedules. Outlook 2000 will search your network for the contacts and their free times. If you are not on a network, you do not have access to the free times of the people you invite.

Click the Appointment tab to complete the dialog box. When you click Send, all recipients (if networked or available by email) get invited to your meeting by being sent the notes you entered on the Attendee Availability page.

Scheduling Events

An *event* is an activity not specifically tied to a time frame, such as a holiday or birthday. When you want to record an event, such as your boss's birthday, perform these steps:

1. Select Actions, New All Day Event. The Event dialog box appears (looking very much like the Appointment dialog box) with the tabbed Appointment page displayed.

2. Schedule the event as you do an appointment, but click the All Day Event check box to show that the event lasts the entire day (otherwise, the event automatically turns into an appointment).

3. Select the Show Time As option if you want your Calendar to show the time as Busy or Out of Office time.

4. Select an appropriate reminder time from the Reminder list, such as two days, to receive an audible alarm and note reminding you of the event so that you can purchase gifts or prepare for the event in some other way.

5. Click the Save and Close button to return to Calendar.

NEW TERM An *event* is a 24-hour activity, such as a birthday or holiday.

If the event is recurring, you can select Actions, New Recurring Appointment to initiate a new recurring event. When you view the event, Outlook 2000 shows it in a banner (a highlighted heading) for that day in the day planner's views.

NEW TERM A *banner* is a highlighted title that signals and describes a day's event.

Managing a Task List

A task is any job that you need to track, perform, and monitor to completion. Outlook 2000 tasks (like appointments and meetings) might be recurring, or they might happen only once. You can manage your Outlook 2000 task list either from the Tasks folder in the Folder list or from the Calendar folder.

NEW TERM A *task* is any job that you need to track, perform, and monitor to completion.

> Unlike appointments, meetings, and events, tasks don't belong to any specific date or time. Tasks are jobs you need to finish but are not linked to a date or time.

To create a one-time task, perform these steps:

1. Click the New Task toolbar button or select File, New, Task. You can create a task even faster by clicking the task list's entry labeled Click Here to Add a Task.

2. Enter a task description.

3. Type the due date (the date you must complete the task, but not necessarily the day you perform the task). If you click the Due Date drop-down list, you can select from a calendar that Outlook 2000 displays. You can enter virtually any date in virtually any format, including Next Wednesday. Outlook 2000 converts your format to a supported date format.

4. Further refine your task (if you need to) by double-clicking the task to display the Task dialog box, shown in Figure 13.9. You can specify recurring tasks and assign priority. Click the Details tab to update the status of the task as you work on it. The Details page even tracks such task-related information as mileage, time involved, and billing information.

5. Click Save and Close to finalize the task.

13

FIGURE 13.9

You can modify the task's specifics and status.

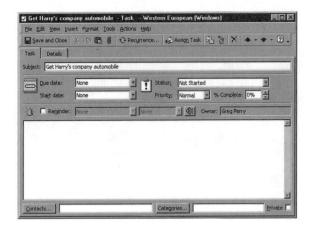

After you complete a task, click the task's check box to cross the task from the list. Delete a task by selecting it and clicking the toolbar's Delete button.

If you want to remind yourself of a task's deadline, make an appointment for the deadline on the task's due date. Set the alarm for 24 hours or 2 days. When the deadline draws near, you are reminded that the task should be nearing completion.

Writing Yourself Notes

Outlook 2000 notes are equivalent to yellow sticky notes. You can post a note inside Outlook 2000 and retrieve, edit, or delete the note later.

To see your notes, click the Notes icon on the Outlook Bar or display the Notes item from the Folder list. Double-click any note to see its contents.

To create a new note, click the New Note toolbar button to display a yellow-note window. Type your note and click the note's Close button to close the note. Resize the note by dragging its lower-right corner. Outlook 2000 tracks the note's date and time. Change the note's font by selecting a new font from the Tools, Options dialog box page and clicking the Note Options button. You can quickly select a different note color by right-clicking the note's icon when you see it in Outlook 2000.

Turn notes into appointments and tasks! Drag a note from the Notes work area to the Calendar or Tasks Outlook Bar icons. Outlook 2000 will open an appropriate dialog box with the note's contents, filling in the task or appointment's description. In the next hour, "Communicating with Outlook 2000," you learn how to work with Outlook 2000's email and journal components—you can drag notes to those Outlook 2000 programs as well.

Quitting Outlook 2000

You can quit Outlook 2000 by performing any of the following:

- Selecting File, Exit
- Pressing Alt+F4
- Double-clicking the Control icon
- Clicking Outlook 2000's Close button

Always quit Outlook 2000 and shut down Windows before turning off your computer; otherwise, you might lose your work. If an email message is in the middle of a transfer and you don't properly exit Outlook 2000, for example, you could lose some or all of that message.

Summary

This hour introduced Outlook 2000 and explained some of the ways you can use Outlook 2000 to check your Calendar; manage appointments, meetings, and events; track tasks; keep notes; and explore your computer. If you have used any other personal-information management program, you will really like the integration of Outlook 2000 into the Office 2000 and Windows environment.

13

The next hour shows you how to use the Contact List to find your associates quickly and easily. Additionally, the Journal tracks events as they happen, including incoming mail and faxes that you receive inside the Inbox.

Q&A

Q How can I assign a task to a specific day?

A You cannot assign tasks to days. Tasks transcend days because tasks are one-time or recurring items that you must accomplish within a certain time frame, but not on a particular day. Perhaps you are only confusing Outlook 2000 terminology. If you want to assign a particular event to a time and day, assign an appointment or meeting. Tasks are items that you must accomplish and that you can track and assign to other people, but tasks are not tied to a specific time and date.

Q After I set a reminder, how does Outlook 2000 inform me of the appointment, meeting, or event?

A You must continually run Outlook 2000 during your computing sessions for Outlook 2000 to monitor and remind you of things you have to do. Outlook 2000 is one program that you probably want to add to your Windows StartUp group so that it always starts when you start Windows. Outlook 2000 cannot remind you of pending appointments if you are not running it.

Outlook 2000 tracks incoming and outgoing events. Also, as you learn in the next hour, Outlook 2000 monitors your electronic mail, faxes, and network transfers, and keeps an eye on your reminders to let you know when something is due. The only way Outlook 2000 can perform these tasks is to keep it running during your work sessions.

HOUR **14**

Communicating with Outlook 2000

This hour concludes coverage of Outlook 2000 by showing you how to use the Journal, Contacts list, Inbox, and Outbox. The Inbox and Outbox components are central to using Outlook 2000 as a repository for your entire data throughput; these mailboxes constitute your computer's Grand Central Station. One of the most common tasks performed on the PC is the exchange of email, and Outlook 2000 makes that exchange simple.

Part of the effectiveness of Outlook 2000 hinges on how well you keep your Contacts list organized. Use Outlook 2000 to keep track of clients, friends, employees, and anyone else you contact. Outlook 2000 tracks not only routine name and address information, but email addresses as well. After you set up your Contacts list, other Outlook 2000 programs (such as the Inbox) refer to the list when an address is needed. You learned in the preceding hour how to use Outlook 2000 to schedule meetings, and you can easily schedule those meetings with the contacts you record.

The highlights of this hour include the following:

- What a contact is
- How to maximize your use of the Outlook 2000 Contacts database
- When the Journal tracks items automatically
- How to enter items manually into the Journal
- How to send and receive messages
- When to use the Outlook 2000 Deleted Items folder
- How to read and reply to messages

Keeping Contacts

The Outlook 2000 Contacts database keeps track of your *contacts* so that Outlook 2000 has a central, uniform repository of information to use when you send email, hold meetings, and record calls. You can add new contacts, delete old ones you no longer need, and change a contact's information from the Contacts folder. The Contacts folder maintains name, title, address, phone, and email information on your contacts, and it offers fields that you can use for additional information, such as notes, family information, and more. In addition to the recording of contact information, Outlook 2000 uses a smart name and address formatter to help ensure that your names and addresses are uniform for more accurate searching.

 A *contact* is a person or organization that you correspond with, either by mail, email, phone, or in person.

Recording Contacts

When you first use Outlook 2000, you have no contacts entered in the Contacts folder except for a sample contact that you can click to highlight and press Delete to remove. To record a new contact, perform these steps:

1. Click Contacts on the Outlook Bar, select Go, Contacts, or select Contacts from your Folder list if you have chosen to display the Folder list.
2. Click the New Contact toolbar button on the Contacts screen to open the Contact dialog box (shown in Figure 14.1).

FIGURE 14.1

Outlook 2000 formats the entry of contact data for you.

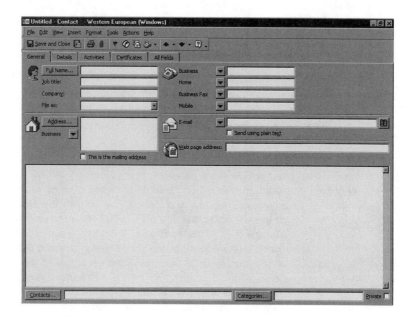

3. Type the contact's full name. If you click the Full Name button, Outlook 2000 displays the Check Full Name dialog box, shown in Figure 14.2, to maintain separate fields for each part of the name (such as title, first name, and last name). The time you take to separate parts of names pays off if you use your contact information in form letters and database work.

Outlook 2000 automatically displays the Check Full Name dialog box if you enter a name that does not follow a typical name pattern. (Outlook 2000 displays this dialog box automatically until you uncheck the option at the bottom of the box.) If you enter only one word for a name, for example, Outlook 2000 displays the Check Full Name dialog box so that you can specify whether the word is the first or last name.

FIGURE 14.2

The Check Full Name dialog box ensures that your names are entered properly.

14

4. Enter the rest of the contact's information. Click the Address button to track separate parts of the contact's address using a Check Address dialog box similar to the Check Full Name dialog box. Click the Address drop-down list to record separate addresses for the same contact. You can record a business, a home, or another address, for example, by clicking the appropriate Address drop-down type before entering the address. Open the phone number drop-down lists as well to store different kinds of phone numbers for your contacts.

Notice how many phone number fields Outlook 2000 gives you to use. Although you see only four on the form, a phone number field for Business, Home, Business Fax, and Mobile, you can click the down arrow inside each of these fields to display a list box full of additional numbers such as Business 2, TTY/TDD, and Pager. Today's communication needs often require multiple phone numbers for the same contact, and Outlook 2000 provides all the number fields that you might need. Any of the list boxes on the Contact form drop down to provide additional choices. You can enter multiple addresses and email accounts for each contact, for example, although only one physical address and one email address show at any one time.

5. After you enter the phone numbers and email addresses, you can enter a Web page site address in case you want to record the contact's Web page or the contact's company Web page.

6. The large text box toward the bottom of the New Contact window holds any notes you want to keep for this contact.

7. Click the Details tab to record other information, such as a spouse name, with the contact. The other tabs are for advanced purposes such as keeping digitally signed security IDs, and the All Fields tab enables advanced users to rearrange the fields on a contact's form. For most Outlook 2000 users, the General and Details tabbed pages are more than adequate to hold the information a contact requires.

8. Click the Save and Close buttons to save the contact information and display a blank dialog box for your next contact.

The contact's data page acts like an Internet Web page browser as well as a repository for contact data. If a contact has a Web page, enter that Web page's address in the Web Page field. When you return to the contact information and click the toolbar's Explore Web Page button, Outlook 2000 locates and displays the contact's Web page using whatever Web browser (such as Internet Explorer) is installed on your system.

Be on the lookout for shortcuts as you work with Outlook 2000. Generally, you can drag and drop information instead of re-entering data when you need to transport information from one Outlook 2000 area to another. You don't even have to type in all of a client's contact information if you have that information elsewhere in Outlook 2000. Suppose, for example, that you wrote yourself a quick note with a new client's name and phone number using Outlook 2000's notes. (You learned how to take notes with Outlook 2000 in the preceding hour.) You can transfer the client's information from the note to your Contacts list by dragging the note to the Contacts icon on the Outlook Bar. Outlook 2000 sets up the initial client name and number information, to which you then can add more information. Conversely, you can drag a contact to a note to place that contact information on the note.

When you close the Contacts dialog box, your first contact appears in the Address Book. As you add more entries, your Contacts list grows, as shown in Figure 14.3. After you build a collection of contacts, you can click the alphabetic tabs to the right of the Address Book to locate specific contacts.

FIGURE 14.3

Your contacts appear in Outlook 2000's Address Book.

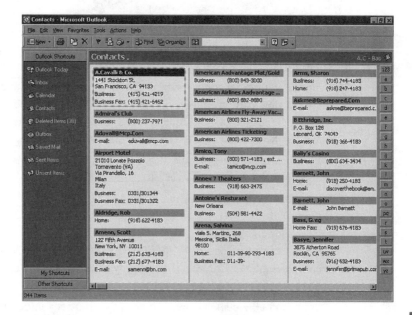

Selecting Contacts

To select a contact, display the contact name in the Address Book. After you select a contact, you can do the following things:

14

- Directly edit the addresses, phone numbers, and email addresses displayed on the page by clicking the appropriate fields.

- Double-click the name to open the Contact dialog box, which displays the contact information, enabling you to edit or view more detail.

- Right-click the contact name, select Call Contact, and dial the contact's phone number from the New Call dialog box (shown in Figure 14.4). If you click the Journal option, Outlook 2000 adds the call to this contact's Journal; the Journal records the call! Use the Journal to track calls such as payment requests so that you have a record of who you called and when you placed the call. The next section explains all about the Journal feature.

FIGURE 14.4

Outlook 2000 automatically dials your selected contact.

- Right-click the contact name and click the Explore Web Page button to see the contact's Web page from within your Web browser.

- Drag the column separators right or left to see more or less of each column. If you prefer to view narrow columns in the Contact folder, you see more contacts but not the full Phone Number and Address field. If you widen the columns, you see more detail for the contacts (but fewer of them at a time).

- Right-click the contact name and select New Message to Contact to write and send an email message to the contact's first email address.

- Right-click the contact name and select the New Contact from Same Company option. Outlook 2000 creates a new contact entry and transfers all the business-related addresses and phone numbers to the new contact. You need only fill in the new contact's name and other specifics. Likewise, Outlook 2000 enables you to create an employee Contacts list easily by transferring similar company data to each new employee you enter.

- After you double-click a contact to open that contact's information window, you can click the toolbar's Display Map of Address button (also available from the Actions menu) to see a graphic map of the contact's general address. Outlook 2000 goes to the Web (assuming that you have Internet access) and locates the contact's address on a Microsoft Expedia Web map and shows that location, such as the one shown in Figure 14.5. Not only does the map pinpoint the address, it also includes links to Web sites related to that area of the country.

FIGURE 14.5

View a map where your contact resides.

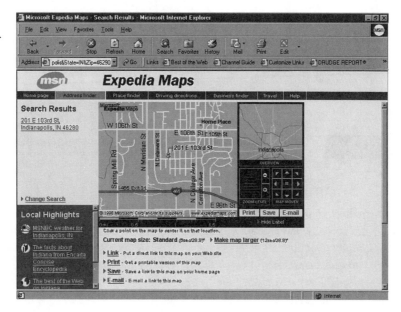

As you get acquainted with Outlook 2000, you will learn more features that will streamline your work. The Organize toolbar button, for example, enables you to view your contacts in a variety of ways, even in a spread-sheet-like format to see more contacts at one time. In Hour 18, "Office 2000's Synergy," you will learn how to write a contact a pre-addressed letter quickly and easily from the Contacts folder.

Keeping a Journal

The Outlook 2000 *Journal* keeps track of all your interactions with contacts, Outlook 2000 items, and activities. Although you can make manual entries, the real power of the Journal appears when you automate Outlook 2000 to record the following types of Journal entries:

- Track and record all items (such as email) that you send to and receive from contacts. Depending on the option you selected when you set up a contact, the Journal can automatically record all interactions with that contact, or you can record interactions selectively.

- Keep track of all Office 2000 documents that you create or edit. Browse the Journal to find a summary of the documents you created and the order in which you created (and edited) them.

14

- Track all meetings automatically.

- Track all appointments and tasks manually. (Outlook 2000 does not track appointments and tasks automatically; you must enter them yourself every time you add an appointment or task.)

- Manually record any activity in your Outlook 2000 Journal, including conversations around the water cooler.

 The Outlook 2000 *Journal* keeps track of all your interactions with contacts, Outlook 2000 items, and activities.

Setting Automatic Journal Entries

Have you ever wished that you had recorded a complaint call you made when you received a bad product or poor service? Let Outlook 2000 track all your calls automatically! The Journal records times, dates, and people you called. As you use Outlook 2000 to make calls, record notes about the calls and track those notes in your Outlook 2000 Journal. After you open the Journal by clicking the Journal icon on the Outlook Bar or selecting Journal from the Folder list, you see a blank Journal entry such as the one shown in Figure 14.6. (Beneath the Journal's date line reside several collapsed Journal entries that you can expand to see details.)

FIGURE 14.6

Your Journal is ready for entries.

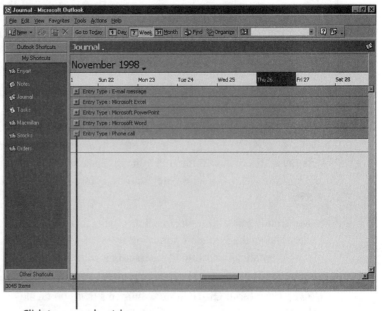

Click to expand entries

The first thing you want to do with your Journal is to designate all items that you want the Journal to track. Select Tools, Options and click the Journal Options button. Select each item from the list that you want Outlook 2000 to track. Select E-mail message, Fax, Meeting request, and Meeting response if those are the items you want the Journal to track automatically. In addition, select one or more contacts from the Contacts list, and Outlook 2000 records all activity for those specific contacts.

If you want Outlook 2000 to track document files from another program, such as Word 2000, just select that program from the list. Outlook 2000 tracks all Office 2000 document activity (if you select this option) as well as other Office 2000-aware software documents and data files. (Note that not all Windows programs are Office 2000-aware.)

Adding Journal Entries Manually

As mentioned earlier in this section, the Journal cannot automatically record all activities in your life; however, you can add manual entries for any activities you want recorded. If you want to record an appointment, open that appointment (from within the Calendar). If you want to record an item not related to Outlook 2000, such as a conversation, create a note for that item (see Hour 13, "Outlook 2000 Basics," for help with the note feature) and transport the information from the note to the Journal.

To record a manual Journal entry from an existing item (such as a new contact you just entered), perform these steps:

1. Double-click the item you want to record to display the Edit dialog box for the item.

2. Select the item's Actions, New Journal Entry option. The Journal now contains an icon that represents the item, such as a phone call to the contact. Double-click the Journal's icon to display the item's details.

Suppose that you wrote a letter to your phone company, for example, and you want to record the complete document in your Journal. If you have set up your Journal to track all Word 2000 documents automatically, the document appears in your Journal. If you have not set up the Journal to track Word 2000 documents automatically, however, just display the document's icon in the My Computer window on the Outlook Bar and drag the document to the Journal icon on the Outlook Bar.

You also can add a new Journal entry of any item type before you create the item. Display your Journal and select File, New. Select Journal Entry to display the Journal Entry dialog box (shown in Figure 14.7). Type a subject and select the type of Journal entry. When you click the Save and Close button, Outlook 2000 saves your entry in the Journal.

14

FIGURE 14.7

Manually enter a new Journal entry.

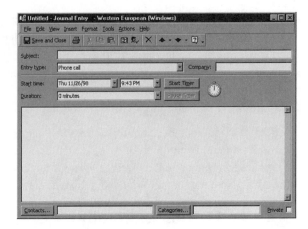

Reviewing Journal Entries

After you set up the automatic recording, Outlook 2000 begins logging those activities. When you open the Journal for days during which some activity occurred (automatically or manually recorded), you see the Journal entry. Suppose that you want to work on files you created a few weeks ago during an end-of-month accounting close period. Open your Journal and scroll back to the date of the close. You see a list of all files that you worked on, whether those files are email messages you sent or received, notes, Word 2000 documents, or Excel 2000 worksheets.

Outlook 2000 compacts entries within the same application. Instead of seeing every Word 2000 document that you worked on this week, for example, you see a band labeled, Entry Type: Microsoft Word. Click the plus sign (+) on the band to expand the entries and see the individual Journal entries recorded for each Word 2000 file you worked on. Double-click any of the files you see to open that file. If you double-click a Word 2000 document, Word 2000 is activated and loads that document. If you double-click a contact you entered, Outlook 2000 displays that contact information.

Periodically, delete older entries from your Journal that you no longer need. The Journal entries add up quickly. When you delete a Journal entry, the files the Journal entry describes are not deleted, only their entries in the Journal are.

Mastering Outlook 2000 Mail

The Outlook Bar displays the following labeled icons:

- *Inbox*. Holds incoming email and faxes.
- *Sent Items*. Displays mail items you have sent to others.
- *Outbox*. Holds items you have queued up to send.
- *Deleted Items*. Holds items, such as email messages, that you have deleted but not removed from Outlook 2000. Select Tools, Empty Deleted Items Folder to remove the Deleted Items folder contents.

> When you remove an item from the Deleted Items folder, Outlook 2000 does not send the item to the Windows Recycle Bin; Outlook 2000 deletes the item completely from your system.

New Term The *Inbox folder* holds messages that you have received.

New Term The *Outbox folder* holds all your outgoing messages until you send them.

New Term The *Deleted Items folder* holds items you have deleted from Outlook 2000 but not completely erased from the disk. The Deleted Items folder is to Outlook 2000 what the Recycle Bin is to Windows 95.

If you want to save messages from your Inbox, move them to a different location. You can also right-click the message to move it to any folder, even a folder not currently listed on the Outlook Bar. You can select and drag any message from the Inbox to another folder on the Outlook Bar. If you change your mind about getting rid of a message stored in your Deleted Items folder, you can move that message to a different folder. Only when you delete a message from within the Items folder is that message completely deleted.

Creating and Sending Messages

One task you probably perform quite often is sending a message to a recipient across the Internet. To create a message, perform these steps:

1. Select File, New, Mail Message to display the Message dialog box (shown in Figure 14.8). (You can also click the New Mail Message toolbar button to open the Message dialog box more quickly than selecting from the File menu.)

14

2. Enter the recipient's name in the To (your primary recipient) field. If you enter a name in the CC (carbon copy) field, Outlook Express sends a copy to that recipient and places a CC before the name. Click these buttons if you want to select a contact in your Contacts list (highly recommended because your Contacts list holds email addresses). If you have not entered the recipient in your Contacts list, add the information now, and then close the Contacts list to return to the mail message.

   If you want to send the same message to multiple recipients, select multiple recipients from the Select Names dialog box when you click the To button to see a list of contacts. If you want to enter email addresses directly in the To field, you can separate multiple addresses with a semicolon (;).

3. Enter the message subject. Your recipient sees the subject in the list of messages that he receives.

Always enter a subject for your email messages so that your recipient knows at a glance what your message is about. This also makes it easier for you to track sent messages.

4. Type your message in the large message area at the bottom of the Message dialog box. To spell check your message, type your message, click your cursor at the beginning of the message and then select Tools, Spelling. You can activate automatic spell checking (so that Outlook 2000 checks your spelling as you type) by selecting the appropriate option in the Options dialog box's Spelling page.

5. Click the Options tab to select certain message options (such as the message importance level and a delivery date). The recipient, like you, can order received mail by importance level when reading through the messages.

6. Click the Send button. Outlook 2000 sends the message to your folder named Outbox. If you are logged on to the Internet, Outlook 2000 sends your message immediately.

7. Select Tools, Send and Receive to send your Outbox messages. If you are logged on to the Internet when you click the Send button in step 6, Outlook 2000 finishes sending your mail and also collects any incoming messages waiting for you. If you are not logged on to the Internet, Outlook displays the Logon dialog box. Always check your Inbox for mail after sending mail from the Outbox using Tools, Send and Receive in case new mail was delivered to you.

FIGURE 14.8

Enter the message you want to send.

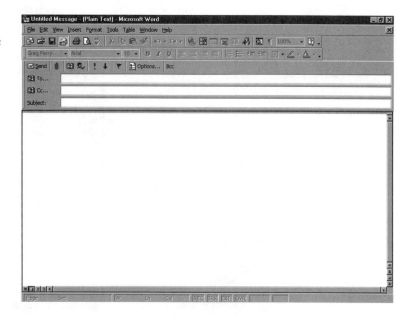

Not all messages are text-only, and Outlook 2000 works with all file types. To attach another document file to your message, such as a Word 2000 or Excel 2000 document, click the Insert File toolbar button and select a document file from the Open dialog box that appears. The file that you attach follows any text that you typed.

Checking Mail

Regularly, you need to check your Inbox folder to see what items await you. As mentioned in step 7 of the preceding section, you must select Tools, Send and Receive to send Outbox items and receive Inbox folder items. Outlook 2000 logs you on to your Internet provider if needed. Your Inbox folder on the Outlook Bar displays a number if you have unread messages that require your attention.

If you use multiple email accounts, select the Tools, Send and Receive option and select the email account that you want to check. You might use Microsoft Network at home and a local Internet provider at work, for example. You can set up both accounts on your home and office computer and select which account's email to retrieve when you select the Tools, Send and Receive option. To add a new email account to Outlook 2000, select Tools, Accounts, Add and select the appropriate account. You may need to contact your Internet service provider to set up the appropriate properties to work with Outlook 2000 after you add an account.

14

If you find that Outlook 2000 logs you off your Internet service provider after you retrieve your email, but you often want to remain logged on to check the Web, you can request that Outlook 2000 stay logged on. Select Tools, Account and select your Internet account. Click the Properties button and uncheck the Disconnect After Transferring Mail from Remote Mail option.

When you display your Inbox folder (by clicking the Inbox icon on the Outlook Bar), you see a list of incoming message headers like the ones shown in Figure 14.9.

FIGURE 14.9

Outlook 2000 gives you a glimpse of each message.

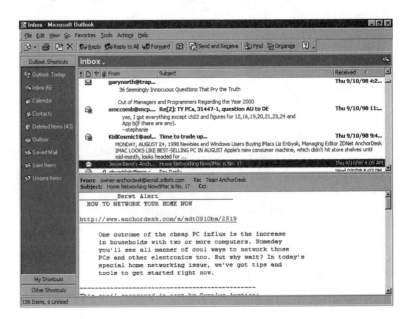

 Outlook 2000 uses icons to let you know what is happening. As you read each message, the message icon changes to show that the message has been read. Revert the read message flag back to an unread state by right-clicking the message and selecting Mark as Unread from the pop-up menu. A paper clip icon appears next to each message that contains an attached file. When you open a message with an attached file, Outlook 2000 shows the attachment as an icon that you can right-click to save or open it.

To read a message, just double-click it. To reply to the sender (in effect, sending a new message to your Outbox folder), click the toolbar's Reply button and enter a reply. You can reply to the sender and all CC recipients of the sender's message by clicking the Reply All toolbar button.

Summary

This hour explained the remaining Outlook 2000 features. You now understand contacts and the importance of entering as much information as you can about them into Outlook 2000. All Office 2000 products use the Contacts list for names and addresses. When you automate your journal, the journal contains all contacts you have elected to track.

One of the busiest Outlook 2000 areas is the messaging Inbox and Outbox folders. Outlook 2000 organizes incoming and outgoing messages and makes it easy for you to respond to messages that you receive.

The next hour, "Power Calendaring," explores the powerful calendar features of Outlook 2000.

Q&A

Q What if I don't have a Web browser?

A You do have a Web browser because Office 2000 comes with one. You might not have Internet access, however. You must sign up with an Internet service provider to use any Internet-based features. Hour 19, "Office 2000 and the Internet," discusses the Internet in more detail.

Q How does a message reply differ from a forwarded message?

A When you reply to a message, you create a brand new message that contains new information about the recipient's original message. If you forward a recipient's message, you send the message exactly as you first read it to another recipient (or to a list of recipients).

Q Why doesn't Outlook 2000 send my messages immediately after I complete them?

A Outlook 2000 does not send messages until you select Tools, Send and Receive (F5 is the shortcut key) unless you are already logged on to your Internet account. If you use the Internet in an office setting with a T1 or satellite connection, you are probably logged on to the Internet most of the time. If you use a modem to access the Internet, however, you have to initiate the logon sequence when you want to check for email.

Dialing and logging on takes time. Instead of logging on to your Internet service provider every time you create an Outbox folder message, Outlook 2000 waits until you request to check for new mail to get your waiting mail and to send your outgoing mail. By waiting, Outlook 2000 only has to log on to the Internet one time to send all your messages.

14

HOUR 15

Power Calendaring

When people meet, they share ideas, someone doesn't understand the ideas, and the process starts over again. Of course, some meeting topics do take hold; if they didn't, we'd still be hanging out in caves.

It is that glimmer of hope that keeps the business world always coming back for more. Today, meetings occur in record numbers. No one wants to make decisions alone. Businesses find group contributions valuable and like to build consensus for important decisions. You can actually get a job as a meeting coordinator whose work description includes arranging meetings, setting up the rooms, getting any audio-visual equipment ready, and ordering bagels.

In most offices, however, there may not be a big enough budget or large enough staff to employ a full-time meeting coordinator, so you have to make do on your own. Calendar can give you a lot of help with meetings, from initial scheduling to inviting the attendees and making your schedule available to others.

The highlights of this hour include the following:

- Setting meetings and sharing calendar information with others
- Creating a recurring meeting

- Publishing your calendar to the Web or intranet
- Working with time zones and printing what you've got

Meeting Basics

You set up a meeting with Outlook 2000 by filling out a form that includes basic meeting details such as attendees requested, the subject of the meeting, the start and projected end times, the location of the meeting, and any other information about the meeting that may be appropriate. The completed form is automatically routed as an invitation to your chosen recipients via Internet or intranet email.

Setting a Meeting

Setting a meeting can be accomplished from either Calendar view or Contacts view, although it may make more sense to set the meeting from Calendar view because you can initially focus on the meeting time in Calendar's appointment grid.

To plan a meeting, follow these steps:

1. On the Outlook 2000 Shortcut Bar click Calendar. Click once on the Appointment grid to select a start time for the meeting. Select Actions, Plan a Meeting to display the Plan a Meeting dialog box, as shown in Figure 15.1.

FIGURE 15.1

You use the Plan a Meeting dialog box to schedule a meeting.

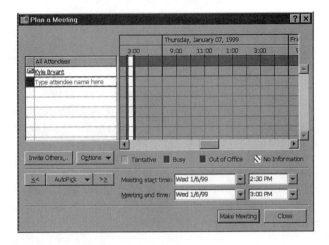

2. Click the Invite Others button.
3. Highlight the desired attendees, and then click the Required button. Click OK to return to the Plan a Meeting dialog box.

4. Click the Make Meeting button to display the Untitled - Meeting form, as shown in Figure 15.2.

FIGURE 15.2

You use this form to fill in specific meeting details.

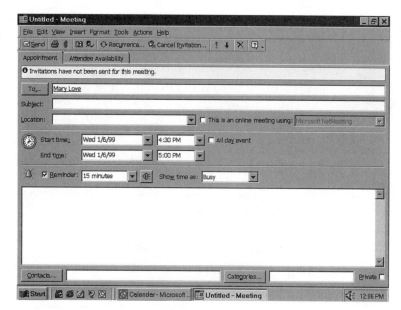

5. Fill out the Subject and Location fields. Adjust the End Time field as appropriate. You can leave the other fields at their default values; however, fill out the free-form text field to advise your attendees of any special requirements.

6. Click the Send button to send the meeting invitation to your designated recipients. The meeting now appears in your Calendar grid.

Changing a Meeting

When scheduling a meeting, sometimes circumstances dictate change. Perhaps someone was inadvertently left off the invitation list, the conference room was flooded, the CEO announced that he will be at your site that particular day, or one of the recipients hates cream cheese. (The list of possibilities is endless.) Here you learn how to adjust a meeting that you have scheduled.

To make changes to a meeting, follow these steps:

1. From your daily calendar, double-click the meeting item in which you need to make changes. The Appointment form for that meeting is displayed.

2. After making modifications, click the Save and Close button. Outlook 2000 prompts you to send the changes to the other invitees.

Sometimes you may discover that more (or fewer) people need to be invited to a meeting, or that your resource needs have changed because you need a larger meeting room. To make these changes, follow these steps:

1. Open the meeting item by double-clicking it.

2. Click the Attendee Availability tab.

3. Click the Invite Others button. After selecting additional attendees or removing them, click OK. Outlook 2000 will then prompt you to re-send the invitations.

Canceling a Meeting

If you want to cancel a meeting, open the meeting item and then choose Actions, Cancel Meeting. You will see the Microsoft Outlook dialog box shown in Figure 15.3. You will typically leave the default option, Send Cancellation and Delete Meeting; however, you should choose the Delete Without Sending a Cancellation option if your prospective attendees already know about the cancellation.

FIGURE 15.3

You should select the type of meeting cancellation desired.

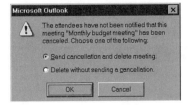

Creating a Meeting from an Appointment

If you have an appointment scheduled, and then you realize that you need to include other associates, Calendar can easily change the appointment to a meeting. Open the appointment by double-clicking it and selecting the Attendee Availability tab. Follow the steps in the section "Setting a Meeting" to set up the meeting time and to invite attendees. After you invite your first attendee, you will notice that the Save and Close button changes to the Send button on the toolbar. After you have listed all attendees, you can click the Send button and notify everyone.

Creating a Meeting from a Contact

As mentioned previously, you can also schedule a meeting from Contacts view. You probably first think about the fact that you need the meeting, then you decide who needs to attend the meeting, and finally, you focus on a meeting time. If this is the case, you can preselect attendees from Contacts view and then proceed to meeting planning.

To schedule a meeting from Contacts view, follow these steps:

1. On the Outlook 2000 Shortcut Bar, click Contacts.

2. Highlighting each contact that you want to attend the meeting. Use the Shift key as you point to contacts to contiguously highlight a range of contacts, or the Control key to selectively highlight noncontiguous contacts. Notice in Figure 15.4 that only two of the three displayed contacts have been selected.

FIGURE 15.4

You can preselect contacts to speed up meeting planning.

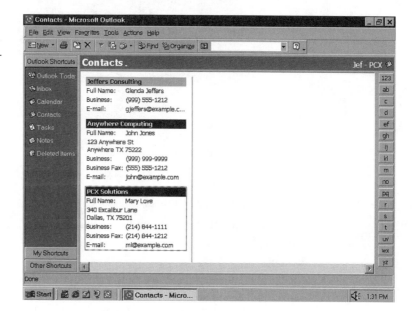

3. Select Actions, New Meeting Request to Contact to begin scheduling the meeting as outlined previously in this chapter.

Creating a Recurring Meeting

Any meetings that you have on a regular basis at the same time on the same day of the week or month are called *recurring meetings*. For instance, the staff meeting every Friday from 9 a.m. to 11 a.m. is a recurring meeting. Outlook can schedule each one of these meetings in one action so that you don't have to schedule them individually.

To create a recurring meeting, follow these steps:

1. From Calendar view, choose Actions, New Recurring Meeting. The Appointment Recurrence dialog box appears, as shown in Figure 15.5.

FIGURE 15.5

Setting appointment (meeting) recurrence frequency.

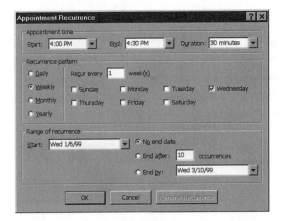

2. Set the frequency requirements for appointment time, recurrence pattern, and range of recurrence.

3. Click OK when finished, and then click Send.

If you want to make an existing meeting recurrent, perform the following steps:

1. Open the meeting item by double-clicking it.

2. Click either the Recurrence button on the toolbar or choose Actions, Recurrence. Complete the necessary fields in the Appointment Recurrence dialog box. Click OK when finished.

3. Click the Save and Close button. You will then be prompted to send the updated meeting information to your attendees.

Getting Meeting Requests

By now you should be a real pro at creating meetings. But what do you do if you're on the receiving end of one of those meeting requests? Meeting requests are received as messages in your Inbox. Like many choices in life, you have the option of saying yes (Accept) or no (Decline), or being wishy-washy (Tentative). Before you decide, click the Calendar button to see how the appointment fits into your schedule.

After you make your choice, a message is returned to the meeting's organizer stating your decision. If you choose Accept or Tentative, the meeting is automatically added to your calendar.

If you receive a meeting cancellation notice, click the Remove from Calendar button to remove the meeting from your schedule and acknowledge the message's receipt to the meeting organizer, with just one mouse click.

Allowing Others to Access Your Calendar

15

Why would you allow other people to have access to your calendar? If you do that, they'll know whether you really have an appointment at the same time they want you to attend their meeting, and you won't be able to bow out gracefully with a little white lie about a conflicting meeting. However, giving colleagues access to your calendar means that they don't have to call you every time they need to set up a meeting. You have to balance privacy with convenience to decide whether to give others access to your schedule.

It is a good idea for your department's administrative assistant to have access to your calendar so that your life can be properly scheduled and you can be located in case of an emergency.

Publishing Your Calendar to the Web or Intranet

New to Outlook 2000 is the capability of publishing your calendar to the World Wide Web or to your workgroup's intranet. When you publish your business calendar to the Web, you can access it from home or while out of town on a business trip via your Web browser.

To publish your calendar, follow these steps:

1. From Calendar view, click File, Save as Web Page. The Save as Web Page dialog box appears, as shown in Figure 15.6.

FIGURE 15.6

Preparing to publish your calendar.

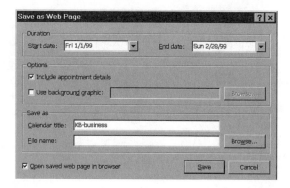

2. Set the Duration Start Date and End Date.
3. Leave the Options section defaults as they are.

4. In the Save As section, provide a Calendar title and File name. See the completed dialog box in Figure 15.7.

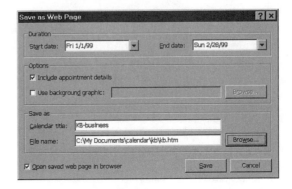

5. Click the Save button to save and publish your calendar. When it is complete, Internet Explorer will launch to display your calendar, as shown in Figure 15.8.

An icon in the lower-right of a date block means that more entries are included on that day. Click the icon to see a summary of details in the Appointment and Event Details pane at the right of the screen. If a detail includes a right-pointing arrow, click the arrow to see even more detail.

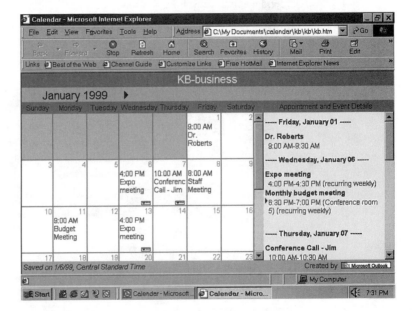

In this example, the calendar is published to a local hard disk. To publish your calendar to your World Wide Web site, fill out the File Name field of the Save as Web Page dialog box by using the following syntax:

```
http://www.example.com/calendar/kb_business.htm
```

Next, click the Save button, and Outlook 2000 establishes a connection to the Internet to connect you to your Web site. Your usual site access rights apply; you will typically be prompted for a user name and password, and then your calendar will be published to the designated preexisting Web directory (folder).

Looking at Calendar a Whole New Way

There are seven different views packaged with Calendar. You can change them by adding or subtracting the amount of information displayed, removing the view altogether, or creating your own view from scratch. We will look at the most common views in this hour.

The Daily/Weekly/Monthly View Set

The first three views are grouped into one category, the Daily/Weekly/Monthly (D/W/M) view set.

So far, all the work we have done in Calendar has been completed in the Daily view. There are, however, two variations of the Daily view we haven't seen: the addition of time zone information and reformatting of the time intervals.

Just to the left of the daily calendar box are time intervals. Calendar defaults these intervals to 30 minutes. However, when you right-click anywhere in the time interval area, a pop-up menu appears that enables you to set the intervals from 5 to 60 minutes (see Figure 15.9).

Changing or adding time zone information is a little more involved. By default, Calendar displays times based on the time zone specified when you first installed Windows. Suppose, however, that your office is in New York and there is a branch office in London that you contact daily. It would be handy to be able to see two time zones on your calendar to ease the scheduling of teleconference meetings that fit the hours of both locations. Here's how you work with time zones:

1. Choose Tools, Options, and then click the Calendar Options button. Next, click the Time Zone button. The Time Zone dialog box appears, as shown in Figure 15.10.

FIGURE 15.9

You can reset your time intervals.

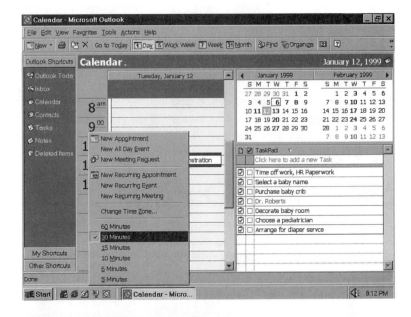

FIGURE 15.10

You can configure time zones in the Time Zone dialog box.

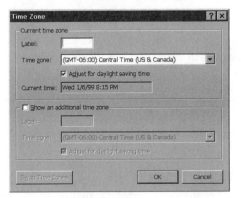

2. Open the Time Zone drop-down box by clicking the arrow to the right of the Time Zone field. Your time zone should already be highlighted and correct.

3. Click the Show an Additional Time Zone check box.

4. Type London Office in the Label field.

5. In the Time Zone drop-down box, choose London's time zone, which is (GMT) Greenwich mean time.

6. Click OK three times to return to your calendar. The two time zones display on the left side of the appointment grid, similar to those shown in Figure 15.11.

FIGURE 15.11

Now you can be sure that meetings don't intrude on tee times.

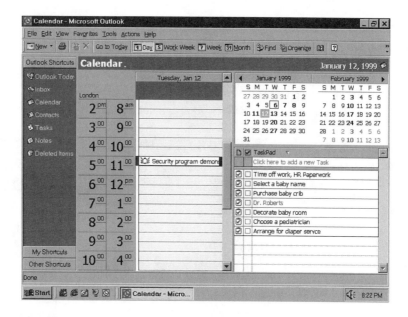

Work Week View

Another useful calendar view is Work Week. You can select this view by choosing View, Work Week. As shown in Figure 15.12, the Work Week view shows only the days that you have set up as your official work week. This view helps you spot calendar openings during a busy week.

FIGURE 15.12

Too many meetings this week? You can more easily find an open slot in Work Week view.

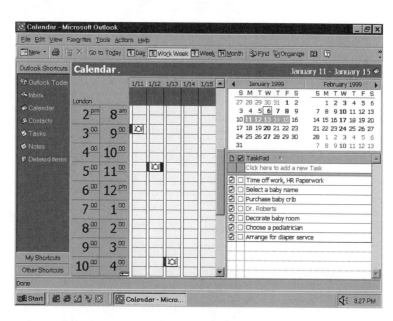

By clicking the Week button in the toolbar or selecting View, Week, you can see the entire week instead of a single day. Notice in Figure 15.13, however, that the folder area (also called the Calendar page) on the left side of the screen is the only part that changes. The toolbar, the TaskPad, and the Date Navigator remain the same. The daily calendar has been replaced with the weekly calendar. Each appointment is still marked by times and reminders, but the color-coded appointment status bars are missing.

FIGURE 15.13

Week view helps you plan your week.

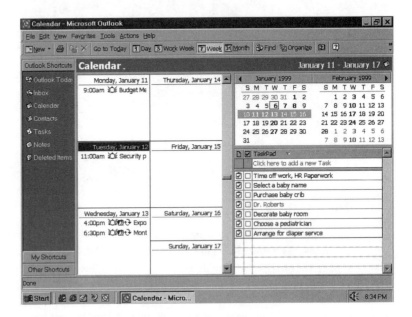

When you select Month view, the Calendar page gets a more dramatic makeover, as shown in Figure 15.14. Now, only the current month is visible and only the subject of each appointment or event is shown. No times, locations, or symbols are used. If the appointment labels don't fit entirely within a single day's cell, a tiny yellow arrow/ellipsis symbol (shown in the margin) is used to indicate a continuation of the day's appointments. Clicking this symbol returns you to Daily view for that day.

FIGURE 15.14

Monthly view displays an entire month at a glance.

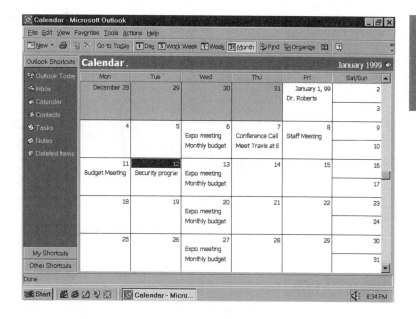

Printing What You've Got

Throughout this hour you may have been wondering how you can keep track of your appointments when you are away from your computer. At any point, you can click the Print button on the toolbar to get the information down on paper so that you can carry it around with you.

The Print dialog box, as shown in Figure 15.15, is similar to the standard Windows Print dialog box; however, you can choose to print daily, weekly, monthly, tri-fold, or calendar details style calendars. Try a test print of each print style to determine which one best meets your needs. It's a matter of personal preference. I prefer the tri-fold style because it also lists my current tasks and appointments for the entire week.

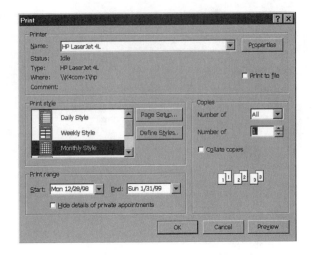

FIGURE 15.15

The Print dialog box provides options for printing your calendars.

Summary

Now that you have finished this hour's look at Calendar, you can see that it can be a simple or very complex tool. Like any other part of Outlook 2000, Calendar's functionality is determined by how you want to use it.

The next hour will help you understand the structure of your personal folders and show you how to archive old data and transfer files between computers.

Q&A

Q If I publish my calendar to my Web site, can I keep it confidential?

A Keeping your calendar confidential is not a function of Outlook, but depends upon how your Web site is set up. If you use a program such as Microsoft FrontPage 2000 to manage your Web site, you can restrict access to your calendar page.

Q Do I have to always show seven columns when printing monthly calendars?

A No, you can suppress Saturday and Sunday by clicking File, Page Setup, Monthly Style, Don't Print Weekends.

Q When in Calendar, can I see a specific type of task in the TaskPad?

A Yes. Choose View, TaskPad View, and select from All Tasks, Today's Tasks, Active Tasks for Selected Days, or several other views.

HOUR 16

Keeping House

If you are obsessive about neatness and filing, this hour is critical to your use of Outlook 2000. If you are just a normal person, then this is still an important hour for you to understand. Earlier in this book, you learned to make Outlook 2000 automatically record a journal entry of the files you use, the phone calls you make, and the email you send and receive, as well as complete a variety of other tasks. After you use Outlook 2000 for an extended period, it will slow down if you don't use some kind of file management.

Managing your file folders in Outlook 2000 is a very important task. By performing tasks such as archiving your data and importing and exporting files, you can save time, make your data transferable, and conserve valuable hard drive space.

This hour helps you understand the structure of your personal folders and shows you how to archive old data and transfer files between computers.

The highlights of this hour include the following:

- How to archive the information stored in your Outlook personal folders file
- How to restore a file from an archive
- How to export a Personal Folders File and other file formats
- How to make your Outlook 2000 files as small as possible

Where Are My Personal File Folders?

All your personal file folders by default are stored in a single file, outlook.pst. To properly maintain your personal file folders, it is important that you know where this file is stored on your computer. To find its location, on the Outlook 2000 Shortcut Bar, right-click the Outlook Today icon, and then choose Properties and click the Advanced button. The Personal Folders dialog box is displayed, as shown in Figure 16.1. The Path field shows the location of your outlook.pst file. By default the path location is c:\Windows\Local Settings\Application Data\Microsoft\Outlook\.

FIGURE 16.1

The outlook.pst file stores all the information you enter into Outlook 2000.

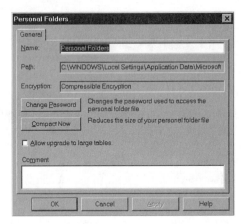

Outlook 2000 has no built-in provision for backing up the outlook.pst file; therefore, it is your responsibility to perform periodic backups. The size of the PST file will grow dramatically as you add new contacts and tasks, send and receive email messages, and use Outlook 2000 in other ways. You will find that backing up the PST file to disk is impractical. If possible, you should back up to tape, a removable medium such as a zip disk, or a network drive.

Because many entries are added to and deleted from the PST file, over time, the structure of the PST file can become scattered, contributing to a larger-than-necessary file size. You can reduce the file size of the PST file by compacting it. On the Outlook 2000 Shortcut Bar, right-click the Outlook Today icon, and then choose Properties and click the Advanced button. Click Compact Now to begin the compacting operation.

Don't Lose It: Archiving

16

At times, you may need to remove old and seldom-used files from Outlook 2000 by archiving some of the information stored in your Outlook personal folders file. Archiving is a manner of removing old data from your Outlook 2000 file in such a way that you can get it back any time you need it. It's an operation that can be compared to filing old bills and receipts. You probably don't refer to them very often (if at all), but you have to keep them somewhere in case the IRS ever wants to audit you.

Similarly, you may have Outlook 2000 files from past projects or previous years. You don't want to delete these files, but you also don't want Outlook 2000 to have to sort through the information every time you instigate a Search or Filter operation. The best way to take care of these files is to archive them. This removes old data from your Outlook 2000 database and stores it in an archive file, usually called `archive.pst`, which can you can access through Outlook 2000 whenever you want to refer to the data.

Setting Up AutoArchive

Realistically, most of us don't have time to sit around and sift through our files to see what needs to be archived and what doesn't. Fortunately, we have Outlook 2000 to do this for us.

You can choose to allow Outlook 2000 to automatically archive your old files, based on a schedule that you designate. You can schedule an archiving session to take place as often as every day or as infrequently as every 60 days. This really depends on how you work and how much hard drive space you have available.

Follow these steps to set up AutoArchive:

1. Open Outlook 2000 if it is not already open.

2. To configure the AutoArchive feature, choose Tools, Options, and click the Other tab, as shown in Figure 16.2.

FIGURE **16.2**

*Accessing the global
AutoArchive settings.*

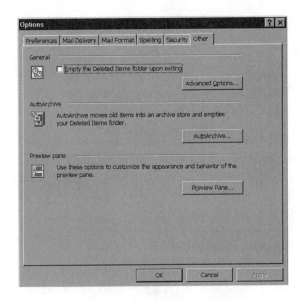

3. Click the AutoArchive button. As shown in Figure 16.3, the AutoArchive dialog
   box provides you with the capability to customize AutoArchive's settings.

FIGURE **16.3**

*Choosing global
AutoArchive settings.*

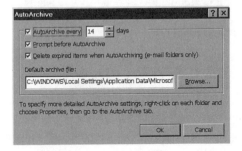

4. When you have specified the desired frequency of your AutoArchive, the location
   of the archive file, and the various other options, click OK. Click OK again to close
   the Options dialog box.

Before Outlook 2000 performs its archive operations, a notice appears onscreen to alert
you that Outlook 2000 is ready to begin archiving. You can choose to accept or decline.
If you decline, the notice appears each time you open Outlook 2000 until you accept the
operation or until you reset the AutoArchive schedule in the AutoArchive dialog box.

Archiving Manually

If you prefer to archive your Outlook 2000 files manually, you can do so by choosing File, Archive. The Archive dialog box enables you to archive according to the AutoArchive settings, which can differ from folder to folder, depending on how you set the properties. Otherwise, you can choose to archive entire folders by the same standard, such as archiving all items older than October 6, 1998.

To manually archive a folder, follow these steps:

1. Choose File, Archive.
2. In the Archive dialog box, highlight the Inbox folder. As shown in Figure 16.4, you can specify the age the messages must be in order to be included in the archive. In the Archive Items Older Than text box, either type a specific date or click the down arrow to drop down the calendar and choose a date.

FIGURE 16.4

Manually archiving a folder.

3. If you would like to differentiate this archive file from your usual AutoArchive files, choose a new filename by clicking the Browse button, specifying the location for the archive file, and typing a filename.
4. When you are ready to archive your files, click OK.

Removing a Folder After Archiving

If you archive all the items in a folder, the empty folder remains in the personal folders file. If you no longer have any use for the folder and would like to remove it, right-click the folder and choose Delete.

16

Restoring from an Archive

You can restore a file from an archive by using two methods: Either open the archive as a separate personal folders file or import the archive. Chances are you will want to open the archive just to retrieve needed information rather than import the entire file.

To open an archive file, click File, Open, Personal Folders File (.pst). Navigate to your archive file, select it, and click OK.

To import an archive file, click File, Import and Export, choose Import from Another Program or File, and then click Next. Choose Personal Folder file (.pst), click Next, and then use the Browse button to select your archive file. Click Next once again, and then click Finish.

Exporting Items

The difference between exporting and archiving items is that archiving removes them from your personal folders file and exporting makes a copy of them in a new file. Exporting also gives you the option of exporting the data as a personal folders file (which can be read by Outlook 2000), as a Windows Messaging file (readable in Microsoft Exchange), or as another file type, such as a text file, an Excel spreadsheet file, or a database file.

Exporting to a Personal Folders File

Exporting is a good way to share Outlook 2000 items with other Outlook 2000 users or between computers. For instance, if you work with Outlook 2000 at work and home, you can export items—such as your contacts list or email messages—to a file and then import them into your Outlook 2000 folders at home.

To export email to a personal folders file, follow these steps:

1. Select your Inbox.
2. Click File, Import and Export.
3. In the Import and Export Wizard, choose Export to a File. Click Next.
4. In the Export to a File dialog box, as shown in Figure 16.5, select Comma Separated Values (DOS). Click Next.
5. In the Export to a File dialog box, as shown in Figure 16.6, choose the folder that you would like to export from, and click Next.

FIGURE 16.5

Exporting email messages for use on another PC.

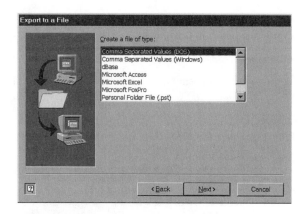

FIGURE 16.6

Choosing the file folder to be exported.

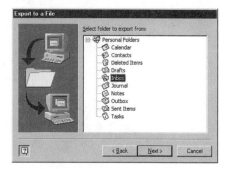

6. Specify a directory and a name for the file you are creating. Click Next and then click Finish to begin the export operation.

Exporting to Other File Formats

At times, you may want to transfer your Outlook 2000 data to another file format. For instance, suppose you want to give your Contacts file to a friend, but he or she does not have Outlook 2000. To accomplish this task, you can export your Contacts list as an Excel spreadsheet, which can be opened just like any other Excel file. To do this, follow these steps:

1. Click the Contacts icon on the Outlook 2000 Shortcut Bar.

2. Choose File, Import and Export.

3. In the Import and Export Wizard, choose Export to a File, and click Next.

4. In the Export to a File dialog box, choose Microsoft Excel and click Next.

5. The Contacts folder should already be highlighted. Click Next.

6. Select the location and filename for the newly exported data. Click Next.

7. Outlook 2000 specifies the actions that will be taken in the exporting process. As shown in Figure 16.7, Outlook 2000 will export the Contacts file from the Contacts folder. Click Finish.

FIGURE 16.7

Exporting Outlook 2000 contacts to another file format.

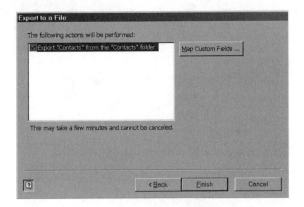

8. Outlook 2000 indicates the progress of the file transfer. When it is finished, your file is ready to be given to your friend.

Tips on Making Your Outlook 2000 Files as Small as Possible

There are a few things you can do periodically to save hard drive space on your computer while you use Outlook 2000. The following are some suggestions:

- By default, items that you delete from all folders other than the Deleted Items folder are not actually deleted. The items are simply moved to the Deleted Items folder when you delete them. You should frequently empty the Deleted Items folder by selecting it and choosing Tools, Empty "Deleted Items" Folder. You can also right-click the Deleted Items Folder and choose Empty "Deleted Items" folder.

- If you want the Deleted Items folder to automatically empty each time you exit Outlook 2000, choose Tools, Options, and select the Other tab. Select the Empty Deleted Items Folder Upon Exiting check box.

- Turn off the option to save messages that you send. To do this, select Tools, Options, and choose the Preferences tab. Click the Email Options button and uncheck the option to save messages in the Sent Items folder (this should be the default, but make sure it is indeed set). You can always specify on an individual basis when you want to save a message that you are sending.

- Be conservative in choosing options to be tracked as automatic Journal entries. Choose Tools, Options and select the Preferences tab. Click the Journal Options button and deselect any unnecessary automatic journal entries.

- Archive frequently either by choosing AutoArchive or by archiving manually, as described at the beginning of this hour.

- Compact your personal folders file frequently, as discussed earlier in this hour.

- Back up your PST file regularly. Every Outlook 2000 item you enter and message you send and receive is maintained in the PST file.

Summary

Managing your data effectively can save you both time and space on your hard drive. Outlook 2000's compaction and archiving features, along with the import and export tools, should enable you to reduce the amount of space your personal folders occupy and give you the ability to transport files between users and computers. And backing up your personal file folders is essential in case of a systemwide failure.

In the next hour, you'll learn how to use Outlook 2000 to manage your tasks and time. You'll learn new ways to use Outlook 2000 to track your time, your projects, and those tasks you've delegated to colleagues or family members.

Q&A

Q When I export a file, do I have to save it to my hard drive and then copy it to a floppy disk?

A No. You can export a file directly to a floppy disk by simply specifying your floppy drive as the target for the file when you name the file and its destination.

Q Which is better: AutoArchive or manual archives?

A It depends on your needs. AutoArchive is handy for those who don't want to go to the trouble of periodically freeing up hard drive space. Manual archives, however, let you keep tabs on the amount of space your files are taking at all times. Pick whichever is best for you.

Q Can I specify the time of day that Outlook 2000 archives files?

A No. You can only specify the Outlook 2000 period—on a daily basis or greater (such as, weekly or monthly).

HOUR 17

Getting Things Done

We have become so busy that almost everyone has to-do lists floating around their offices and homes. At work your projects are broken down into specific tasks, and you have daily and weekly routines that seem to include more parts all the time. At home you have lots of family-related tasks, such as the Monday night Scout meeting, the patches that need to be sewn on the shirt before that meeting, the field trip permission slip to return to the school, and the sitter to hire for Saturday night. You also have the home-related tasks, such as mowing the lawn, fixing the toilet, grocery shopping, and picking up the dry cleaning.

Even with to-do lists and sticky notes, how do we manage to find time to get it all done? Despite being scheduled down to our last 15 minutes, we recognize the need for variety, social interaction, and family life. However, the more efficiently we manage our time and our tasks, the more quickly we can move on to the next challenge or reward.

Task management and time management are the focus of this hour. You'll learn new ways to use Outlook 2000 to track your time, your projects, and those tasks you've delegated to colleagues (or family members).

The highlights of this hour include the following:

- How to create tasks manually and automatically
- How to create and finish a task
- How to create a task from a calendar item
- How to check, delegate, and track your tasks

Time Management

There are many tried-and-true methods of time management out there, as well as a crop of new ones each year. Just wander over to the business section of the local bookstore, and you will see a variety of books on how to organize your life, your time, and your files, not to mention every other thing you can possibly organize (even your closets).

Although we don't recommend any specific time management system, the following are some basic ideas that generally seem to work:

- First, do the tasks that accomplish the most with the least energy.
- Be accessible, but firm. Don't let a lot of minor interruptions sidetrack you from your tasks.
- Set aside a few minutes at the beginning of each day to set each day's goals, or a few minutes at the end of the day to set the following day's goals. They don't have to be big—just some things to accomplish each day.
- Do similar tasks together. For instance, return all your phone calls at the same time and schedule another time to do all your computer work. When you leave the office or your home, combine as many errands as you can to avoid needless retracing of your steps later.
- Always make time for yourself and your family. No matter how much you love your job, it's only one part of your life. If it becomes all your life, you're missing out. If you haven't talked to your spouse, parents, kids, friends, or other significant people in your life today, put this book down right now and go do that.

What Is a Task?

If you are among the many skeptics of time management and personal organizers, the tasks feature of Outlook 2000 can make a believer of you by

- Enabling you to create and maintain lists of things to do, as well as track tasks by project, by the people involved, and by priority.
- Letting you maintain lists of recurring tasks that occur either on set dates, or at a certain time after the previous occurrence of the task is completed.

- Enabling delegation of tasks and task management to other people for times when you're too busy to do them yourself.

- Accepting task assignments from others. This is certainly not fun, but at least tasks makes it easy by enabling you to integrate a new incoming task into your list of things to do.

Starting the Tasks Screen

Accessing the Tasks screen in Outlook 2000 is much the same as using any of the other tools.

You can start tasks by

- Clicking the Tasks icon on the Outlook Shortcuts bar
- Clicking the Calendar icon in the Outlook Shortcuts bar to view the TaskPad
- Clicking the Tasks folder in the Folders list
- Choosing View, Go To, Tasks from the Menu bar

And on Your Right, You Can See...

Click the Calendar icon on the Outlook bar. The TaskPad information viewer is not flashy. It appears as a simple-looking table, as shown in Figure 17.1. But you know by now that in Outlook, such things are never quite as simple as they look. If they were, this book would be very short.

FIGURE 17.1

The TaskPad viewer provides one method of inputting tasks. Click the Click Here to Add a New Task text box to enter a new task.

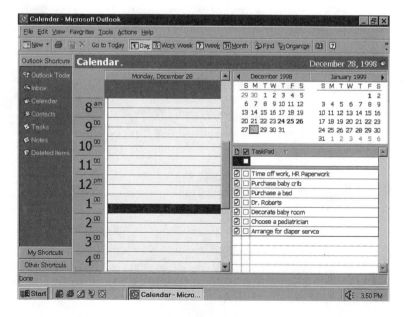

The Icon column shows the type of Outlook item. Most of the time, the Task icon will be present here, although assigned tasks are symbolized in this column as well. We'll take a closer look at assigning tasks later in the hour.

The Complete column is merely a check box that indicates when a task is complete.

The Subject column is where you describe your tasks: "Take out the trash." "Get Dave the Top Ten List by 5:30." "Launch the Mars probe." These are all good examples of task subjects. Just make sure you don't go overboard in this column, because you can add more information to a task by double-clicking on it to open the Tasks window.

Creating a Task

Tasks can help you in both your business life and your personal life. In an example in this hour, your family is soon to be enlarged. Imagine you are a working parent-to-be. For all you men out there, play along. In light of the federal Family Leave Act, fathers, too, are assuming more active roles in planning for a new family member.

Over the next few months, you are going to be very busy preparing for the new arrival. To be able to get everything done without waiting until the last minute, you make a long list of tasks.

To create a task list for the new arrival, click the Task icon on the Outlook Shortcuts bar. Double-click the Click Here to Add a New Task text box. The Untitled - Task window is displayed, as shown in Figure 17.2.

FIGURE 17.2

The Untitled - Task window is used to enter more thorough data than can be entered from the TaskPad view.

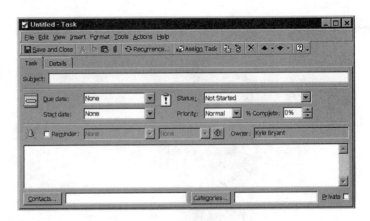

Besides this window's similarity in style to all of Outlook's other tools, notice the small number of fields to fill out. This makes creating tasks quick and painless.

The subject line should be simple and to the point. You can add extra information in the Note box at the bottom of the Task window as you need it.

The next information group is the Due Date field. The default is None. By clicking the drop-down arrow, you see the Date Navigator box (see Figure 17.3). The current date is highlighted. Select the date by which you want to complete the task or leave it at None. For the current date, either click the Today button or click the date on the Date Navigator. To choose another date, use the Date Navigator to click the appropriate date. Also, you can just type the correct date directly over None.

FIGURE 17.3

The Date Navigator in the Task window can be used to specify a due date.

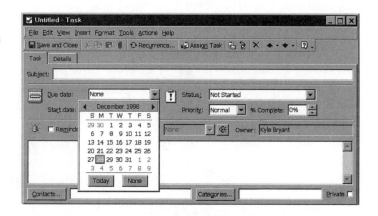

17

The Start Date field is optional, and you may not even find a need for it. You can just type 3 months and press Tab. You can enter the tasks from the TaskPad rather than opening the Task tool for each entry. You input dates by typing 1 mo (or the appropriate number of months). You enter the status by typing the first letter of the status code (Not Started, In Progress, Completed, Waiting on Someone Else, or Deferred). Priority codes can also be entered by typing the first letter (High, Normal, or Low).

The Start Date field works in much the same way as the Due Date field. It is used to establish the date on which the task will begin. This may be immediately, or it may be some time in the near future. If the task is already in progress, the start date may be in the past.

The next field, % Complete, is optional. There are certain situations for which pinning down a percentage value is tricky. When the task is segmented or can be easily measured, then it's helpful to use this field. For instance, when writing a specific number of chapters in a book, an author could change the percentage of chapters completed and submitted to the editor by either directly entering the percentage or using the spin buttons to the right of the field to increase or decrease the percentage.

> If you mark a task as complete, the Status and % Complete fields are auto-matically adjusted.

In the following exercise, you enter several tasks that are related to your expanding family; later, you learn to edit them and add additional ones:

1. Create a new task. An Untitled - Task Window is displayed.

2. Type Purchase baby crib in the subject line.

3. Insert the date three months from now as your due date.

4. Enter today as the start date.

5. Choose the In Progress option for the Status field.

6. Leave Normal as the Priority for now. (Normal is the default priority.)

7. Click Save and Close. Figure 17.4 shows the task you just created.

FIGURE 17.4

A single task has been entered.

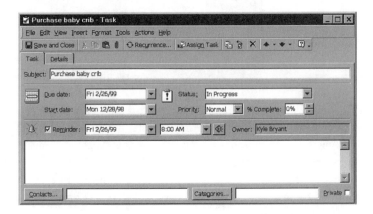

8. Over the course of the next few months you are going to have a lot of other tasks that need to be done before the new arrival comes home. Take the next few minutes and enter the tasks noted in Table 17.1.

TABLE 17.1   DATA FOR TASK ENTRY

Subject	Due Date	Start Date	Status	Priority	% Complete
Arrange for diaper service	3 mo	None	Not started	Normal	0
Decorate baby room	3 mo	Today	In progress	Normal	10

Subject	Due Date	Start Date	Status	Priority	% Complete
Time off work, HR paperwork	1 mo	Today	In progress	High	25
Choose a pediatrician	1 mo	Today	Waiting on someone else	High	25
Select a baby name	3 mo	Today	In progress	High	25

Your tasks should look similar to the ones shown in Figure 17.5.

FIGURE 17.5

You can create, edit, and track task items here.

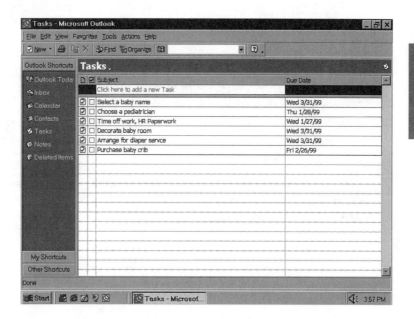

The tasks in Table 17.1 have all been entered. At this point, you may be asking yourself, what's the difference between Calendar and Tasks items? On the surface, not much. They handle different things in a similar way.

When you are not in Tasks view but areclicking the Task command in the Create New drop-down list in the Standard toolbar or by using the shortcut key Ctrl+Shift+K.

As in Calendar view, in Tasks can set reminders for any task you want. However, there are some differences between reminders in Tasks view and reminders in Calendar view.

When you click the Reminder check box, the date field next to it activates, with the default data value as the due date of the task. If there is no due date, the date field will default to the current date. The next field is the Reminder time field, with a default of 8:00 a.m.

Usually, setting the reminder by date is enough, unless you are on a tight schedule. For example, you might have to have a report ready for the quarterly trustees' meeting, and because it contains up-to-the-minute stock prices, you will be working close to the exact time that it is due.

If a certain time of day is better for you to receive task reminders, change the default time:

1. In Tasks, choose Tools, Options.
2. In the Reminder time field, either directly enter or use the list box to set the Reminder time to 7:00 p.m.
3. Click OK.

Learning More About the Task Window

You can double-click to open an existing task. The Owner field is not editable because it shows the user who owns it. When a task is assigned by clicking the Assign Task button, the creator of the task gives up ownership to the person he or she is assigning it to and the reminder time, if set, is turned off.

The large Note box that dominates the lower third of the screen lets you enter as many details about the task as you need. You can keep track of baby names as you and your spouse narrow the choices by putting the top six baby names for each sex in the Note box.

To update a task, follow these steps:

1. Open the Task window for the task Select a Baby Name by double-clicking the task. Resize the window so that you can see the other fields at the bottom of the screen.
2. In the large Note box beneath the Reminder field, enter `Girls' names: Jessica, Ashley, Kristen, Emily, Holly, Traci` and `Boys' names: Kristopher, Scott, Jason, Jonathon, Zachary, James.`
3. Change the % Complete to 50%. Your screen should be similar to the one shown in Figure 17.6.
4. Click Save and Close.

The final field in the New Task window is the Private check box. This is used when a task is created that not everyone needs to know about, such as any information in your personal folder. After all, you don't want everyone to put in their two cents' worth regarding baby names.

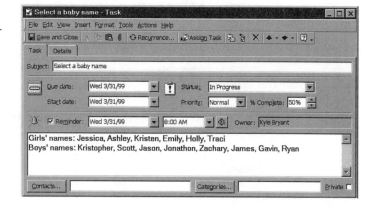

FIGURE 17.6

The enlarged Task window shows additional fields at the bottom of the screen.

Creating a Task Automatically

If you are like me, you get a lot of email that contains urgent matters that you must efficiently deal with to keep the world safe for democracy. You know, things like, "Could you get me a copy of that report?" and "Can you find a way to deal with that knucklehead Lex Luthor?" Such messages can be converted to a task quite easily:

1. Click Inbox and select the appropriate message. Drag and drop the message onto the Tasks icon on the Outlook Shortcuts bar.
2. When the Task window appears, fill in the appropriate information (priority, due date, and so on).
3. Click Save and Close.

Calendar offers another clever way to automatically create a task: by associating a task with a calendar item. This is helpful, for instance, if you have an appointment or meeting that you need to prepare for. For example, you need to have all the hospital pre-registration forms filled out by the next doctor's appointment, so the doctor's office can get them processed. To help you remember this, create a task from the appointment on the Calendar:

1. Click the Calendar icon on the Outlook Shortcuts bar.
2. Create an appointment for next Friday at 9:00 a.m. with Dr. Roberts and save it.
3. Highlight the appointment item in the calendar. Drag and drop it onto the Tasks icon on the Outlook Shortcuts bar.
4. A new Task window appears, with the appointment in the Note box (see Figure 17.7).

17

FIGURE 17.7

*Making sure you're
prepared for an
appointment.*

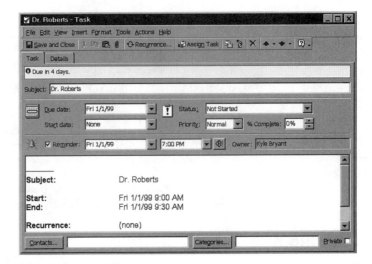

5. The Reminder time is set for 7 p.m. (because you changed the default). Change it to 7:30 a.m., or you may be late for the appointment.

6. Click Save and Close.

Finishing a Task

There's no greater satisfaction than a job well done, but how do you tell tasks that you're done with them? There are four ways:

- When the Complete column is in view, as in Simple List view, click the check box next to the finished task to mark that task as completed.

- When the Status field is in view in the Information viewer (the Detailed List view), enter Completed in the Status field to indicate that the job is done. You can also enter this value in a Task Detail window.

- In the Task window, enter 100% in the % Complete field. Or enter 100% in the % Complete field for Detailed List view.

- On the Menu bar, click Actions, Mark Complete.

After you have marked a task as complete, it does not disappear from the Simple List view. Rather, it changes to a lighter, strikethrough text. This helps you keep track of the recent things you've accomplished.

In the Active Tasks view, however, tasks disappear as soon as they are marked as complete. Although the tasks are still in the folder, to see them you must switch to Simple List view. Later in this hour, you will learn to completely delete a task.

Editing a Task

Editing a task is not difficult. If the item you want to edit is visible in the Information viewer, you can edit the subject directly without opening the Task window by clicking once on the desired task to be edited. In the next exercise, you learn to add a reminder date.

When you want to do more detailed editing, you can double-click any task in the Information viewer. This opens that task's Task window. Editing any of the fields on the Task tab is the same as creating the task.

To edit a task, follow these steps:

1. In any of the Information Viewer views, open the Time Off Work, HR Paperwork task.

2. Add a reminder date of one week prior to the due date.

3. Click Save and Close to exit this item and the change is saved.

After the doctor's appointment, you and your spouse have found out that you are having a baby boy. Now you can delete all the girls' names and add two more boys' names:

1. Open the Task window for the task Select a Baby Name.

2. Delete the girls' names and add two more boys' names: Gavin and Ryan. Your screen should be similar to that in Figure 17.8.

FIGURE 17.8

The girls' names have been removed, and two more boys' names have been added.

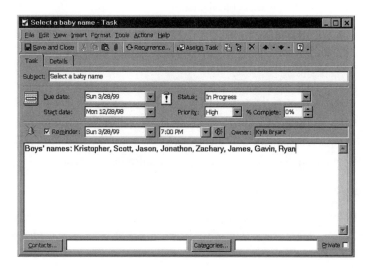

3. Click Save and Close.

Other fields can be edited as well—fields on the Details tab that deal with many things that come up during a particular job. Take a look at the Details tab, as shown in Figure 17.9. There's lots of room for information here! Let's look at what each field can record for you.

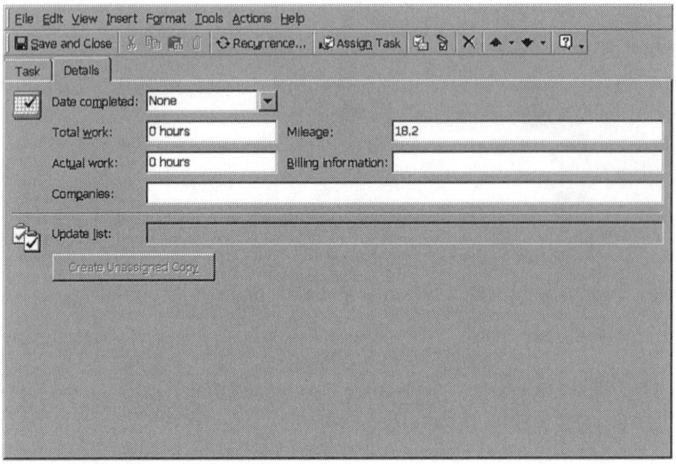

FIGURE 17.9

The Details tab in the Task window can be used for tracking additional information.

The Date Completed field is automatically filled when a task is marked as complete. This is helpful when the task is part of an overall project and you need to know who finished what and when it was completed.

The Total Work and Actual Work fields are sort of misnomers—at least the Total Work field is. It should be called the Estimated Work field because you enter the *estimated* number of hours you think a task will take to finish. In the Actual Work field, you enter the number of hours the task really took to complete. (If this task had been assigned, this would be a great way of monitoring someone's performance level.) The values of the field automatically change to day or week values if you enter more than eight hours.

The next three fields are self-explanatory: Mileage, Billing Information, and Companies. If you need to track any of this type of information, here's where you do it.

Copying a Task

If you need to create a task that is nearly identical to another, you can make a copy. Try this with Purchase a Baby Crib because you've decided you also need a new bed. A copy is born!

To copy a task, follow these steps:

1. In any of the task lists shown in the Information viewer, select the task (or tasks) you need to copy—in this case, Purchase a Baby Crib.

2. Choose the Edit, Copy menu command.

3. Choose the Edit, Paste menu command. A duplicate task appears.

4. Open the newly copied task and change the subject to Purchase a Bed.

5. Click Save and Close when you are finished.

An even faster way of doing this is to highlight the task, press the Ctrl key, and drag the task somewhere else in the Information viewer. As soon as you release the mouse button, the task is copied to the new location.

Deleting a Task

As mentioned previously, when tasks are completed, they do not just vanish into the air. They stick around, reminding you of all the work you've accomplished.

You can keep tasks around until they are autoarchived, but you may want to clean house and sweep out these old tasks sooner than that. You may even need to delete a current task if someone else has taken it over and you are no longer responsible for its completion. In any case, to delete a task, just highlight it, and then press the Delete key.

Checking Task Status

Usually the status of tasks is best used at work because work tasks tend to be more segmented and easier to track than those in your personal life. If your boss has access to your calendar, he can use the Status section to check the progress of a task he has assigned to you without having to call you into his office.

Delegating and Tracking a Task

In the past you may have asked a coworker to do a project and then forgotten that you gave it to her. It doesn't happen often, thankfully, but it always tends to happen at the worst times.

17

With Outlook you can create a task that needs to be done, assign it to someone to be completed, and be able to find out the status of it at any time without having to call the person. In the following exercise, you assign a task to another person:

1. Open the Task window to arrange for a diaper service by using one of the methods you've learned this hour.

2. Click the Assign Task icon on the toolbar. This displays a window for you to complete.

3. Click the To button to bring up the Select Task Recipient dialog box.

4. Choose the person you are assigning the task to, and click the To-> button.

5. Click OK. You are now back at the Task tool, with the recipient's name in the To: field.

6. Make sure the check boxes are marked where it says Keep an Updated Copy of This Task on My Task List and Send Me a Status Report When This Task Is Complete.

7. When finished, click Send. The task will be emailed to the assigned person.

Summary

During this hour, you learned some ways to manage your time and your life better. You will find that tracking all your tasks will become a habit and you will be much more organized after using it for a while. Not only will you know what you need to complete and what you have already done, you will also be able to keep a close eye on all those tasks and projects you ask other people to take care of.

The next hours will get you started on the road to utilizing Office 2000 products as a suite—and with the Internet. Hour 18, "Office 2000's Synergy," explores how Office 2000 products work together and how Office 2000 Small Business Edition programs are integrated.

Q&A

Q When editing a task, do I lose the information if I accidentally close the window?

A If you have made any changes to the task and click the Close button instead of the Save and Close button, Outlook will prompt you, asking if you would like to save your changes.

Q **I have 10 items included in a task and have completed one of them. Do I have to enter 25% because that's the lowest percentage the % Completed field gives me?**

A No, you can manually enter 10% into the % Complete field.

Q **How can I see additional tasks in the TaskPad list?**

A Use the scrollbar to scroll through the tasks. Double-click a specific one to open it.

Tasks do not focus on a certain point in time as does a meeting or an appointment. After you set a reminder and that date is reached, tasks will keep reminding you each day until the task is complete (unless you dismiss the reminder). If you are using task subfolders, reminders are not active. Reminders only activate from the primary Tasks folder. In the Task window, next to the time field is a button with a speaker icon on it. Click this button to open the Reminder Sound dialog box. This contains the path to the sound file (usually in WAV format) that will sound when the Reminder time begins.

17

PART V

Combining the Office 2000 Products and the Internet

Hour

Hour 18

Office 2000's Synergy

This hour explores how Office 2000 products work together and how you can enhance your documents. Office 2000 programs integrate so well that it is hard to know where to start describing the possibilities. Generally, if you need to work with two or more Office 2000 program documents together, you are able to load or embed one document within the other even though the Office 2000 programs that created the two documents are completely different.

The highlights of this hour include the following:

- Why drag-and-drop operations work so well between Office 2000 programs
- How to control a drag-and-drop operation to produce a copy, a move, a link, or a shortcut
- How to edit and break links between Office 2000 documents
- How to write letters to Outlook 2000 contacts quickly
- How to add your own art (or sound or video) clip files to Office 2000's Clip Gallery

- When the AutoShapes toolbar comes in handy
- How to select WordArt styles when you want to add fancy text titles and banners to your Office 2000 documents

Sharing Data Among Applications

Office 2000's cornerstone is data sharing among its programs. Office 2000 offers several ways to share data among products. The Office 2000 products almost all support the inclusion of other Office 2000 documents. Word 2000 includes the Insert Microsoft Excel Worksheet toolbar button that inserts any Excel 2000 worksheet in a Word 2000 document, for example.

Besides inserting full documents, you may want to insert a part of a document in another Office 2000 application. The following sections explain the most common methods to embed part of one application's document inside another.

Drag and Drop

Suppose you want to use part of an Excel 2000 worksheet a Word 2000 document. If you have both Excel 2000 (with the relevant data loaded) and Word 2000 running at the same time, perform these steps to drag the worksheet to the Word 2000 document:

1. Resize your Excel 2000 and Word 2000 program windows so that you can see both the *source document* (the Excel 2000 worksheet) and the *destination document* (the Word 2000 document).

NEW TERM The *source document* is the document that holds an item that you want to drag to another location.

NEW TERM The *destination document* is the document that receives the object that you drag from a source document.

2. In the Excel 2000 worksheet, select the cells that you want to copy and transfer to Word 2000.

3. Hold the Ctrl key and drag the edge of the highlighted cells to the location in your Word 2000 document where you want to place the table.

4. Release the mouse to anchor the table. (Figure 18.1 shows the result of such a copy.)

FIGURE 18.1

Word's table came from Excel 2000.

From here in Excel...

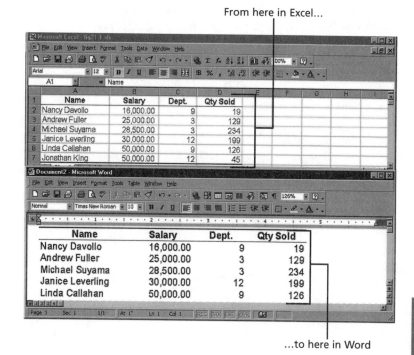

...to here in Word

18

If you did not first press Ctrl before dragging the cells, Excel 2000 would have *moved* the table from the Excel 2000 worksheet to the Word 2000 document instead of *copying* the table.

Depending on the size and style of your Word 2000 document, you might want to format the copied table differently from Excel 2000's format. Right-click the table and select Format Object to display the Format Object dialog box. You can apply colors, lines, shading, and other formatting attributes to the copied object from the Format Object dialog box.

Creating Links

Suppose that you create a monthly sales report using the same Word 2000 document and the same Excel 2000 worksheet every time. Only the details in the Excel 2000 worksheet change (obviously, you have created templates for these files long before now). You don't have to drag the updated Excel 2000 table to your Word 2000 document before printing the Word 2000 document each month. Instead of copying or moving the cells, you can create a *link* to the cells.

NEW TERM A *link* is a cross-reference to another file. Instead of copying or moving the contents of one file to another, the link maintains a live connection to the other file. Therefore, if the source file changes, the destination file always displays those changes. The destination file does not actually hold the source file's data, but displays the data as though it resided in the destination file.

As long as you have inserted a link to the Excel 2000 worksheet, you need only change the Excel 2000 worksheet each month, start Word 2000, load the report document, and print the document. You won't have to copy or move the actual Excel 2000 cells into the report. The report always points to the worksheet cells via the link that you inserted when you created the Word 2000 document.

To create a link, perform these steps:

1. Arrange and resize your two program windows so that you can see both the source document (the Excel 2000 worksheet) and the destination document (the Word 2000 document).

2. Select the cells in the Excel 2000 worksheet that you want to link and transfer to Word 2000.

3. With the right mouse button, drag the edge of the highlighted cells to the location in your Word 2000 document where you want to place the table.

4. Release the right mouse button. Word 2000 opens a pop-up menu with these options: Move Here, Copy Here, Insert Excel Object Here, and Create Shortcut Here.

5. Select Insert Excel Object Here to indicate to Word 2000 that you want to create an object link (as opposed to a move or a copy of the cells). Although the cells appear as though Office 2000 copied them into the Word 2000 document, the cells represent only the link that you created between the Excel 2000 source and Word 2000 destination document.

> The destination document (in this case, the Word 2000 document) always reflects the most recent changes to the source document (in this case, the Excel 2000 worksheet). Therefore, if you must keep archives of old reports with the previous monthly values, you want to copy the cells instead of creating a link.

To see the interactive nature of the links, change a value in the source Excel 2000 worksheet. The Word 2000 document immediately reflects your change.

After inserting one or more links, select Edit, Links to open the dialog box shown in Figure 18.2. The Links dialog box contains every link in your document and enables you to change, break, or lock any link. When you break a link, the data becomes embedded in the document and no longer updates when you update the source. When you lock a link, you temporarily prevent the link from being updated when its source is updated.

FIGURE 18.2

Use the Links dialog box to manage your document links.

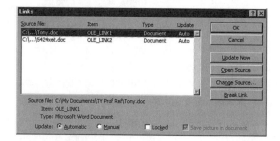

Creating Shortcuts

Instead of inserting a copy or a link, you can insert a *shortcut* in the destination document.

A *shortcut* is an icon inserted in your document that you can double-click to access data from a document stored elsewhere.

You probably use shortcuts less often than links and embedded copies when producing reports because you usually want the reports to show actual data and not icons. If you often work with data from one program while in another program, however, the shortcuts are nice. The data does not get in your way until you are ready to work with it because you see only icons that represent the shortcut data.

If you create a shortcut from one Office 2000 program to another, Office 2000 actually displays the data and does not display a shortcut icon. If you double-click the data, Office 2000 opens the appropriate program and enables you to edit the original data using the source program that created the data. If you insert a shortcut into a non-Office 2000 program, however, Office 2000 inserts a shortcut icon that represents the data. If you double-click the icon from within the other program, the appropriate Office 2000 program begins, and you can edit the data.

18

Consider this scenario: You are working in Excel 2000, modifying weekly salary figures for a large worksheet that you maintain. Each week you must study the salary amounts and enter a 10-line explanation of the salaries. Instead of typing the definition each week or (worse) using Excel 2000 as a limited word processor and editing the text each week, you could embed a shortcut to a Word 2000 document that contains a template for the text. When you double-click the shortcut, Excel 2000 starts Word 2000, which automatically loads the template. You can create the final text in the template, copy the Word 2000 text into your salary worksheet (replacing the shortcut), and save the worksheet under a name that designates the current week's work.

To insert a shortcut, perform these steps:

1. Arrange and resize your program windows so that you can see both the source document (the Word 2000 template document) and the destination document (the Excel 2000 worksheet).

2. Select the Word 2000 template text that you want to use for the shortcut. (Press Ctrl+A if you want to select the entire Word 2000 template document.)

3. With the right mouse button, drag the edge of the highlighted template text to the location in your Excel 2000 worksheet where you want to place the shortcut.

4. Release the right mouse button.

5. Select Create Shortcut Here from the pop-up menu. Office 2000 creates the shortcut. As with a link, the shortcut data does not actually appear in the destination document. Unlike a link, you can drag the shortcut to your Windows desktop, to Explorer, or to another program to create additional copies of the shortcut.

Outlook 2000 Letters

Users often keep Outlook 2000 loaded throughout the day, making appointments, calling contacts, and planning meetings. Outlook 2000 includes a handy feature that enables you to write a letter to any contact quickly and easily. A wizard makes the connection between Outlook 2000 and Word 2000. The following steps explain how to access this often-overlooked feature from Outlook 2000:

1. Click to select any Outlook 2000 contact.

2. Select Actions, New Letter to Contact to start the Word 2000 Letter Wizard shown in Figure 18.3.

FIGURE 18.3

The Letter Wizard takes care of the letter's formatting and address details.

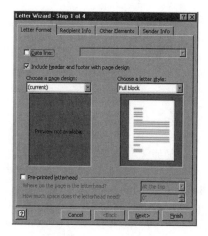

3. Select a page design and letter style from the dialog box.

4. Click the Recipient Info tab to display the letter's recipient information. The wizard fills in the contact's name and address.

5. Click the Other Elements tab to define other aspects of the letter such as the reference line and subject if those items are to appear.

6. Click the Sender Info tab to enter information about you, the sender. You can put your return address information as well as a company name and closing, such as "Best Wishes."

7. Click Finish and Word 2000 builds the letter using the elements you selected. Your only job now is to fill in the details, such as the body of the letter, and to complete the elements, such as the attention and subject lines.

Enhancing Your Office Documents

Office 2000 enables you to insert images and other objects into your documents. Graphics spruce up newsletters and other documents that require eye-catching images.

In both Word 2000 and Excel 2000, the Insert, Picture commands produce a menu that includes the following options:

- *Clip Art*. Enables you to insert an image from the Clip Gallery.

- *From File*. Enables you to insert an image from any graphics file. Use this option when you don't want to confine your images to the ones supplied in the Clip Gallery.

- *AutoShapes*. Inserts one of Office 2000's *AutoShapes*, which you can manipulate.

18

NEW TERM *AutoShape* is a ready-made shape that you can use in a document. After you insert a shape, you can resize, rotate, flip, color, and combine that shape with other shapes. The Drawing toolbar contains an AutoShape section, which produces the AutoShapes floating toolbar. Use the AutoShapes floating toolbar to insert and edit AutoShapes.

- *WordArt*. Displays the WordArt Gallery of WordArt styles (shown in Figure 18.4). WordArt enables you to convert text into shapes. Despite its name, WordArt is available from all Office 2000 products, not just Word 2000.

- *From Scanner or Camera*. Enables you to scan an image into the Office 2000 document or receive a digital camera's image. You must have a TWAIN-compliant scanner or digital camera attached to pull such images into Office 2000. (Most scanners follow the PC scanner standard called TWAIN; your scanner's documentation should indicate whether your scanner is TWAIN-compliant.)

- *Organization Chart*. Starts an Office 2000 add-in application that creates organizational charts (available only in Excel 2000).

- *Chart*. Displays a small Excel 2000-like worksheet (called a datasheet) in which you can enter data. The datasheet offers a sample set of cells in which you can enter your own values or import data from Excel 2000. When you close the datasheet, the resulting bar chart appears in your document (available only in Word 2000).

FIGURE 18.4

You can select a WordArt style from the WordArt Gallery.

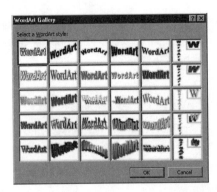

The next three sections describe the most common graphics insertions you can make into your Office 2000 documents from the Insert, Picture menu.

Inserting Images from Files

To add an image (or sound or video) clip-art file to a document, select Insert, Picture, From File to display the Insert Picture dialog box. Locate the image on your disk (or on your network, or the Internet by selecting the source from the Look In list box) and click Insert to insert the image.

If you often insert the same image, sound, or video clip, consider adding the clip to your Office 2000 Clip Gallery. The Clip Gallery makes common clips easy for you to find, thus eliminating the need for you to search your disk drive every time you want to insert a clip file.

To add a clip file to your Clip Gallery, perform these steps:

1. Display the Clip Gallery by selecting Insert, Picture, Clip Art.

2. Click the Import Clips button.

3. Locate the clip-art file that you want to import. When you locate the file and press Enter, Office 2000 displays the Clip Properties dialog box (shown in Figure 18.5), which shows a thumbnail sketch of the image along with the image's details.

4. Select the category and add a keyword or two (to help with subsequent searches for the image).

5. Press Enter to add the image to the proper Clip Gallery category.

FIGURE 18.5

Add a description for the image you want to add to Office 2000's Clip Gallery.

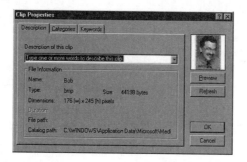

Using OfficeArt Tools

Office 2000 introduces a completely revamped set of *OfficeArt* tools. Instead of just upgrading previous Office drawing tools, Microsoft rewrote them for Office 2000 to improve performance.

OfficeArt is the general term applied to the Office 2000 drawing tools such as AutoShape and WordArt.

OfficeArt provides a single drawing interface for all the Office 2000 programs. If you learn how to use AutoShape inside Word 2000, you also know how to use AutoShape in Excel 2000. Although you might expect such an integrated and consistent drawing system, Office 2000 is the first time Microsoft successfully integrated one consistent drawing interface into all the Office 2000 products.

 Unlike the other Office 2000 products, Outlook 2000 contains no OfficeArt tool support.

 OfficeArt's drawing tools work with all the applicable Office 2000 features. Therefore, you can spell check the text in an AutoShape drawing.

Not only did Microsoft help you learn the OfficeArt tools more quickly, but Office 2000 includes only one set of OfficeArt code. Therefore, whether you install only Word 2000 or the entire set of Office 2000 programs, Office 2000 installs a single shared copy of the OfficeArt code. As a result, the drawing tools work quickly and efficiently, consuming much less disk space than if each program contained its own drawing code.

Inserting WordArt

WordArt displays text in several shapes, colors, and styles to add pizzazz to your documents. You can add an eye-catching title at the top of an Excel 2000 worksheet, for example, to grab the reader's attention.

To add a WordArt image, perform these steps:

1. Select Insert, Picture, WordArt to display the WordArt Gallery dialog box.

2. Select the WordArt style that you want to use by double-clicking the style. Office 2000 displays the Edit WordArt Text dialog box (shown in Figure 18.6).

3. Enter the text that you want to format as WordArt and select the proper font and point size. The WordArt style that you select follows your font and size request as closely as possible.

4. Click OK to insert the WordArt text. Office 2000 displays resizing handles around the WordArt image, which you can use to resize or move the image. In addition, the WordArt toolbar that appears provides several editing techniques that you can apply to the image, such as rotation and color.

FIGURE 18.6

Provide text for WordArt to format.

Figure 18.7 shows a sample WordArt image inserted at the top of a small imported Excel worksheet.

FIGURE 18.7

A sample of WordArt's appeal.

18

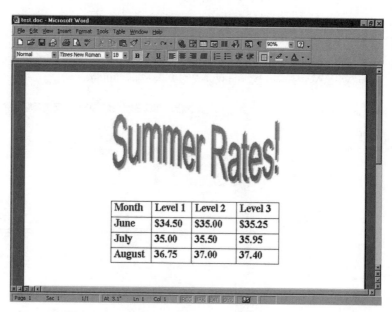

Inserting AutoShapes

The AutoShapes toolbar that appears when you insert an AutoShape provides numerous drawing tools for creating line drawings inside Word 2000 or Excel 2000. When you click one of the toolbar options described next, Office 2000 opens a set of drawing tools for that option. If you click the Basic Shapes tool, for example, Office 2000 displays a drop-down selection box of about 30 shapes. After you select a shape, you can continue drawing with that shape until you select a different shape or another AutoShape tool. To draw a shape, drag the mouse over the editing area.

The following list describes the AutoShape tools you find on the AutoShapes toolbar:

- *Lines*. Provides straight, curved, and freeform lines that you can draw with the mouse.
- *Basic shapes*. Provides circles, ovals, rectangles, and other shapes that you can select and draw with.
- *Block arrows (Word 2000 only)*. Provides several connecting arrows that you can use for pointing parts of a drawing to each other.
- *Flowchart*. Draws various flowcharting symbols.
- *Stars and Banners*. Places stars and various banners on the editing area.
- *Callouts*. Draws spoken and bubble-thought cartoon callouts so that the figures you draw can be made to speak.
- *Connectors (Excel 2000 only)*. Draws several kinds of lines that connect one AutoShape image to another.

Figure 18.8 shows how you can have fun by combining AutoShape and OfficeArt images with WordArt to spruce up a Word 2000 document.

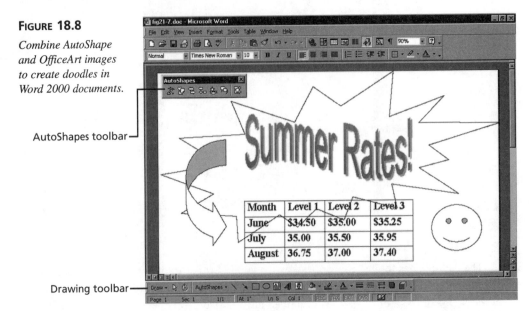

FIGURE 18.8

Combine AutoShape and OfficeArt images to create doodles in Word 2000 documents.

AutoShapes toolbar—

Drawing toolbar—

AutoShape offers two ways to add text to your image:

- *Placing text in a callout.* As soon as you add an AutoShape callout to your drawing, Office 2000 enables you to enter text for that callout.

- *Placing text anywhere on the AutoShape image.* Right-click anywhere over the AutoShape area and select Add Text from the pop-up menu to place text on any AutoShape image.

> When you click any AutoShape image that you draw, resizing handles appear so that you can resize the image. In addition, you will see the image's yellow adjustment handle. Drag the adjustment handle to change the shape's most prominent feature, such as the smile on the happy face.

When you add an AutoShape to your document, Office 2000 displays the Drawing toolbar on your screen. Select from the Drawing toolbar to change the orientation of any selected AutoShape image. You can vertically or horizontally flip an image, for example. Any text you have placed on the image retains its original orientation.

Summary

This hour described how to integrate Office 2000 products by sharing data files among the programs. One of the easiest ways to copy or move data from one Office 2000 program to another is to use drag and drop. By holding your right mouse button, you can control how the drag-and-drop operation sends the data from one document to another.

Word 2000 and Excel 2000 share data files easily as long as you use the proper heading styles. Presenters often use Word 2000 documents as a basis for a presentation, and you will appreciate the automation Office 2000 provides.

This hour also explained how to use the graphics-related tools to insert art and draw pictures inside your Office 2000 documents. As you might expect, the Office 2000 tools are easy to use and appear (along with their toolbars) when you request them, but stay out of the way when you don't need to work with art.

The next hour, "Office 2000 and the Internet," introduces the Internet and shows you how to access Web pages using the Internet Explorer Web browser included with Office 2000.

18

Q&A

Q What format does my data take when I drag and drop something from one Office 2000 product to another?

A Office 2000 provides excellent intuitive conversions when you combine data from more than one Office 2000 product. When you drag a worksheet from Excel 2000 to Word 2000, for example, the worksheet becomes a Word 2000 table. You then can use all the standard table-editing tools in Word 2000 to modify the appearance of the worksheet. Excel 2000 converts Word 2000 text to text-cell entries.

Q What is the advantage of a shortcut over a link?

A If you are sticking with Office 2000 products only, you probably want to use links to embed live connections from one document to another. If you share Office 2000 documents with other programs, however, those programs probably recognize shortcuts and present your Office 2000 document as an icon. If you use a stand-alone email program (such as Eudora) to send a Word 2000 document, for example, the Word 2000 document appears in your email note as a Word 2000 icon. If you double-click that icon (or if your email recipient double-clicks the icon after receiving the email), Word 2000 starts (assuming Word 2000 resides on the system), and you (or the recipient) are able to edit the document.

Q Why would you ever want to copy data and not create a link to another document?

A When you copy data, it is copied into the destination document, so the data resides in both the destination document and the source document. If you were to take the destination document to another computer, the document could not access its original link (if you had used a link). In addition, you may not want the destination document's data being hooked "live" to the source data. If you are creating archive files of older data, for example, you always want to copy the data and not form a link or shortcut to the original source data.

Q What is the difference between AutoShape, WordArt, and OfficeArt?

A AutoShape is the general term applied to all the drawing tools provided when you insert an AutoShape picture into an Office 2000 document. The AutoShapes toolbar appears when you draw AutoShape graphics to help you with freeform drawings and to supply common shapes that you might need. WordArt is a feature that manipulates and colors text to turn standard text into various eye-catching 3D colorful styles. The term *OfficeArt* is a general term applied to all the graphics and drawing tools you find in the Office 2000 suite of products, including AutoShape and WordArt.

Q What is the difference between an adjustment handle and a resizing handle?

A Adjustment handles change the *form* of shapes; resizing handles change the *size* of shapes.

Hour 19

Office 2000 and the Internet

If you are new to Internet technology, this hour introduces you to a whole new world. The Internet is much more a part of computer users' lives than ever before. Microsoft recognizes this and includes Internet access capabilities in Office 2000. The individual Office 2000 products include Internet connections and Internet Explorer, an Internet browser that enables you to access the Internet from within Windows. Microsoft is committed to integrating Internet access more completely into future Office and Windows releases—you see that commitment already in Office 2000.

If you have used the Internet before, you may want to skim this hour to see how the Office 2000 products and Internet Explorer connect you to the Internet.

The highlights of this hour include the following:

- Why the Internet and the Web are so important
- How to start and use Internet Explorer

- How to surf the Internet to find and view multimedia information
- How to use search engines to locate the exact Internet information you need
- How to access the Internet from within an Office 2000 product
- How to view Office 2000 documents from within Internet Explorer
- How to include Web links in your Office documents

Introducing the Internet

The *Internet* began as a government- and university-linked system of computers that has since turned into a business and personal system that contains a seemingly infinite amount of information. The Internet is a worldwide system of interconnected computers. Whereas your desktop computer is a standalone machine, and a network of computers is linked together by wires, the Internet is a worldwide online network of computers connected to standalone computers through modems.

NEW TERM The *Internet* is a worldwide network connection of computers that provides information and offers electronic mail services to the users who access the Internet from their own computers.

The Internet offers the most unique research and information-access tools ever invented. You can get up-to-date news, stock quotes, and sports scores. You can locate product information, purchase everything from cars to airline tickets, play games, listen to music, view videos, and chat with other Internet users around the world via your keyboard or microphone.

That vast amount and format of Internet data requires a standard so that all may share in the Internet's content. Users all over the world send electronic mail to each other, view each other's Internet material, send files back and forth, conduct business over the Internet, research from the Internet, keep up with the latest news, sports, entertainment, and business headlines, and chat with each other through the keyboard, voice, and video.

Introducing the Web

The *Web*, or *World Wide Web (WWW)*, is a collection of Internet pages of information. Web pages can contain text, graphics, sound, and video. Figure 19.1 shows a sample Web page. As you can see, the Web page's graphics and text organize information into a magazine-like readable and appealing format.

FIGURE 19.1

Web pages provide Internet information in a standard format.

The term *Web*, or *World Wide Web (WWW)*, is given to the interconnected system of Internet information pages that you can access to read specific information. Many of the Web pages are connected with hypertext links that enable you to more easily traverse the pages that you view.

Generally, a Web site might contain more information than fits easily on a single Web page. Therefore, many Web pages contain links to several additional extended pages, as well as other linked Web pages that may be related to the original topic. The first page you view is called the *home page*, and from the home page you can view other pages of information.

19

A *home page*, also called a *start page*, is the page you have requested Internet Explorer to show first when you sign on to the Internet.

The Internet has standardized Web page locations with a series of addresses called *URLs*, or *uniform resource locators*, that are formatted like this: www.microsoft.com. You can view any Web page if you know its URL. If you do not know the URL, the Internet provides several search engines that find Web pages when you search for topics. You learn how to search the Internet later this hour in the "Searching for the Information You Need" section.

Using Internet Explorer

Internet Explorer is a *Web browser* (also called a *browser*) that brings Web data to your desktop. Microsoft's Web browsing program, Internet Explorer 5, comes with every version of Office 2000. Therefore, you already have the tools you need to access the Internet if you have Office 2000.

 A *Web browser*, or *browser*, is a program you use to access the Internet and display Web data.

If your company offers cabled Internet access, you need the interface card in your PC that can accept the cable. If you use the Internet from home, or from an office that does not provide cabled Internet access, you need to get Internet access through an *ISP*, an *Internet service provider*. One of the easiest ways to get access is through the Microsoft Network or America Online services, which have access programs that are available with all Windows 95 and Windows 98 installations. If you want Internet access through another ISP, such as a local Internet provider, your provider will tell you how to use Internet Explorer or another Web browser to access the ISP's Internet system. You will also need modem access (28.8Kbps is the minimum recommended speed these days) or another Internet connection that might be available in your area such as a cable modem, ISDN, or satellite access. Check your phone book for options that you can get locally.

 An *Internet service provider*, or *ISP*, is a company that provides you with a phone number that you can command Internet Explorer to dial for Internet access.

 Although Internet service is relatively inexpensive, it is not free. Most ISPs charge a flat rate, such as $19.95 a month, for unlimited Internet usage.

Starting Internet Explorer

Internet Explorer is easy to start. You literally can access the Internet with one or two clicks by running Internet Explorer. After you sign up with an ISP and get the Internet phone number to access the Web, you are ready to navigate the Internet.

To start Internet Explorer, double-click the Windows desktop icon labeled Internet Explorer. If you get an Internet Connection Wizard dialog box, you must contact your service provider to learn how to hook up Internet Explorer to the Internet. Internet Explorer prompts you for the username and password that you selected when you signed up for your Internet service.

Assuming that you have Internet access and have been set up with a provider, Internet Explorer dials your provider and displays the page set up to be your initial browser's home page. If you have high-speed, constant access, through a company connection or through cable modem service, you may not have to log on to the Internet to use it. Depending on the amount of information and graphics on the page, the display may take a few moments or may display right away.

The Home button on the Internet Explorer toolbar displays your home page. You can return to the home page by clicking the Home button. You can change your home page address by entering a new home page address within the Tools, Internet Options dialog box's General Tab. When you enter a new home page address, Internet Explorer returns to that page whenever you click the Home toolbar button or start Internet Explorer in a subsequent session.

Managing the Internet Explorer Screen

You can navigate Internet pages easily with Internet Explorer. If you are new to the Internet, study Figure 19.2 to learn the parts of the Internet Explorer screen. Internet Explorer displays your home page and lists the home page's address in the address area.

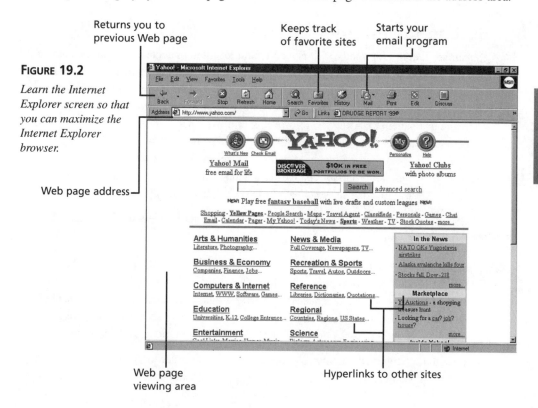

FIGURE 19.2

Learn the Internet Explorer screen so that you can maximize the Internet Explorer browser.

19

Use the following guidelines to familiarize yourself with the Internet Explorer screen:

- Some Web site addresses are lengthy. Drag the Address bar left or right (giving more or less room to the link buttons) to adjust the address display width.
- Click the down arrow at the right of the address entry to open a list of recently traversed site addresses. If this is the first time you or anyone has used your computer's Internet Explorer, you may not see sites other than the current home page sites.
- Use the scrollbar to see more of your home page. Most Web pages take more room than fit on one screen.
- Use the View menu to hide the toolbar and status bar so that you have more display room for the Web page. The Address list box can be hidden as well. You can still enter site addresses that you want to traverse from the File menu.
- Display the toolbar and status bar again by clicking the appropriate View menu options.

You will probably spend a lot of time on the Internet, so the better you understand Internet Explorer, the more effective you will be online.

Surfing the Internet

Remember that the Internet's Web is a collection of interconnected Web pages. As you *surf* the Internet using Internet Explorer, you run across Web pages that contain *links* to other sites. These links (often called *hot spots* or *hypertext links*) may be underlined, appear in different colors from the surrounding text, or even be activated by clicking on an image or imagemap. After you click a link on a Web page, if you return to that Web page, the link appears in a different color to let you know that you have already gone there. You can locate these links by moving your mouse cursor over the underlined description. If the mouse cursor changes to a hand, you can click the hand to move to that page. After a brief pause, your Web browser displays the page.

NEW TERM To *surf* the Internet means to navigate the Internet by viewing Web pages that interest you.

NEW TERM A *link*, *hyperlink*, or *hot spot*, is nothing more than a URL to another Web site embedded on a Web page. The link often displays a description and not a technical URL. (As you move your mouse cursor over a link, your Web browser's status bar displays the actual URL to the link.) Therefore, you can traverse related Web pages without worrying about addresses; just click link descriptions to move to those sites.

Suppose that you view the home page of your financial broker to update an Excel 2000 investment worksheet that contains your stock portfolio. The page might include links to other related pages, such as stock quotation pages, company financial informational pages, and order-entry pages in which you can enter your own stock purchase requests.

One of the most useful features of Internet Explorer and every other Web browser is the browser's capability to return to sites you have visited both in the current session and in former sessions. The toolbar's Back button takes you back to a site you just visited, and you can keep clicking the Back button to return to pages you have visited in the current session. The Forward toolbar button returns you to pages from where you have backed up. Because this back-and-forth feature is so popular with Web browsers, Microsoft chose to add the Back and Forward buttons to all Windows 98 windows.

At any point, you can click the Address drop-down list box to see a list of URLs you have visited. You find addresses from the current as well as previous Internet Explorer Web sessions.

If you know the address of a Web site that you want to view, you can type the site's address directly in the Address text box and click Go. Internet Explorer takes you to that site and displays its Web page. In addition, you can select File, Open to display an Open dialog box in which you can enter an address. When you click OK, Internet Explorer displays the page associated with that address.

If you find a location you really like, save that location in Internet Explorer's Favorites list. If you run across a site that discusses your favorite television show and you want to return to that site again quickly, for example, click the Favorites toolbar button to add the site to your Favorites list. The Address history does not keep track of a lot of recently visited addresses; you can store your favorite sites in the Favorites folders, however, so that you can quickly access them during future Internet sessions.

As you familiarize yourself with the Internet, you will want to visit Web pages that interest you. After you visit a site, you can easily return to that site. Use the following steps to become comfortable surfing Web pages:

1. If you have not started Internet Explorer, start it and log on to the Internet.

2. Click the Address list box to select the URL of your home page.

3. Type the following Web page address: **www.mcp.com**. You see Macmillan Computer Publishing's home page appear, as shown in Figure 19.3. (Depending on the changes that have been made to the site recently, the site may not match Figure 19.3 exactly.)

19

FIGURE 19.3

Practice surfing the Web to Macmillan Computer Publishing's home page.

Often, you see Web addresses prefaced with the text `http://`. This prefix indicates both for you and your browser that the address to the right of the second slash is a Web page's URL. This prefix is optional for today's Web browsers. If you type the prefix, be sure to type forward slashes and not the MS-DOS or Windows backslashes you may be used to typing for PC folder locations.

4. Click any link on the page. After a brief pause, you see the linked Web page.

5. Click the toolbar's Back button. Almost instantly, the first page appears.

6. After you are back at Macmillan Computer Publishing's home page, practice building a favorite site list by clicking the Favorites toolbar button.

7. Click the Add to Favorites option. Internet Explorer displays the Add to Favorites dialog box.

8. Enter a description for the page. Make the description something you can remember the page by (such as **Macmillan Computer Book Publishing**).

9. Click OK.

10. Click the Favorites toolbar button again. You see the new entry. When you select the favorite entry, Internet Explorer looks up that entry's stored URL address and goes to that Web page.

If you add too many favorites, your favorites list might become unmanage-able. As you add to your favorites list, you can create folders using the Create In button in the Add to Favorites dialog box. By setting up a series of folders named by subjects, you can group your favorite Web sites by subject so that they are easier to manage and find.

Some Web pages take a long time to display. Often, Web pages contain a lot of text and graphics, and that data takes time to arrive on your computer. Therefore, you might click to a favorite Web site but have to wait a minute or longer to see the entire site.

To speed things up, Internet Explorer attempts to show as much of the page as possible, especially the text on the page, before downloading the graphic images. Internet Explorer puts placeholders where the graphic images are to appear. If you view the page for a few moments, the placeholders' images begin to appear until the final page, with all graphics, displays in its entirety.

Searching for the Information You Need

How can you expect to find any information on a vast network of networks such as the Internet? Web pages offer linked sites in an appealing format that enable you to comfort-ably view information and see related pages, but you must know the location of one of the site's pages before the links can help.

Fortunately, Internet Explorer offers a searching mechanism that helps you locate infor-mation on the Web. By clicking the Search toolbar button, you can access a search page, such as the one shown in Figure 19.4. As you can see, the search page consumes the left pane of your Internet screen. You can still see the Web page you were viewing while you perform a search. The resulting search page that you find will appear in the right pane when you make the search. You can easily return the browser to a single-pane Web view by clicking the X in the upper-right hand corner of the Search pane.

19

The Internet Explorer 5 search page offers the benefit of multiple search engines. The accuracy of the search depends on the words and phrases you enter, as well as the capa-bility of the search engine. Some search engines you can choose from search only Web pages, for example, while others search *newsgroups*. To search with a different search engine, click the search pane's Customize toolbar button. The right pane displays a list of search engines that you can use for subsequent searching.

Click to change search engine

FIGURE 19.4

Locate data on the Web.

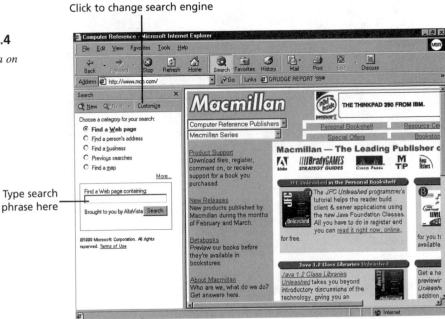

Type search phrase here

NEW TERM A *search engine* is a Web program that enables you to enter words and phrases for which to search, and then scans the vast information on the Web to locate sites that contain the words or phrase.

NEW TERM *Newsgroups* are Internet discussion areas that hold files and messages related to topics. You can read messages and download files, as well as post your own messages and files for others to see. Outlook Express, a program that comes with Internet Explorer 5, enables you to read newsgroups.

After the search engine locates its information, Internet Explorer displays from zero to several address links in the left pane that you can click to find specific Web-based information about your topic. (Figure 19.5 shows the result of one search.) By scrolling down the page (and by clicking the additional pages of links if your search turns up a lot of sites), you can read the descriptions of the pages. The descriptions often contain the first few lines of the located Web page text.

FIGURE 19.5

The results of a search might produce several pages of Web sites.

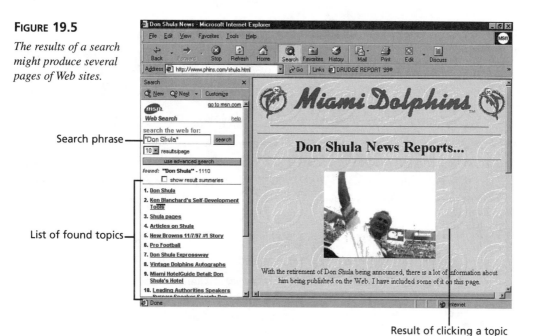

Search phrase

List of found topics

Result of clicking a topic

Each search engine locates information differently and each also has its own rules for the words and phrases you enter. Keep in mind that the more specific your search phrase is, the more accurately the search engine can find information that helps you.

Generally, you can use these guidelines with most search engines:

- Enclose a multiple word phrase in quotation marks if you want the search engine to search for those words in the order in which they are listed. If you enter "West Virginia", for example, the search engine searches for that specific name. If you enter West Virginia (without the quotation marks), however, most search engines locate every site that contains the word *West* and every site that contains the word *Virginia*, most of which would have nothing to do with the state you originally wanted to locate.

- Place a plus sign (+) before each word for which you want to search. Entering +Tulsa +oil would find only those sites that contain both the word *Tulsa* and the word *oil*.

Remember that these search criteria rules are only guidelines that usually work well with the most popular search engines. Some of the search engines follow slightly different rules and you have to look up that search engine page's help references for specific information if the previous rules do not seem to work the way you expect.

19

Office 2000 Products and the Web

Office 2000 offers a complete set of tools that integrate the Office 2000 products and the Internet. From any Office 2000 product, you can access files and Web pages on the Internet. The following sections describe how you can access the Web from Office 2000.

Viewing Web Pages Within Office Products

You don't have to start Internet Explorer to view a Web page from within an Office 2000 product. All you need to do is display the Web toolbar and type the address you want to see. While creating an Excel worksheet, for example, you may need to locate financial information from your company's Web site. Follow these steps to surf the Web from Excel:

1. Select View, Toolbars, Web to add a new Web-browsing toolbar to Excel.

2. Click the address area of the Web toolbar.

3. Enter the Web address that you want to see. (Alternatively, you can click the Favorites list on the Web toolbar to select the Web page that you want to view.) If you access the Internet from a modem, Excel dials your Internet service provider to get Internet access.

4. Excel's menus and toolbars change to match that of Internet Explorer. Excel then displays the Web site that you want to view. You can switch between the Web and Excel by pressing Alt+Tab. In addition, you can copy and paste information from Web pages to your Excel worksheet.

Viewing Documents in Internet Explorer

In addition to starting Internet Explorer from an Office 2000 product, you can view Office 2000 documents directly from within Internet Explorer. Whenever you are browsing the Internet, select File, Open and type the full path (or click Browse to locate the path) and filename you want to view from within Internet Explorer.

Internet Explorer opens the file and displays the file within the browser window. Not only does Internet Explorer display the file, but all Internet Explorer menus change to enable full editing capabilities for that Office 2000 document. If you open a Word 2000 document, for example, Internet Explorer menus change to Word 2000 menus; you can then insert a table or format the text as if you were using Word 2000. If you click the Internet Explorer Tools toolbar button while viewing the Office 2000 document, the Word 2000 toolbars appear beneath the Internet Explorer toolbar so that you have full Word 2000 toolbar capabilities from within Internet Explorer.

If you click the Back button, Internet Explorer displays the preceding Web page or whatever else you were viewing from Internet Explorer, and the menus change so that you can surf the Web normally.

> You might wonder why Excel 2000 seems to become Internet Explorer. A Web page does not actually appear inside the Excel 2000 worksheet window when you use the Web toolbar to request the Web page. Excel 2000 cannot access the Web; for that, you need a Web browser. Nevertheless, the Web toolbar that you find in all the Office 2000 products does enable you to navigate between Office 2000 documents without changing programs, as you will learn toward the end of this hour.
>
> Perhaps someday, the only program you will need is a Web browser! The browser menus and toolbars can change depending on the document with which you want to work. Internet Explorer 5 integrates with Windows itself so that the browser becomes part of your Windows environment. The Internet is so important to computing today that companies such as Microsoft are incorporating Web technology into all products, as well as operating systems.

Creating Links in Office 2000

As you learned how to use Office 2000 products throughout the previous hours, you learned that you can type a Web address in an Office 2000 document to create a link to that address. When you type a Web address in a PowerPoint 2000 presentation, for example, that address becomes a link to an active Web site address. If you click that address, the Office 2000 product starts Internet Explorer, logs you on to the Internet if needed, and displays the Web page located at that address.

> You don't have to use Web addresses for hyperlinks in Office 2000 documents. You can enter path and filenames that reside on your own PC. When you or another user clicks the link, the Office 2000 product displays that link's file. Therefore, you can easily link documents together, even documents from different products within Office 2000.

Upgrading to Internet Explorer 5

Like most Office 2000 users, you probably had Internet Explorer 4 already installed on your PC. When you installed Office 2000, the installation routine offered to install Internet Explorer 5. To take advantage of all of Office 2000's Web-related features, and to use

Internet Explorer's latest and greatest operations, you should upgrade to version 5. If you chose not to upgrade but stayed with version 4, you can still use most features in Office 2000. Unless you upgraded to 5, however, some of the remaining portions of this lesson will be different for you and your screens may not match exactly the book's figures.

Use Internet Explorer 5 More Effectively

Now that you have gotten a taste for what Internet Explorer 5 can do (in this and the past two lessons), you are ready to take the browser to the next step so that you can utilize Internet Explorer 5, along with Office 2000, at their fullest potential.

Managing Favorites

You will add to your Favorites list as you find more Web sites that interest you. By adding Web sites that you visit frequently to your Favorites list, you receive these advantages:

- You can quickly return to these sites as you surf the Web, by clicking the Internet Explorer 5 Favorites button and selecting from the list.
- You can return to these sites even if you are not surfing the Web in Internet Explorer from one of the Office 2000 applications' Web toolbar or from the Start menu's Favorites option.
- You can manage your favorites list to keep your favorite sites organized for fast access and review.

To add a site to your Favorites list, select Favorites, Add to Favorites to display the Add Favorite dialog box shown in Figure 19.6. To add the current site to the Favorites list, you only need to click OK and Internet Explorer 5 adds the site to your list. You will almost certainly want to add your own name for the site (the default name is the site's title provided by the site authors) and store the site in a folder that exists or that you create to organize your favorite sites by subject. You might want to store a movie review site in a folder named Entertainment, for example.

FIGURE 19.6

You can easily add and organize your Favorites list.

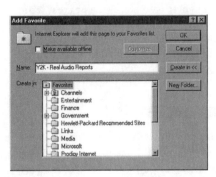

When you click the Favorites button on the toolbar, a left pane opens with your Favorites list displayed. If you click the X in the Favorites list area, the Favorites list goes away, giving you more room to view the Web page content.

In addition to your Favorites list that you maintain, Internet Explorer 5 keeps track of your recently visited Web site addresses. If you click the History button on your toolbar, Internet Explorer 5 adds a History list in a left pane (where the Favorites list resided) so that you can select from a list of Web site addresses you have visited in the past few days.

Keeping Links

If you want your most important Web sites located even closer than the Favorites list, add the site to your Links bar. At the top of Internet Explorer, as well as on your Windows taskbar if you choose to display the Links toolbar, resides a series of links to Web sites. As Figure 19.7 shows, your links are always on your screen ready for your click to jump to that site.

FIGURE 19.7

Your links are ready for one-click access.

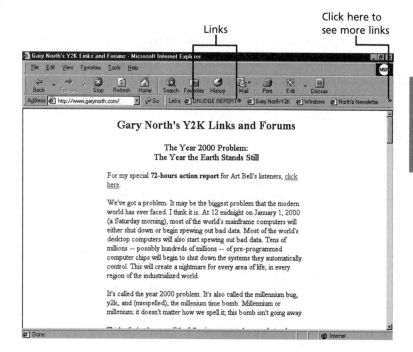

Links

Click here to
see more links

19

To remove or change a link, right-click over the link and select the appropriate menu item from the pop-up menu. To add a link, drag its Web site icon from the Internet Explorer 5 Address text box to the Links bar. You can rearrange links by dragging them to a different location. To see the links that don't fit on the Links bar, click the arrow at the far right of the Links bar.

Internet Explorer 5 helps improve the way that you view Web pages with graphics. Some Web pages take several seconds, and possibly longer, to display. Although the text appears right away, the graphics take some time to load. Internet Explorer 5 puts a status bar at the bottom of the browser so that you know how much (by percentage) of the current page is loaded and how much is left. If you don't want to wait on a long load, you can load another page.

Using Shortcut Keys

Internet Explorer 5 supports these two shortcut keys that will save you time:

- *F4.* Opens the Web address's drop-down list box so that you can quickly jump to a site you have visited recently.
- *F5.* Places the text cursor in the Web address list box so you can type a Web address to display.

If a Web address meets this common format: `http://www.`*SiteAddress*`.com`, all you need to type is *SiteAddress* and Internet Explorer searches for the correct site using the fully formatted Web site address.

As Internet Explorer searches and locates Web sites, Internet Explorer produces sounds. A bell rings when a Web page you search for appears in the browser window, for example. The sounds are helpful when you work in multiple open program windows simultaneously. You can enter a Web address and press Alt+Tab to switch to Word 2000 and type more of a letter. When Internet Explorer locates and begins to display that site, you will hear the bell ring and know that it is time to return to Internet Explorer to view the Web page.

One final tip can provide multiple Web pages from one browser. Suppose you are viewing a Web page with links to another page. You want to read both pages, perhaps to compare notes in resized windows. You can open a second Internet Explorer browser window by right-clicking over the hyperlink and selecting Open in New Window from the pop-up menu that appears. A second Web browser window opens with that linked Web site there, but your original browser window will still be open displaying the Web site you started from. By judiciously opening new Web sites in additional windows, you can view several Web pages at the same time without having to browse between them each time you go back to one.

Summary

This hour introduced you to the Internet, the Web, Internet Explorer, and how Office 2000 and the Internet work together. The Internet is a vast collection of networked computers all around the world. You can access the Internet as long as you have access through an Internet service provider. Although Internet information appears in many forms, the most useful Internet information often appears on Web pages that contain text, graphics, sound, and video.

Internet Explorer includes searching tools as well as a history system that keeps track of recent Web pages. Not only can you view Web pages with Internet Explorer, but you can also view other kinds of files on your computer. As the Internet becomes more organized and Internet access gets faster and cheaper, the Web browser will become part of your daily computing routine. One day, you will find that you do most of your work from Web browsing software such as Internet Explorer.

The next hour continues the Internet discussion by explaining how to create Web pages from within the Office 2000 products.

19

Q&A

Q I have clicked the Internet Explorer icon, but I don't see Web pages. What do I have to do to get on the Internet?

A Do you have Internet access from Microsoft Network or from another Internet service provider? Generally, unless you work for a company that offers Internet access to its employees, you have to sign up for Internet access, get the access phone number, pay a monthly fee (most Internet service providers offer unlimited access for a flat monthly rate), and set up a browser, such as Internet Explorer, to access that provider.

Q Does all Internet information appear on Web pages?

A The Internet's information appears in many forms, sometimes in a form known as an FTP site or a newsgroup. The Web page standard, however, has become one of the most popular ways to organize and view Internet information. As more people used the Web-page standard, more modern technology enabled that standard to evolve into a uniform container of multimedia-based information. Therefore, with a Web browser, you can view all kinds of information over the Web.

Hour **20**

Creating Web Pages with Office 2000

You don't have to be just a user of Web pages. You can create them yourself with the tools available in Office 2000. By utilizing the Office 2000 wizards and design tools, you can quickly create Web pages that equal those made by the pros. With Office 2000, you can hone text, graphics, and data tables, and present that data to the world on the Web.

Most Office 2000 users use Word 2000 as their primary Web page development tool and import other Office 2000 product data into their Word 2000 Web pages. All the Office 2000 products are Internet aware; they all enable you to convert their data to Web pages.

The highlights of this hour include the following:

- What you need to publish pages on the Internet
- How to save Word 2000 documents as Web pages
- When to use the various Office 2000 wizards to generate your initial Web pages
- How to export Excel 2000 to your Word 2000-based Web pages

Preparing to Publish Web Pages

Before you can publish pages on the Web, you must have access to a *Web server*. Perhaps your company uses a Web server for its site; if so, you can store your Web pages on that computer. If you have access to an online service, such as CompuServe, it may offer an area for one or more Web pages that you can copy to the online site's Web server for a small charge, or even for free.

NEW TERM   A *Web server* is a computer dedicated to presenting Web pages on the Internet.

You may want to publish a personal Web page for fun, so you can enjoy telling the world your stories and sharing your family photos with others. If you want to start a business on the Internet, however, or offer timely information that you want others to visit often, you need to be aware that Web page *maintenance* is costly and time-consuming. You don't just create a Web page, load the page on the Web, and expect to keep people's interest if you don't keep the material up-to-date. In addition, performing *e-commerce* often requires the help of an outside agency such as a bank or credit card service, so you may want to get help when you first go online with your organization.

NEW TERM   *Maintenance* is the process of modifying and updating Web page information.

NEW TERM   *E-commerce*, or *electronic commerce*, is business conducted over the Internet and includes transactions such as online banking and buying and selling transactions using credit cards.

Office 2000 Small Business Edition and the Web

One of the reasons you should consider using Office 2000 to create Web pages is that you already have the Office 2000 tools. Office 2000 offers several wizards and templates that you can use to create your Web pages. Office 2000 offers good tools with which you can create and maintain a Web page. Nevertheless, Office 2000 is not necessarily the best tool you can use to create Web pages. If your Web page generates a lot of interest, you may want to use a more specific tool for Web page creation such as Microsoft FrontPage 2000 or Internet Explorer. FrontPage 2000 offers specific Web page tools that create advanced Web pages with very little effort on your part.

Although FrontPage 2000 is not a part of Office 2000 Small Business Edition, Internet Explorer does include a "lite" version of FrontPage 2000 called FrontPage Express. FrontPage Express is basically the portion of FrontPage 2000 that deals with page editing only, without FrontPage 2000's Web management environment and other tools.

All the Web material in Office 2000 supports both the Internet and *intranets*. Therefore, if your company maintains an intranet, you can save Web pages to that intranet as easily as (and sometimes more easily than) on the Internet.

NEW TERM An *intranet* is a local area network of computers whose users use Web pages and Internet technology to communicate with each other on the network. Instead of dialing up an Internet service provider and accessing a Web page from another location, you just access a Web page from a coworker's PC.

The following sections describe how you can use Word 2000, Excel 2000, and FrontPage Express to generate Web-page information.

Once you see how these individual Office 2000 products support Web pages, you will be ready to publish your own Web pages.

Most of your early Web page creation will probably take place in Word 2000 until you master a more full-featured Web-page creation program such as FrontPage 2000. Even if you embed an Access database on a Web page, you will probably do most of that Web page design in Word 2000. Therefore, most of this hour focuses on Word 2000's Web-editing tools. The final sections describe how to integrate the other Office 2000 products into your Word 2000 Web pages, and they give a brief introduction to FrontPage Express.

Word 2000 and Web Pages

Word 2000 offers two ways to create Web pages: You can save Word 2000 documents in a Web page format or you can create a Web page using one of the Word 2000 wizards. The following two sections explain each method.

20

Saving Word 2000 Documents as Web Pages

One of the easiest ways to create a Web page from a Word 2000 document is to save the document in *HTML format*. Suppose you create a company report that you want to publish on your Web server. All you have to do is select File, Save as Web page, and then click OK. Word 2000 saves the file in an *HTML* Web page–compatible format that you can transfer to the Web server.

NEW TERM   *HTML*, or *Hypertext Markup Language*, is the name of the language format used by Web pages. HTML pages contain formatting codes that define how the page looks from within a Web browser such as Internet Explorer or Netscape Navigator.

After Word 2000 converts your document to HTML format, you can view your document from the Internet Explorer Web browser by selecting File, Web Page Preview. By viewing the document from the Web browser, you'll see how your Web page will appear to other Internet users. Notice that the format differs somewhat from the format of the Word 2000 document (especially italicized fonts).

When working with an HTML document in Word 2000, Word 2000 changes its toolbars to provide better tools for Web page editing. You can also choose to display the Web toolbar from the View menu. When formatting your Web page, keep your end user in mind and write for the largest audience possible. You can select a fancy font for your Web page text. If you stick with the standard fonts that come with Windows (such as Courier, Times New Roman, and Arial), however, you ensure that all viewers of your Web page will have those same fonts and the page will look the way you intend it to look on their browsers.

Keep in mind that Web pages are often colorful. Color fonts can spruce up a Web page dramatically as long as you don't overdo the colors. Use the toolbar's Font Color button to select a new font color quickly.

If you have written HTML code before, you can embed HTML commands in your Web page from within Word 2000. Format your HTML code with the HTML markup style, and Word 2000 embeds it as HTML code. The code does not appear on the Web page, but formats the page according to your instructions. All HTML markup text is hidden, but you can display the text by clicking the Show/Hide button on the Word 2000 toolbar.

Actually, Word 2000 converts your Web page elements to HTML code as soon as you add something to a Web page. You can, at any time during the development of your Web page, select View, HTML Source to see the HTML code behind your Web page. Word 2000 starts a new environment known as the *Microsoft Development environment*. Figure 20.1 shows HTML code for a Web page being displayed for editing inside the Microsoft Development environment. Inside the Microsoft Development environment, you can return to the formatted Web page by selecting File, HTML. Although the Microsoft Development environment's features are beyond the scope of this book because they require skills the average newcomer to Office 2000 need not master, the Microsoft Development environment provides a platform from which you can develop and manage Web pages.

 NEW TERM The *Microsoft Development environment* is a program that enables users to manage HTML code from Web pages.

FIGURE 20.1

You can view the HTML code for your Web page.

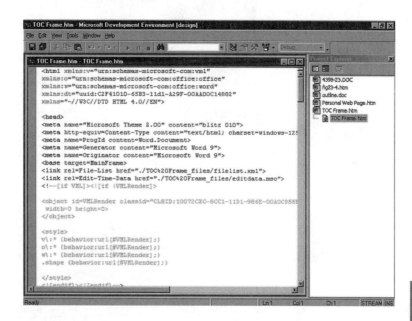

Using the Web Page Wizard

When you create a new document by selecting File, New, Word 2000 offers a dialog box with a series of wizards and templates. If you click the Web Pages tab, you find Web options such as the following:

- Column with Contents—A Web page designed for informational purposes with topics at the left, and hyperlinked details from those topics in the right pane.

- Frequently Asked Questions—A Web page designed to ask a series of questions at the top of the page and include hyperlinked answers to those questions for the remaining portion of the page.

20

- Left-Aligned Column—The left-aligned column format in Figure 20.2 includes an image in the page's left pane and information flowing down the right pane. As with all the samples from the Web Page Wizard and templates, you can easily replace the figure and placeholder text in this sample.

FIGURE 20.2

Word 2000 produces a clean sample you can work from.

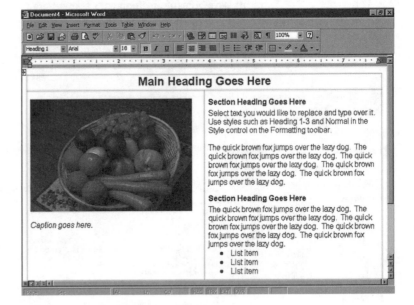

- Personal Web Page—A Web page that is simple and laid out well for personal, non-business informational home pages. A family might use this type of page to provide news to other family members living elsewhere.
- Right-Aligned Column—A Web page that is the mirror-image of the left-aligned column page, with the figure in the page's right pane and information flowing down the left pane.
- Simple Layout—A Web page with its information down the middle column of the page.
- Table of Contents—A Web page with a table of contents section flowing down its middle.
- Web Page Wizard—The step-by-step wizard that creates a Web page according to your specifications.

The easiest way to create a Web page according to your specifications is to start the Web Page Wizard. Figure 20.3 shows the wizard's opening screen.

FIGURE 20.3

Word 2000 builds a Web page as you respond to the wizard.

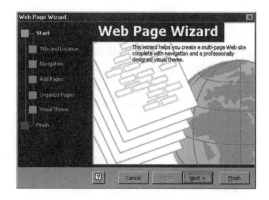

Microsoft's Web site, www.microsoft.com, includes several additional Web-specific Word 2000 templates that you can download.

As you follow the wizard, you see the underlying Word 2000 Web page take shape. The wizard prompts you for the style of the Web page. Figure 20.4 shows how fun making personal Web pages can be.

FIGURE 20.4

The Web Page Wizard generates many varieties of Web page styles.

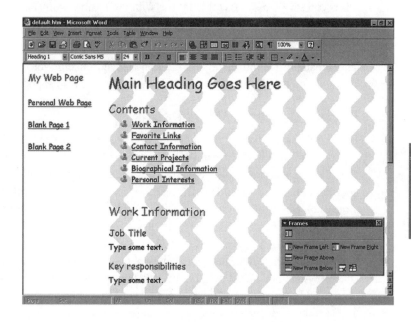

20

After the wizard does its job, you can edit the Web page and change the general text to the specific text you want on the page. As you edit, check out the Web Tools toolbar that you can add from the View, Toolbars option, as well as the Insert menu. When you're working with a Web page in Word 2000, the Insert menu and Web tools toolbar include several items you can insert in your Web page, including pictures, videos, text boxes, background sounds, scrolling text, and hyperlinks.

> If you want to add callout graphics to your Web page, Word 2000 offers all the drawing tools you learned about in Hour 18, "Office 2000's Synergy," including the AutoShape tools.

Now that you have seen how to use Word 2000 to create Web pages, you already know much about how the other Office 2000 products create Web pages. Many of the Web page features in the other Office 2000 products work the same way as those in Word 2000. For example, you can save an Excel 2000 worksheet as a Web page. When saving Office 2000 documents as Web pages, most of the formatting and editing features you get with the products' native formats remain. In other words, an Excel 2000 worksheet that you save as a Web page contains all the same elements that the worksheet contains when you save it as an Excel 2000 file with the normal worksheet extension, .xls. Revision markings do not appear in Web pages, but all other Office 2000 document elements do appear in the Web page.

The remaining sections build on your knowledge of using Word 2000 and the Web by showing you how Excel 2000 and FrontPage Express also support the Web.

Excel 2000 and Web Pages

Excel 2000 supports most of the same Web features that Word 2000 does, including the capability to save worksheets in HTML format. After you create the worksheet, select File, Save as Web Page to save the worksheet in a format readable to any browser. In addition to the Web-based HTML format, Excel 2000 also supports the Web toolbar, which you can display by selecting View, Toolbars, Web. From that toolbar, you can select other Office 2000 documents to display and edit from within Excel 2000, as well as enter an Internet Web site address to view. Because Office 2000 products all support the Web toolbar, and because you can display any document from Internet Explorer 5.0 (the browser engine used by all Office 2000 products when you work with Web-based objects and pages), all Office 2000 products enable you to view any of the other Office 2000 products' documents or any Web page; all you have to do is type that document or Web page address in the address text box of the Web toolbar.

If your company stores worksheets on the Internet or on an intranet, the File, Open option in Excel 2000 can open those worksheets. When you select File, Open and then enter the URL and filename, such as http://www.mycompany.org/accts.xls, Excel 2000 opens that worksheet. (Excel 2000 offers you the Internet Log On dialog box if you are not already logged on to the Internet.)

If you type a hyperlink Web address or a hyperlink to another Office 2000 document in an Excel 2000 cell, Excel 2000 takes you to that document and displays the Web toolbar automatically (if the toolbar is not already displayed). When you click the Web toolbar's Back button, Excel 2000 takes you to the preceding Web page.

Rarely does a Web page contain just an Excel 2000 worksheet. Web pages usually contain other text and graphics; that's why you probably want to create the general Web page in Word 2000 by using the Web Page Wizard and then import (using the Windows Clipboard or Insert menu) your Excel 2000 data into the Web page. If you insert a link to your Excel 2000 data instead of inserting a copy of the worksheet, your published Web page always contains "live" worksheet data that changes as you update the worksheet.

If you use an online service to publish your Web page and not a local Web server networked to your PC, you have to update the Web page manually each time you want to update the worksheet data.

Introduction to FrontPage Express

FrontPage Express comes with Office 2000 as part of Internet Explorer. With FrontPage Express, you can create and edit your own Web page in a separate, HTML-specific editing environment.

20

Before Web page editors such as FrontPage 2000, you'd have to master the HTML language before you could create or edit a Web page. Fortunately, FrontPage Express and other programs like it enable you to bypass HTML by putting a buffer between you and the underlying HTML code. If you want to draw a line or place a graphic image in a particular location on the Web page you're designing, you'll be able to drag that item onto the page with your mouse and a little help from FrontPage 2000.

Summary

This hour showed you how to use Office 2000 products to create Web pages. Word 2000 certainly offers the advantage in your initial Web page design, as does Excel 2000 for publishing your worksheets. And FrontPage Express is a quick solution for editing pages on-the-fly.

You can use Word 2000 as your primary Web page development tool and import other Office 2000 products as needed to add their elements to the Web page that you save from Word 2000.

Now that you have a solid foundation for combining Office 2000 products and the Internet, you are ready to move on to one of the most powerful of Office 2000 Small Business Edition's applications: Publisher 2000. The next hour will get you started.

Q&A

Q Can I use my Windows 95 or Windows 98 PC as a Web server?

A You can, but you probably don't want to tie up your PC by using it as a Web server. Windows NT-based computers are better equipped to be Web servers. If you want to try, however, you can use a Windows 98 program called Personal Web Server. This program provides the tools needed for your PC to operate as a Web server. If you use a slow PC and if you use a dial-up Internet connection, your PC offers slow Web page viewing. Therefore, no matter how effective your Web page content is and no matter how well you used the Office 2000 tools to develop an attention-getting Web page display, your Windows 98-based Web server is probably too slow to keep your viewers' interest.

Q Can I include Excel 2000 graphs on my Web pages?

A Certainly. You can copy the graph to the Windows Clipboard, and then paste the graph directly into your Word 2000- or PowerPoint 2000-based Web page. An Excel 2000 graph is no different from any other kind of data that you can copy and paste into a Web page from any of the Office 2000 products.

Windows supports OLE (object linking and embedding) technology, which enables you to insert virtually any object inside any other kind of document. If you want to insert an Excel 2000 graph or a video file with sound into a Web page, you can do so by using the Insert menu from the Office 2000 product's menu bar.

PART VI
Publisher 2000

Hour

HOUR 21

Publisher 2000 Basics

This hour introduces Publisher 2000 and gets you started on the road to turning the documents you created in other Office 2000 products into polished, professional publications. Publisher 2000 is the latest in a series of Publisher versions that Microsoft has produced over the years. In keeping with Publisher's tradition, Publisher 2000 offers new and simpler ways of producing documents that look better than ever before.

Publisher was the first product to offer wizards, the technology that all who are familiar with Microsoft products have used. You've worked with wizards already in this book (in Hour 3, "Introducing Office 2000 Small Business Edition's Powerful Features") and you know how wizards can help guide you through the document creation process. Publisher 2000 provides wizards that help you create almost any publication you need; you may never have to create a document from scratch again. Once you create a publication, you can apply wizard technology to change that publication's design.

The highlights of this hour include

- When to use Word 2000 and when to use Publisher 2000 for your publications
- How to use the Publisher 2000 wizard technology to create an initial publication design

- When to add details to the publication's design
- Why to use a text frame to hold text you'll need to edit later

Why Publisher 2000 and Not Just Word 2000?

Microsoft put both Word 2000 and Publisher 2000 in Office 2000 because these products work so well together. If you want to create attention-getting publications that contain exactly the information that's important to you, first write your publication's text (perhaps more than one article, if your publication requires multiple articles), use Word 2000's powerful word-based editing tools, and hone your words to perfection. After you are satisfied with your writing, import that Word 2000 document into Publisher 2000. Publisher 2000 then takes over and, with Publisher 2000's help, you can turn your words into a publishable product.

Getting Acquainted with Publisher 2000

Start Publisher 2000 by selecting Microsoft Publisher from the Start, Programs menu. The opening screen, shown in Figure 21.1, displays a catalog of wizards that create various kinds of publications for you. The catalog's left pane lists the types of publications you can create and the right pane displays samples from each type available. Scroll through the wizard samples to see all that Publisher 2000 can do for you.

FIGURE 21.1

From the start, Publisher 2000 offers wizards that help you create eye-catching publications.

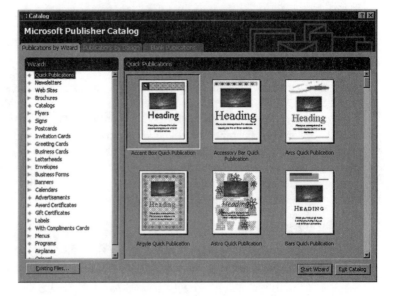

If you have children, you may want to scroll down to the Airplanes and Origami wizards. Publisher 2000 creates documents that include folding instructions for airplanes and other creations, such as birds and boats.

Creating Your First Publication

You'll use a wizard to create almost every publication in Publisher 2000. The wizards handle most needs and, once you create a publication with a wizard, your job will be to enter the text, import the graphics, and fine-tune the publication to meet your needs.

Get acquainted with a publication wizard by following these steps to create your first publication:

1. If you've already started Publisher 2000 and closed the Catalog dialog box shown in Figure 21.1, you can start a new publication by selecting File, New and clicking the Publications by Wizard tab.

2. Select the second wizard option, Newsletters. Publisher 2000 displays a list of newsletter design choices in the right pane. More choices appear than will fit inside the dialog box, so you can scroll down the dialog box's scrollbar to see additional newsletter designs. The dialog box's preview area shows what the design will look like after you create the publication.

3. For this example, select the Floating Oval Newsletter design and click the Start Wizard button. Publisher 2000 starts the wizard, prepares your publication for the Floating Oval design, and displays the wizard's opening window with the publication's initial design, as shown in Figure 21.2, after prompting you for name and address information that subsequent wizards will use.

4. You can click Finish at any time before completing the wizard and finish individual wizard steps later. Click Finish now to see the wizard's steps appear in the upper-left hand corner.

At the bottom of the screen is a series of pages with page numbers. Many of your publications will span multiple pages, and you traverse through the pages by clicking on the page number you want to see.

21

5. Click the Zoom control's plus sign to zoom closer to your publication and see the details better. The minus sign takes you further out so you can see the overall design once again.

6. The wizard's steps appear in the pane labeled Newsletter Wizard. Click Color Scheme to select colors for the newsletter's elements.

7. Click different color schemes to see the effects of the color schemes applied to the sample newsletter in the right pane. For this example, select the Prairie color scheme to apply the Prairie color scheme to your publication.

FIGURE 21.2

The wizard generates an initial design and helps you finish the publication.

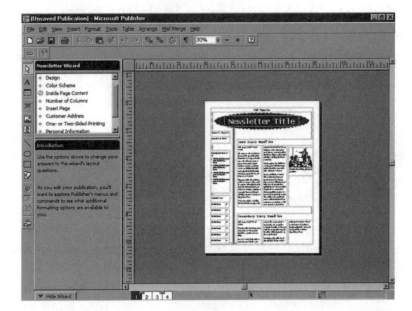

8. Click the Newsletter Wizard's option labeled Number of Columns and then choose 2 Columns in the pane below. The preview changes to show what the two-column newsletter would look like, as Figure 21.3 shows.

9. You can continue selecting options from the Newsletter Wizard pane and specifying the options' details in the lower pane. The publication in the right pane always reflects your latest selections.

If you want detailed help on a particular Publisher 2000 topic, select Help, Publisher Tutorials to display the tutorial topic window, shown in Figure 21.4. When you click on a topic, Publisher walks you through a brief, graphical tutorial of that topic.

FIGURE 21.3

Publisher 2000 can convert your newsletter to multiple columns.

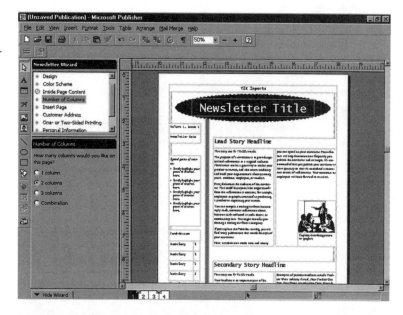

FIGURE 21.4

Publisher 2000 offers self-guided tutorials from the Help menu.

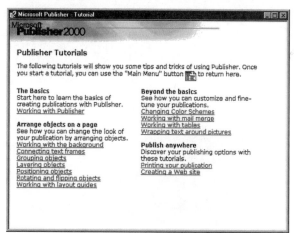

Filling in the Details

After Publisher 2000 lays out the newsletter's design, the Newsletter Wizard offers to help you more. The Newsletter Wizard's steps always remain on the screen in the Newsletter Wizard pane, along with your publication, as you've seen. You can change any part of your newsletter's design, such as the color scheme, by selecting that wizard topic and changing that option.

21

Now that you've laid out your publication with the help of the wizard, your publication is ready for details. Those details are the pictures and text in your newsletter.

Adding Text

One of the first elements you'll add to any design is the text. The simplest text to add is the text that you type directly into your publication. Click over the newsletter's left column to highlight the column. When you begin typing, the highlighted text automatically disappears.

Now that you've selected the first newsletter column, you can begin typing the text that you want to appear in that column. The first thing you'll notice, as soon as you begin typing, is that you cannot read what you are typing! That's okay because you can press F9 or the toolbar's + button at any time to zoom into the text that you type. Figure 21.5 shows zoomed text being entered into the first column. Use the horizontal and vertical scrollbars to bring into view whatever zoomed text area you want to work with.

FIGURE 21.5

Press F9 to zoom into your publication and make the text readable.

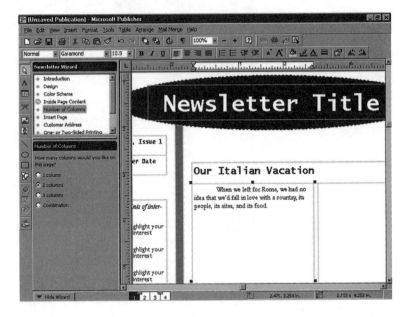

Publisher 2000, like Word 2000, supports paragraph indentation. Select Format, Indents and Lists to open a dialog box from which you can set the spacing for each paragraph's first-line indentation.

As you type, you'll notice that Publisher 2000 automatically hyphenates for you. You can turn off the automatic hyphenation by selecting Tools, Language, Hyphenation. In addition to turning on and off automatic hyphenation, you can control when the hyphenation occurs from the Hyphenation dialog box.

Publisher 2000 performs background spell-checking as you type, the same way that Excel 2000 and Word 2000 do. Also, you can select Tools, Spelling, Check Spelling (F7 is the shortcut key) to check the spelling of the entire document one final time. Publisher 2000 has no grammar checking abilities. If you create the text in Word 2000, however, you can use the Word 2000 writing tools to create accurate text and then bring the text into your publication once you've designed the publication with a wizard. If you make a mistake while typing, Publisher 2000 supports multiple levels of undo, just as Word 2000 and Excel 2000 do.

Continue entering text, and you'll notice that Publisher 2000 supports the same AutoCorrect entries you set up in Word 2000. Use the F9 key to zoom in and then back out of Publisher 2000. When looking at the overall publication, you can click on any column, title, or banner with text and type new text. If you click over an area where you've already entered text, Publisher 2000 lets you edit that text.

All the character formatting options from Word 2000 and Excel 2000 are available in Publisher 2000. If you don't like Publisher 2000's default font, select Format, Font and choose a new one.

If you want to add a *drop cap* to a paragraph, select Format, Drop Cap. (The drop capital letter cannot follow a tab.) Select the type of drop cap that you want to see, click OK, and you'll see the drop cap, which should be similar to the one shown in Figure 21.6.

NEW TERM A *drop cap* is a large character that begins a paragraph's first sentence.

21

FIGURE 21.6

Adding pizzazz to your introductory paragraphs with a fancy first letter.

Getting Text from Other Sources

You won't always want to type text directly into a publication. As a matter of fact, you'll often create the text in Word 2000 and then transfer that text to Publisher 2000. To bring text from other sources, you'll almost always do one of two things:

- Copy text from the Windows Clipboard
- Import the text from its native application

Suppose you write a travel book that teaches people how to travel through Europe the fun way, as a traveler who meets the people and not as a tourist who views the sites from a bus 50 yards away. To help promote your book, you create a newsletter that acts as a sales flier for your book. You may want to copy some text from the book's manuscript into the newsletter. You certainly don't want to copy the entire book, but just a paragraph or two.

Start Word 2000 (you don't have to exit Publisher 2000 to start Word 2000, of course; just click the Start button and start Word 2000 as you normally do). Load the book's document into Word 2000, select the paragraph you want to copy to the newsletter, and select Edit, Copy (Ctrl+C) to copy that paragraph to the Windows Clipboard. Switch to Publisher 2000 (press Alt+Tab to switch to Publisher 2000, or click the Publisher 2000 button on your Windows taskbar), click the area that is to receive your text, and select Edit, Paste (Ctrl+V) to put the Clipboard's text into your publication.

Although the Clipboard is useful for copying small portions of text into your publication, you may want to import long columns of text into Publisher 2000 from a full Word 2000 document. If you work with others who write for the publications you produce, you will be able to use the wizard to lay out the publication and then import the other writers' document files directly into the newsletter columns that are to receive the writing.

To import a file from Word 2000, select Insert, Text File from the menu to display the Insert Text File dialog box. Move to the folder that contains the text document and double-click that file to import the text directly into your publication. You can then format the drop cap as well as the font and character spacing if you wish.

Text Frames

As you type, you enter text into publication elements called *text frames*. If you use the wizard to create all your publications, you don't need to be as concerned about adding text frames as you have to be if you create a publication from scratch or if you modify a publication that a wizard designs for you. The wizard adds text frames where text is to go so that you can easily type or insert text into the frames. The frames keep the text in columns within your publication.

NEW TERM   A *text frame* holds text that you can edit.

By putting text in a text frame, and by separating the text from the other elements such as the art, Publisher 2000 lets you return to that text and edit the text by using the standard insert and delete text-editing tools you are accustomed to. You can format the text, spell-check the text, and so on.

If Publisher 2000 did not put your text into a special text frame, but simply put the text in your publication without distinguishing text from art, you would not have text-editing access to the text. Some art, such as fancy lettering boxed within a flowery border, is textual in nature. You would only be able to edit such text as you might edit artwork, one *pixel* (a screen's dot from the word's picture element) at a time.

NEW TERM   A *pixel* is a dot on your screen; many pixels work together to make up the pictures and text you see.

To add a text frame to a publication, as you would do if you were to create a publication without the help of a wizard, click the Text tool on the toolbox at the left of the Publisher

21

2000 screen. (The Text tool is the button with the letter *A* showing.) After you select the Text tool, drag your mouse anywhere inside a publication to create a rectangular text frame that works just like the text frame you used to enter text in the previous section. You can add multiple columns inside a single text frame or use a different text frame for each column in your publication.

To add multiple columns to a text frame, right-click over a text frame and select Change Frame, Text Frame Properties to display the Text Frame Properties dialog box, shown in Figure 21.7. Notice the options labeled Include "Continued on Page" and Include "Continued from Page" that add connecting messages to columns that continue on subsequent publication pages.

FIGURE 21.7

Specifying the number of columns you want in a text frame to make text wrap from column to column inside the frame.

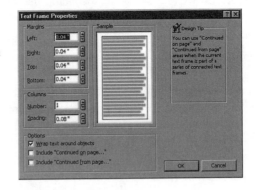

If you want text to wrap across columns, continuing into subsequent columns as you type, you need to connect two text frames together. Select Tools, Text Frame Connecting to display a small Connect Frames toolbar. Click the Text Frames button (the button with two chain links) to change the mouse cursor to a pitcher shape, and click on the text frame that is to connect to the original frame. (Select the frame's page number if the text is to continue into a text frame on a different page.) When the frames are connected, Publisher 2000 ensures that overflowed text from the first text frame flows into the connected text frame, even if that text frame is on a different page.

Summary

This hour introduced Publisher 2000 to you and showed you how simple creating a publication can be with the wizards. The Publisher Wizard lets you design the overall publication, and the Design Assistant Wizard guides you through the individual steps you need to finish your publication with text and art.

Enough wizards exist to help you create just about any kind of publication you need to create. Rarely, if ever, will you need to create a publication from scratch. By adding text and art frames, you can customize any publication the wizards create. Publisher 2000 is more than a simple publication design tool, however. Publisher 2000 goes the next step and lets you add professional touches to your publication.

The next hour will show you how to access the versatile design elements of Publisher 2000.

Q&A

Q Can I create Web pages with Publisher 2000?

A Certainly. The wizard named Web Sites gets you started. As you'll learn in Hour 24, "Creating Web Pages with Publisher 2000," FrontPage 2000 is perhaps the best tool within Office 2000 to create and manage Web pages, but you can develop the initial Web page in Publisher 2000, and then later import it into FrontPage 2000.

Q How many different kinds of text can be converted to a picture?

A Fancy formatted text is converted to a picture, so that it still looks the way you want it to online. The types of text that turn into pictures include

- WordArt (which is basically a picture anyway)
- Text in table cells
- Text in a frame with a fill color or shading in it
- Rotated text
- Text that overlaps another object
- Text in a frame that is very close to another object

21

HOUR 22

Designing Professional Publications

This hour wraps up your introduction to Publisher 2000 by describing many of the publications that Publisher 2000 can help you create. When you understand the basics of how to use Publisher 2000, you can let Publisher 2000 do most of the initial design work for virtually any publication you want to create, including mass mailings and Web pages.

The highlights of this hour include

- How to place art in your publication
- How to use wizard technology to modify your publication after you've created it
- Where to use the many kinds of publications that Publisher 2000 helps you produce
- How to get extra wizard help when you want to design publications from scratch

Your Publication's Art

Working with art is actually simpler than working with text. Art resides inside art frames, just as text resides inside text frames. You can change, resize, and move art within its frame.

When a wizard finishes designing your publication, you'll need to change the wizard's sample art to the artwork you want to use. Publisher 2000 makes replacing artwork simple. Double-click the artwork to open the Clip Gallery, shown in Figure 22.1. When you select the replacement art from the Clip Gallery by double-clicking the image, Publisher 2000 places the image. You can then resize the image to fit the publication's boundaries as needed.

FIGURE 22.1

The Clip Gallery holds art that you can place in your publication.

If you want to use artwork from another source, such as a scanned image, you can select Insert, Picture, From File. Publisher 2000 inserts all major picture formats, including GIF, JPEG, Kodak Photo CD, TIFF, and CorelDraw images.

After you load the image you want to place in your publication, you can move or resize that image. When you click inside an art frame, eight black *sizing handles* appear around the frame's borders. By dragging any of the resizing handles in or out, you can shrink or expand the art frame, and the image size changes along with the frame.

NEW TERM *Sizing handles* are black squares that appear around an art frame that you can drag to resize an image.

If you point to the art frame's edge, without pointing to a resizing handle, the mouse cursor changes to a Move cursor. You can use the Move cursor to drag the image (and its frame) to any location on the publication. If you move the art frame over text, Publisher 2000 formats the text around the art frame so that the art does not cover up the text, as Figure 22.2 shows.

Justify both margins to get newspaper-like columns, where the text aligns evenly on both sides of the column. When you move artwork into the text, as shown in Figure 22.2, the text flows more gracefully around the artwork.

FIGURE 22.2

When you move an art frame into text, Publisher 2000 wraps the text around the art.

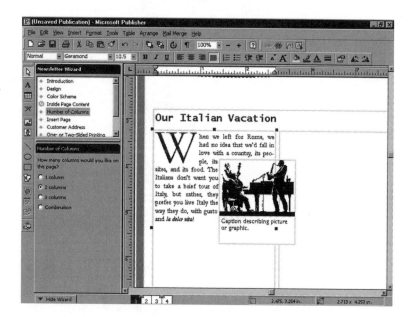

As with text, you can copy pictures from the Windows Clipboard that you have copied there from another application.

Extra Shapes

The Publisher 2000 toolbox (the set of tools on the left side of your screen) includes a few drawing tools with which you can add shapes to your publication. Although these tools are not good enough to use for most original artwork, you can use the drawing tools to add lines, circles, boxes, and other simple shapes to your drawing. Many of these shapes make good borders for special text, such as for emblems and callouts that you want to add to your publication.

To access the shapes, click the line, oval, or box drawing tools. A collection of special shapes appear when you click the Custom Shapes tool, as shown in Figure 22.3. To draw any shape, from lines to the custom arrows, click and hold your mouse at the shape's starting point and drag the mouse to size the shape where you want it.

FIGURE 22.3

Selecting a custom shape from the collection of shapes available from the toolbox.

Custom shape tools

Designing with the Design Gallery

Publisher 2000 includes a design feature called the *Design Gallery*. The Design Gallery acts as a repository of predesigned elements that you can place in your publications. For example, you may need a special banner to spruce up a newsletter's featured column. Although you can design your own eye-catching banner, why not check the Design Gallery to see if you like an example that's already there?

NEW TERM The *Design Gallery* is a collection of predesigned objects, grouped by publication style, that gives you easy access to graphic elements such as banners, sidebars, called-out quote bubbles, and even table of contents styles.

You can explore the Design Gallery contents by following these steps:

1. Click the Design Gallery button on the toolbox. The Design Gallery button is the extra-large button at the bottom of the toolbox. The Design Gallery window opens, as shown in Figure 22.4.

Like the Clip Gallery, the Design Gallery is organized in categories listed on the left side of the Design Gallery window. (When you add your own items to the Design Gallery, you can create new categories that appear on the tabbed page labeled Your Objects.) Each category has its own design.

2. Click on different Design Gallery categories to see the designs available in them.

3. When you locate the picture that represents the Design Gallery item you want to insert, double-click the item to add it to your publication. Publisher 2000 places the item on the Publisher 2000 editing area and closes the Design Gallery window. You can move, resize, and edit the item as if you had designed and drawn the item yourself using the shape and text tools on the toolbox.

FIGURE 22.4

The Design Gallery contains graphic elements you can include in your publication.

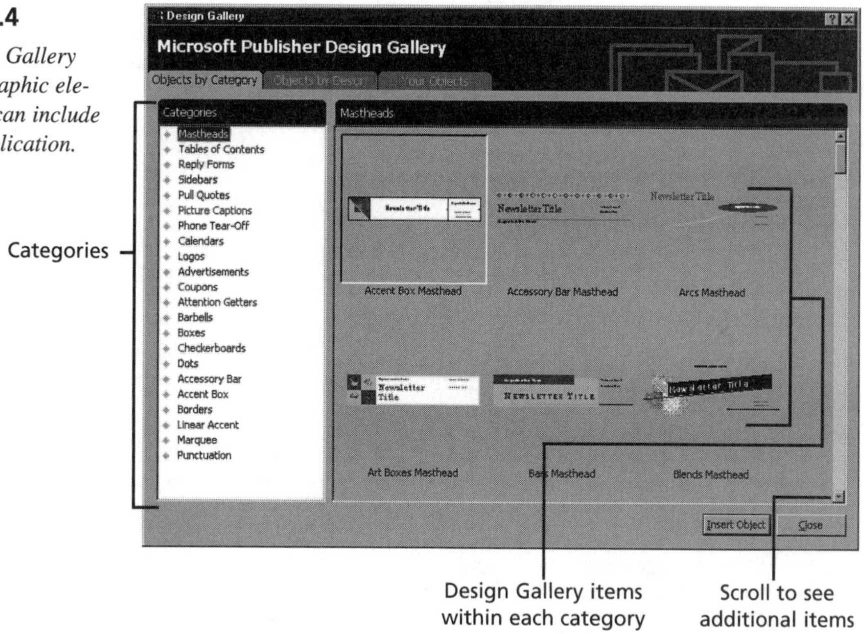

Categories —

Design Gallery items within each category

Scroll to see additional items

Getting Help with the Design Checker

Publisher 2000 includes a design tool called the *Design Checker* that you use after you create your publication. When you select Tools, Design Checker, the Design Checker dialog box appears. To learn what kinds of design elements Design Checker analyzes, click the Options button to display the Options dialog box, shown in Figure 22.5.

The *Design Checker* analyzes your publication and offers suggestions on how to improve it.

FIGURE 22.5

The Design Checker analyzes your publication for common design problems.

As you can see, the Design Checker looks over your publication and searches for the problems listed in the Options dialog box. You can uncheck one or more of the options and click Check Selected Features if you want to limit the Design Checker just to those items you've selected. Click the option labeled Check All Problems if you want the Design Checker to look at all elements of your publication.

The Design Checker does not leave you hanging when it finds a problem. If you click the Explain button, the help window to the right of your editing area gives instructions on how you might go about correcting the problem just found.

Even if the Design Checker finds multiple problems with your publication, you don't have to wait for it to find them all before you correct the problems. You can leave the Design Checker window on the screen but drag it out of the way while you correct a problem. After you fix the problem, click the Design Checker's Continue button to look for additional design problems that might appear.

Putting Borders Around Your Publications

You may want to place a border around your entire publication, or perhaps around a single text or art frame. A border is nice to place around smaller publications you create, such as placecards for dinner guests. You may want to create your own business cards and place a border around your company's name.

To add a border to a publication, follow these steps:

1. Click the rectangle tool on the toolbox to activate the tool. Your mouse cursor turns into a crosshair shape.

2. Draw the box where you want the border to appear. Perhaps you are going to use the border around a headline, a photo, or even the entire publication page. If you don't draw the box the proper size, you can resize the border after you complete it.

3. Right-click over any of the box's edges to display a pop-up menu and select Change Rectangle, Line/Border Style, More Styles. The Border Style dialog box appears. Click the BorderArt tab to display the special border art shown in Figure 22.6.

FIGURE 22.6

The Border Style dialog box determines the size, color, number of sides, and thickness of your border lines.

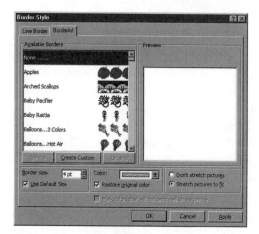

The BorderArt dialog box page lets you specify the size of the border and the color. In addition, you can determine whether artwork that will go inside the border (if you plan to place art inside the border) is to stretch to fit the border or whether the border's picture is to retain its size even if the border is much larger than the figure.

4. You can click the Create Custom button to make your own border art. After you enter the name of a picture (from the Clip Gallery or another image), Publisher 2000 repeats that image to build a border that you can name and save in the list of borders that appear.

5. Click OK to save the border art on your editing area. You now can resize the border as you would any other box or graphic image on the publication.

Summary

This hour showed you how to access the design elements of Publisher 2000. Your small business will be able to use Publisher 2000 to design more than just newsletters; Publisher 2000's wizards help you produce forms, invoices, labels, and even paper-folding projects for children who may want something to do while they wait for you to finish your work at the office.

The next hour will give you the tools you need to manage addresses, and create and print mass mailings by using Publisher 2000.

Q&A

Q How can I place a background on my publication?

A A background image can appear on the back of your publication, acting like a watermark image that shows through. By placing the background on every page in your multipage publication, you can add consistency to your publication's look.

The background remains blank until you add design elements, such as lines and pictures, to the background. To add art to a publication's blank background, select View, Go to Background (Ctrl+M). Publisher 2000 then temporarily hides your publication's foreground (all the elements on top of the background, including all the text and art frames). After you add whatever background images and text you want to add, select View, Go to Foreground (Ctrl+M again). The publication's current page number appears at the bottom of the screen, and when you're working, the foreground is visible.

You can hide the background on any page by selecting View, Ignore Background. The background does not go away, but it does disappear from view and does not appear again until you again select View, Ignore Background to show the background.

Hour 23

Creating and Printing Mass Mailings

Mail merge, as it has been called for many years in word processing programs, is the process of setting up a publication for a form letter, label form, or envelope, and then automatically printing a separate copy (or label) for each entry in a list of names, addresses, or other information. Mail merge enables you, for example, to create a letter and then print out dozens of copies, each personally addressed to a different recipient.

It's a great time saver and an easy way to produce direct-mail advertising, address newsletters or cards, and crank out labels or pre-addressed envelopes.

In Publisher, mail merge happens in four distinct steps or stages, so that's how I'll take you through the process in this hour. It's all pretty easy, actually, but many people get hung up on some of the concepts, so I'll take it slow and steady so you can see exactly how everything comes together. At the end of the hour, you'll be able to answer the following questions:

- How do I create the list of addresses or other information to be used in a mail merge?
- Can I do a mail merge with an address list I already have from a different program?
- If I manage names and addresses in Microsoft Outlook, how do I merge that information in a Publisher mailing?
- How do I attach a list to a publication and decide which information from the list to print?
- How do I choose where in the publication to print each piece of information from the list and format that text?
- Can I preview the results of a merge before printing?
- How do I print the results?

Step 1: Creating a Data Source

Before you can set up a publication for mail merge, you must have the *data source* ready from which Publisher will pull the information to be plugged into the publication.

NEW TERM   A *data source* is a list of names and addresses (or other information) to be used in a mail merge; it's the "source" for the "data" (information) that will be printed in the publication.

Creating a data source can be a bit of a chore the first time around—but don't let that hold you back. After you've created that source, you can use it again and again. The long-term time-savings of mail merge far exceeds the time it takes to set up a list.

There are two ways to create a data source, each of which you'll discover next. You can

- Create a Publisher address list
- Use a list already created in another program

Outlook is Microsoft's all-in-one program for managing your messages, contacts (names and addresses), and schedule. It's included in most versions of Microsoft Office. (Don't confuse Outlook with Outlook Express, the free email program included with the Internet Explorer Web browser.)

If you use Outlook to manage your contacts, note that you can use your Outlook contact list as a data source, easily merging your Outlook contacts into a Publisher mail merge. See "Borrowing a List from Another Program," later in this hour.

Typing a Publisher Address List

To create a new address list in Publisher, begin with any open publication (even Unsaved Publication), and that publication doesn't need to be the one to which you'll attach the list. In other words, the address list you create need not have anything to do with the publication that happens to be open when you create it.

To start, choose Mail Merge, Create Publisher Address List. The New Address List dialog box opens (see Figure 23.1). For the first *entry* in the list, fill in all the *fields* you want to use (you can leave the fields you don't need blank).

23

FIGURE 23.1

To create a new address list, just fill in the fields for each entry.

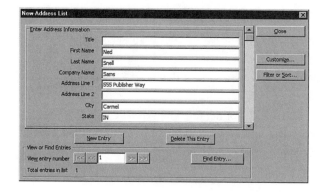

> **NEW TERM** An *entry* is a discrete set of information in the list (a person's name, address, and so on). If your list was stored in a Rolodex file, each card would be an entry.

> **NEW TERM** A *field* is a piece of information within an entry—first name, last name, and so on. To continue the Rolodex metaphor, each line on the card would be a field.

After filling in any fields you want for the first entry, click the New Entry button. The fields clear, so you can type the information for Entry Number 2. To complete your list, just fill in one entry at a time and click New Entry after each.

Note the buttons and number shown at the bottom of the dialog box, under View or Find Entries (refer to Figure 23.1). These controls work exactly like the Page controls you've used in Publisher to move among the pages of a multipage publication. The number shown is the number of the entry in the list; at the very bottom of the dialog box, you'll see a report of the total number of entries in the list. Use these buttons to move back and forth to entries that you've already typed, to check your work, or make changes.

Observe in Figure 23.1 that the New Address List dialog box contains a scrollbar. That tells you that there are more fields available than those you see at first. You can scroll down to reveal such useful fields as zip code, Home Phone, Work Phone, and E-mail Address.

When you finish typing new entries, click Close. A Save As dialog box appears so you can give this list a name. Don't type a filename extension; Publisher automatically gives the list the extension .mdb.

To Do: Make a Short Mailing List

1. Begin in any publication. (It doesn't matter which publication is open when you create a list.)

2. Choose Mail Merge, Create Publisher Address List. The New Address List dialog opens.

3. Fill in the fields for the first entry as shown below (leave any fields not mentioned blank). Remember that you might have to use the dialog box's scrollbar to bring the last few fields into view.

>   First Name: Ned
>
>   Last Name: Snell
>
>   Company name: Sams
>
>   Address Line 1: 555 Publisher Way
>
>   City: Carmel
>
>   State: IN
>
>   ZIP Code: 55555
>
>   Work Phone: 555-555-5555

4. Click New Entry. The fields in the dialog box clear, and the blank fields for entry number 2 appear.

5. Add an entry for yourself (your name and address), filling in only the same fields used in step 3. (After this entry, you can optionally fill in a few more entries for practice.)

6. Click Close. The Save As dialog box opens.

7. Type TestList, and click the Save button. You have created and saved a short list called TestList.mdb, which you will use in a later To Do to merge data with a publication.

A single address list can be used in as many different publications as it's useful for; it's not married to a single publication.

Editing an Address List

You can easily add or change entries in a list at any time. Choose Mail Merge, Edit Publisher Address List to open the Open Address List dialog box, which shows a list of the lists you've saved. Choose a list, click Open, and a dialog box that looks just like the New Address List opens. In that dialog box:

- Click New Entry to add a new entry to the list.
- Use the controls under View or Find Entry to move to an entry you want to change and make any changes you like.
- Move to an entry you want to delete from the list and click the Delete This Entry button to remove it.

Borrowing a List from Another Program

If you already have an address list entered in another program, you might be able to use it in Publisher as a mail merge data source, saving yourself the work of typing a new list and the work of keeping the list up-to-date separately in two programs (Publisher and your other program).

In addition to using Outlook's Contacts folder as a data source for a mail merge, Publisher can use lists from the following types of files (all except dBASE are from Microsoft programs for Windows):

- Word tables or mail merge data documents
- Access databases
- Excel spreadsheets
- FoxPro databases
- Microsoft Works databases (only if the database contains no formulas)
- dBASE versions III, IV, or V

To use a list in one of these file formats, you will select the file when attaching the data source to the publication, as you learn to do next.

Step 2: Attaching a Data Source to a Publication

Before you can begin inserting field data in a publication, you must attach a data source to that publication so that Publisher knows where the information is coming from.

To begin, do most or all the layout and editing of the publication. (You can do more layout and editing work after you add the merge fields, but it's easy when editing to inadvertently delete or otherwise scramble mail merge fields, so it's best to leave them for fairly late in the process of creating a publication.)

When you're ready, open the publication that you want to attach a list to and choose Mail Merge, Open Data Source. The dialog box shown in Figure 23.2 opens.

FIGURE 23.2

Choose Mail Merge, Open Data Source to use an existing name and address list you have in Outlook or another program.

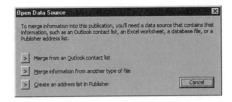

The dialog box offers four ways to attach a data source:

- Merge from an Outlook contact list. Choose this option, and the dialog box shown in Figure 23.3 appears; select the Outlook contact file you wish to use.

Publisher can use contact information from Outlook 97, Outlook 98, and Outlook 2000.

FIGURE 23.3

Outlook contact lists can be chosen here.

- Merge information from another type of file. Choose this option to display the Open Data Source dialog box shown in Figure 23.4, where you may attach a Publisher list you've already created or a list created in another program (except Outlook).

- Create an address list in Publisher. Choose this option to open the New Address List dialog box and start a new Publisher address list, just as you did in step 1 of this hour (refer to Figure 23.1).

If you're attaching a Publisher list or a list from another program (except Outlook), use the dialog box shown in Figure 23.4 to choose the data source.

23

FIGURE 23.4

Use the Open Data Source dialog box to attach a list created in Publisher or in any other program (except Outlook).

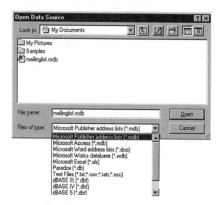

- To use a Publisher address list you've created, select it from the dialog box and click the Open button. (Publisher lists are files with the extension .mdb.)

- To use data from another data file supported in Publisher, drop down the Files of Type list at the bottom of the dialog box and choose the type of file you'll use. Then use the Look In list at the top of the dialog box to navigate to the folder where the data file is stored, choose the file, and click the Open button.

Step 3: Inserting Fields

Now the nitty gritty: choosing where in the publication each piece of information—first name, last name, and so on—will be printed. You do this by inserting fields in your publication.

To insert a field, create or select a text frame or table cell in which you want the field data to appear when the publication is printed. Then choose Mail Merge, Insert Field. The dialog box appears, listing all the fields in the data source that's attached to the current publication.

Choose a field name from the list, and its name appears in the selected frame or cell, surrounded by double carets (<< >>), as shown in Figure 23.5. The carets tell you that what you see in that spot is a field that will be replaced by data from a list when you print. Note that the carets will not appear when you print.

FIGURE 23.5

Pick a field to insert in your publication, where it will appear surrounded by double carets (<< >>).

Apply formatting to the field to control the look of the list text that will be printed in place of the field.

For example, suppose I want the first name to appear in 12-point Arial, in bold. I simply click the field in my publication (<<First Name>>) to select it, and then apply the formatting from the Formatting toolbar.

After the field is in the publication, you can treat it like any other text—move it, format it, delete it, and so on.

To Do: Make Simple Address Labels

1. In Publisher, open the Catalog by choosing File, New.

2. In the list of wizards on the Publications by Wizard tab, choose Labels.

3. Choose the first Labels template, euro7159, and click Start Wizard.

4. Click the wizard's Finish button, and click Yes when asked if you want to skip the wizard's questions. A single label appears on your screen, with placeholder text in a single text frame.

5. Click the placeholder text to select it and press your Delete key. The placeholder text is deleted, but the empty frame remains.

▼ 6. Choose Mail Merge, Open Data Source, and on the dialog box that appears, choose Merge Information from a File I Already Have. The Open Data Source dialog box opens.

7. Choose TestList (the simple list you created in this hour's first To Do) and click Open. TestList has been attached to the new label publication.

8. Make sure the text frame in the publication is still selected, and choose Mail Merge, Insert Field to open the Insert Field dialog box.

9. Click First Name and then click the Insert button. The field <<First Name>> appears in the publication.

10. Press Enter to start a new line.

11. Repeat steps 8, 9, and 10 for the remaining fields of the name and address. Note that in practice, you need not insert all fields in the list; you can select only the ones you want for the publication at hand.

12. Save your new labels publication. When you print this publication on label stock
▲ (as described next), a label will be printed for each entry in the list.

23

You can put a field anywhere—on a line by itself, or run in with other text. For example, you could create the sentence

Dear <<First Name>>, my old friend:

and the printout of the first entry (using our TestList) would read

Dear Ned, my old friend:

If you string fields together, don't forget to insert any necessary spaces between them. The phrase

<<First Name>><<Last Name>>

produces

NedSnell

Putting a space between the fields would get you the necessary space between the words.

Step 4: The Big Merge

Now comes the fun part, the reward for all your efforts—merging (plugging the actual list data into multiple copies of the publication). You can merge data two ways, both of which you discover next:

- Preview the merge results onscreen.
- Print multiple copies of the publication, each containing an entry from the list.

Previewing the Merge

To preview your merge results onscreen (to test them before printing), open the publication and choose Mail Merge, Merge. The onscreen view of the publication shows the first entry in the list as it will appear in print, and the Preview Data dialog box opens (see Figure 23.6).

Use the controls on the Preview Data dialog box to display the other entries and to see how each copy of the printed publication (or each label in a sheet of labels) will appear.

FIGURE 23.6

You can preview the merge to check your results before printing.

Printing the Merge

To print a mail merge publication, you don't need to preview it. Just open it and choose File, Print Merge to open the Print Merge dialog box (see Figure 23.7).

Use the Print Merge dialog box just as you would the regular Print dialog box—just press Enter (or click Print) and a copy (or label) for each entry in the list will print.

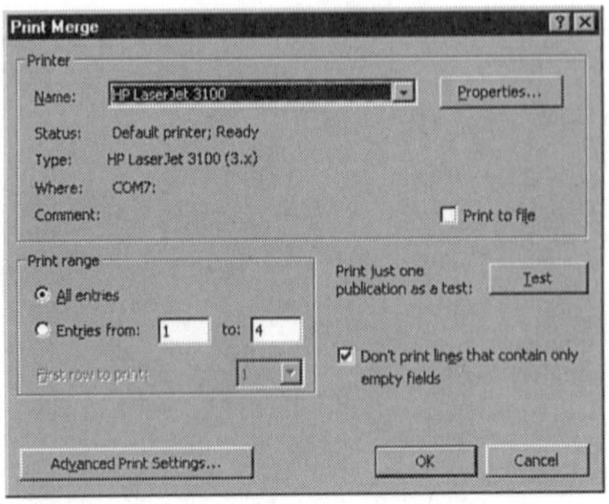

FIGURE 23.7

Choose File, Print Merge to produce a copy (or label) for each entry in the list.

When you need to, though, take advantage of the Print Merge dialog box's special features:

- Under Print range, you can choose to print a copy for all entries (the default setting), or print only selected entries, or a range of entries.

- Click the Test button to print a single copy for a single entry (or a few rows of labels) as a test, to judge the appearance of the results without printing the whole list.

23

Summary

As you can see, setting up for mail merge takes some work. But, if you often address multiple copies of letters, envelopes, and such, the rewards of creating lists and inserting fields are well worth the effort.

That's almost it, but not quite, for printing publications—you're now ready for the wonderful world of Web pages. If you want to create and publish Web pages using Publisher 2000, you're about to make a pleasing discovery.

Q&A

Q What if I need different fields than the ones I see in the New Address List dialog box?

A There's no need to change the standard list of fields in a Publisher address list—Title, First Name, and so on—as long as the list includes all the fields you need. If the list contains fields you don't need, you can just leave those blank, or not insert those fields in the publications where you don't need them.

However, you can optionally customize the names of the fields for a particular list, adding new fields, deleting fields, or changing the names of existing fields. To customize the list, click Customize on the New Address List dialog box to open the Customize Address List dialog box where you can add, delete, or rename fields. After customizing the list, return to the New Address List dialog box and fill in entries as usual.

Q Can I create one address list and then use fields from it in different publications?

A Yes. After you have the list, use it wherever and whenever you need it.

Hour 24

Creating Web Pages with Publisher 2000

For all intents and purposes, creating, editing, and formatting a Web page in Publisher is not really any different from what you do with a printed pub. You create and arrange frames and put text and pictures in 'em. Easy.

All you need to know now is the few simple steps you must take to tell Publisher that the pub is for the Web, not for paper. Doing so instructs Publisher to limit the kinds of formatting choices available in that pub to those that work on the Web (and to add a few Web-specific tools, too). In this hour, you'll discover those steps. At the end of the hour, you'll be able to answer the following questions:

- In what special ways does Publisher manage the fundamental difference between a Web page file and a regular pub?

- How can I create a fully formatted Web site in a flash with a Wizard?

- How do I give my page a title and choose other optional properties for it?

- How can I preview my page in Internet Explorer to see what my visitors will see?
- What special helping tools can I call upon to assist me when editing a Web page?
- Can I convert an existing print pub file into a Web page file?
- How can I design a Web page specifically for display on an 800×600 display?

Understanding the Weird, Wonderful Way Publisher Webs

In Hour 20, "Creating Web Pages with Office 2000," you learned that a Web page file is in a special format called HTML and uses the extension .htm or .html which is different from a regular .pub file.

But Publisher isn't built for editing HTML files, so it cheats a little. When you work on a Web site in Publisher, the whole time you're working on it, it's still a pub file (see Figure 24.1), using the extension .pub. (It's a special kind of pub file, though, that Publisher knows is intended as a Web page.) When you open or save a Web page in Publisher, you open or save a .pub file.

FIGURE 24.1

Publisher's view of a Web site, as you edit it, is not exactly WYSI-WYG; you must preview the file in Internet Explorer to get a real WYSIWYG view.

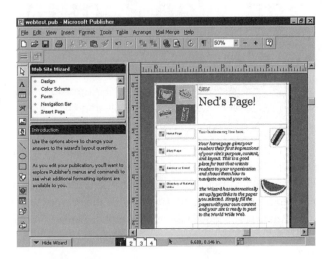

But when you finally publish the file, Publisher then converts the pub file into HTML format, giving it a new filename and extension online. Publisher calls this process of converting the pub file to HTML at publishing time *generating the Web site*.

 A *Web site* is a set of separate Web pages, each in its own file, that are linked together to function as a single, multipart document. Most Web sites have a beginning home or top page containing links that the visitor clicks to jump to the site's other pages. In Publisher, you create, open, or edit whole Web sites at once (as a single pub), and move from page to page just as you'd move among the pages of a print pub. The pages are automatically separated into individual files when published.

There's an advantage to this weird approach. After a pub has been designated as a Web site (either because you created it as such or because you converted it from a print pub), you edit and format it exactly as you would any other pub, adding and positioning frames and formatting their contents. Publisher's cheating enables you to apply your familiar Publisher skills to the new job of Web authoring.

> A Web page does not support all the formatting possible in a print pub, and a Web page does support a few things—such as multimedia—that a print pub doesn't.
>
> But you needn't think too much about those differences because when you're working in a pub file that you've designated as a Web page, Publisher changes the toolbar buttons, menu items, and other options to those required for Web page work. It limits your work to the stuff that can go in a Web page, so you don't have to think about what you can and cannot do.

24

Although Publisher helps you avoid formatting that's not supported in a Web page (especially if you run the Design Checker, as described later in this hour), there are a few big differences you should consider when creating and formatting text and pictures. (These subtle, sneaky differences are one reason it's important to regularly preview your Web page in Internet Explorer, as you learn to do later in this hour.)

Text Tips

You create and edit text frames and text in a Web site exactly as you do in any other pub. But, because the options for text formatting are much more limited on the Web than in print, a few things will happen a little differently in order to best preserve the formatting choices you make while also maintaining Web compatibility.

Fancy formatted text is converted to a picture so that it still looks the way you want it to online. The types of text that turn into pictures include

- WordArt (which is practically a picture anyway)
- Text in table cells
- Text in a frame with a fill color or shading in it
- Rotated text

- Text that overlaps another object
- Text in a frame that is very close to another object

> It's important to know when text is turned into a picture for two reasons:
>
> - The more pictures in a Web page, the larger its files will be and the slower it will materialize on the visitor's screen. When performance is important to you, you must be careful that your pages do not include too many pictures.
> - Some people use text-only Web browsers or switch off picture display in their browsers, and thus see only the text in Web pages. If important text in your page has turned to pictures, it's invisible to these visitors. To make your page work for them, you'll need to simplify the text formatting so that Publisher does not turn text into pictures, or you'll need to repeat any text turned to pictures in simple text elsewhere on the page.

Text not formatted in one of these ways will remain text in the Web page. However, it might not show up in the size or font you selected. The Web supports a limited selection of text sizes, so all text is converted to the closest supported size, which might not match what you intended.

More importantly, the fonts you choose will show up on the visitor's browser only if the visitor also has those same fonts installed on his or her computer. If you set text in, say, the Garamond font, any visitor who does not also have Garamond on his PC will instead see that text in a standard default font selected in his browser. That's not a big deal—your words still get through. But as always with Web pages, you cannot assume that what you create is exactly what the visitor sees.

A few standard fonts are widely supported, so using these most often in your Web pages improves the chances that your visitors will see text as you intend (although there's still no guarantee). In Publisher, you apply the standard Web fonts by using the TrueType fonts shown in Figure 24.2.

FIGURE 24.2

Use these fonts to improve the chances that text will be formatted in the visitor's browser as you intend—or at least pretty close to it.

Arial (and **Arial Black**)
Comic Sans MS
Courier New
Georgia
Impact
Σψμβολ
Times New Roman
Trebuchet MS
Verdana
♦)(■ ℔Ω)(■ ℔♦   (Wingdings)

Pic Tips

Although you can use many different types of graphics files in a print pub, only two types are technically supported in Web pages: GIF (`.gif`) and JPEG (`.jpg`). However, that rule has no effect on what files you can use in a Publisher Web page. You can insert pictures in any of the file formats Publisher supports (including any object from the Clip Gallery or Design Gallery). When it generates the Web site from your pub, Publisher automatically converts all graphics to `.gif` format.

Wizarding Up a Web Page

The best way to create a Web site in Publisher is to start with a wizard; doing this gives you a great-looking Web layout quickly, and helps you avoid adding elements or formatting that won't play well online.

You start a Web Site Wizard from the catalog, like any other wizard. The Web site templates are easy to spot in the catalog, because they all have the words "Web Site" in their names:

- To see all the Web site template previews at once, open the catalog's Publications by Wizard tab and choose Web Sites from the Wizards list (see Figure 24.3).

- To see Web site templates matched with stylistically similar print templates, open the catalog's Publications by Design tab, choose the design set you want, and scroll to the templates that include "Web Site" in their names.

24

FIGURE 24.3

To start a new Web site, choose a template with the words "Web Site" in its name.

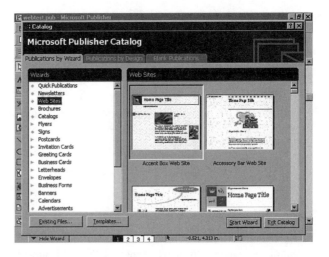

After choosing a template, click Start Wizard to run through a series of questions as you would for any other wizard. The following To Do shows what each of the questions means.

To Do: Run a Wizard to Make a New Web Site

1. Open the catalog's Publications by Wizard tab, and click Web Sites in the column of wizards.

2. In the panel of Web Site template previews to the right, click any one you like (your choice!).

3. Click the Start Wizard button. The Web Site Wizard opens. Click Next to move past the Welcome. (As you perform the remaining steps, click Next after each step.)

4. Choose a color scheme just as you would for a print pub.

5. Check the check box for any pages you'd like in your site. If you check no check boxes, the Wizard will produce a single home page. Check check boxes to add pages with a particular layout: Story is formatted as a general-purpose, text-oriented page; Calendar provides a calendar of events, and so on.

6. The next part of the wizard offers you a chance to add a form, a page containing boxes in which visitors can enter information, as in an order form.

7. When a site contains multiple pages, the wizard can automatically add a navigation bar to every page that provides links for jumping among the pages of the site. You can choose to make those links out of text labels alone (which improves your page's performance by not including a graphical navigation bar), graphics alone

▼   (which adds a spiffy graphical navigation bar), or graphics and text (so that text-only browser users still get links they can use).

8. Next, the wizard lets you add a background sound that plays automatically when the visitor arrives (if the visitor's computer and browser support sound). Click Yes to add the sound.

9. Next, the wizard lets you add a texture covering the background of all pages, which can look pretty neat.

10. Finally, the wizard lets you add a good old personal information set. After choosing one, click Finish and then save your new Web site.

▲

> When looking at your new Web site, keep in mind that some aspects of it won't function properly in Publisher:
>
> - The navigation bar doesn't work; use the regular Publisher page controls to move among pages in the site.
> - Animations and background sounds do not play.
>
> To see how these objects work, you must preview the site, as described later in this hour.

24

Choosing Properties for Your Page

When you create a Web site, there's one property that's never optional.

It's very important that you take a few moments after creating a new Web site to give its top page a title. While on the top page, choose File, Web Properties to open the Web Properties dialog box (see Figure 24.4), where you can enter a title on the Page tab (required) and change other properties on either of the two tabs (optional). When working with properties, remember that

- Items on the Site tab of the Web Properties dialog box affect all pages in the current Web site open in Publisher.

- Items on the Page tab of the Web Properties dialog box affect only the page you were viewing when you opened the dialog box. You can choose these items separately for each page.

FIGURE 24.4

Identify your page to the Web by giving it a title on the Page tab of the Web Properties dialog box.

Giving Your Page a Descriptive Title

The most important item on the Web Properties dialog box—and the only one you absolutely *must* change—is the title that appears on the Page tab. Publisher automatically fills this in with a generic default title, but you should replace that with a short title that concisely, but accurately, describes the contents of your page.

"Ned's Home Page," for example, is too generic—it doesn't tell a visitor enough about what the page contains. Better titles might be "Ned Snell's MS Publisher Home Page," or "Ned's Movie Reviews Page," or "The Snell Guide to Vulgar American Playwrights."

It's important that the title you enter is descriptive and engaging because it identifies your page to the Web in all the following ways:

- When a visitor displays the page, the page's title appears in the title bar of the visitor's Web browser.

- If a visitor uses his browser to create a Bookmark or Favorite for your page (to revisit it easily), the title is what appears in the visitor's bookmarks or favorites list.

- When a search engine that automatically catalogs the contents of the Web, such as Excite or AltaVista (www.excite.com and www.altavista.com, respectively), creates a listing for your page. It will use information from the title to decide under what categories to list your page.

- When a visitor finds your page in a list of pages generated by a search, what the visitor sees in the list is the title.

Besides the title, the other properties a search engine looks for are the keywords and description, both of which you can supply on the Site tab of the Web Properties dialog box.

In Keywords, type one or more keywords that describe the contents of your site. In a search engine, whenever anyone searches for pages that match one of those words, your page will appear among the search results.

For "The Snell Guide to Vulgar American Playwrights," my keywords might be *play*, *playwright*, *theatre*, *drama*. (Note that you separate multiple keywords with commas.)

In Description, type a brief, general description of your site. Some search engines display the description along with the title.

Choosing Other Optional Properties

When you're just starting out, it's best to leave everything else on the two tabs of the Web Properties dialog box—besides Title and maybe the Keywords and Description—alone. But in case you run into problems or get an attack of technical ambition, it's valuable to know what a couple of these other options are about.

Target Audience

Every few years, a new standard is approved for HTML file formats, and the new standard always includes support for new, fancier formatting options. To display those options, however, a visitor must have a newer browser that's compatible with the new standard.

By default, Web pages created in Publisher conform to an older, well-established standard called HTML 2.0, which is supported by virtually every browser around. If you leave this choice in place, Publisher helps ensure that you apply no formatting that isn't supported by HTML 2.0 browsers and all browsers that support more recent standards, too.

If you will publish to a corporate intranet or other environment where you can be certain that all visitors use state-of-the-art browsers that support HTML 4.0, switching to that option allows Publisher to apply some kinds of advanced formatting, such as better font control, that aren't supported in HTML 2.0.

File Name and File Extension

When you publish, new HTML files are generated and copied to the Internet. Publisher automatically assigns filenames to the HTML files it generates: The top page is named `Index.htm` and any other pages are named `page1.htm`, `page2.htm`, and so on.

24

If you have your own private directory on the Web server where you publish your files, these filenames will work fine. However, if you share that directory with someone else, that person might already have published a file named Index.htm. In such cases, you can use the File Name and File Extension options on the Page tab to choose new filenames.

Evaluating Your Page

A Web page is not meant to be viewed through Publisher—it's supposed to be viewed through a browser, such as Internet Explorer or Netscape Navigator. As you've seen, the process of generating a Web page from the pub you see in Publisher brings about several important changes, such as converting fancy text into pictures. More importantly, multimedia in the page—sound and animation—will not play in Publisher.

So you can do broad, general work on your page within Publisher's view of it, but to get a fully accurate view of the way it will appear to others online, you must preview the page through Internet Explorer. In addition to previewing, you have a few other tools at your disposal—the Design Checker and the Troubleshooter—to help you smooth out any problems you might find.

> You must have Microsoft's Internet Explorer installed on your PC to use the preview. See Hour 19, "Office 2000 and the Internet" for more details.

Previewing the Page

To preview your page, open the page in Publisher and click the Web Site Preview button on the Standard toolbar. Internet Explorer opens (see Figure 24.5) and shows your page as it will appear to visitors on the Web—or at least to visitors using Internet Explorer or Netscape Navigator, who together make up the overwhelming majority of Web users.

In the Preview pane, the page behaves exactly as it will online: Navigation buttons work (so you can jump from page to page) and animated graphics and sounds play.

To return to Publisher after previewing the page, close Internet Explorer or click Publisher's button on the Windows taskbar.

24

You can leave Internet Explorer open after previewing and return to Publisher by clicking its button on the Windows taskbar. However, after you make more changes to the page in Publisher, you can't preview the page again simply by switching back to Internet Explorer.

Every time you preview—even if Internet Explorer is already open—you must click the Web Site Preview button so that Publisher can generate a new preview file containing all the changes you've made since the last time you previewed the site.

Displaying the Preview Troubleshooter

Publisher offers a Web Site troubleshooter that's akin to its Print Troubleshooter—only not as useful. Publisher can't show its own help contents atop Internet Explorer, so, to read the Troubleshooter's advice, you must switch back and forth between the preview and Publisher (you can use the button on the Windows taskbar to do this).

Setting Up the Troubleshooter

To set up the Preview Troubleshooter, first open or create any Web page in Publisher. (The option you need in order to enable the troubleshooter is available only when a Web site is the current pub.) Then, open Publisher's Options dialog box (Tools, Options).

On the User Assistance tab, check the Preview Web Site with Preview Troubleshooter check box. As long as you do not later remove that check mark, the Troubleshooter will appear automatically any time you preview a Web page.

Using the Troubleshooter

To use the Preview Troubleshooter, preview a Web page. In addition to the preview, the Publisher Help window opens to show the troubleshooter (see Figure 24.6). Using the buttons on the Windows taskbar, you can switch back and forth between the preview and the troubleshooter to work out any kinks you see.

FIGURE 24.6

Use the Preview Troubleshooter to figure out and fix flaws you see in your Web pages.

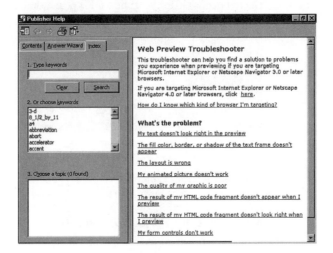

In the troubleshooter, choose the item that most closely describes the problem you observed in your Web page. You'll see another set of more specific problem descriptions. Continue choosing the items that best match your problem until you arrive at help text that tells you how to fix it.

Checking a Web Page's Design

Publisher offers a special Design Checker, different from the regular Design Checker for Print pubs. This Design Checker checks for design problems in a Web site and offers suggestions for improvement.

> The Design Checker is especially helpful when you're starting out because it alerts you to many of the ways a Web page is different from a print pub. For example, it tells you where and when fancy text will be converted into a picture. Knowing such information can help you find and fix problems later.

You can run the Design Checker from time to time when developing a page to help guide its evolution, and you should always run the Design Checker before publishing the page to help perform any final cleanup steps.

To run the Design Checker, choose Tools, Design Checker. The Design Checker at first displays a simple dialog box on which you can choose to check the design of the whole Web site or only selected pages. After you click OK on that dialog box, the Design Checker locates the first object in the page it considers a potential problem, and displays a dialog box like the one shown in Figure 24.7.

FIGURE 24.7

The special Web site Design Checker alerts you to objects and formatting that won't work well online.

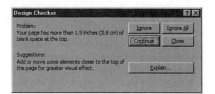

The Design Checker dialog box describes the problem it has found and offers a suggestion for repairing it. While viewing the Design Checker's advice, you can do the following:

- Click in the pub and make whatever change the Checker recommends. Then, click the Checker's Continue button to proceed to the next problem.
- Click Ignore to instruct the Checker to ignore this particular problem and move ahead to the next.
- Click Ignore All to instruct the Checker to ignore this type of problem, both here and anywhere else in the page or site.
- Click Explain to display help text about the problem at hand.
- Click Close to quit the Design Checker.

Wizardless Ways to Start Web Pages

Again, the best way to start a Web page in Publisher is to choose an appropriate Web site template from the catalog—and when you want a Web site, I highly recommend you start that way.

But you do have two other options: You can create a blank Web site into which you can pour whatever contents you like, or you can convert an existing print pub file into a Web site.

Creating a Blank Web Site

When starting from scratch, even hen you don't want to use a wizard, it's important to determine from the outset that the pub you're creating is a Web page, so that Publisher can present you with the proper tools and options for Web work.

To create a new, blank Web page, open the catalog's Blank Publications tab, choose Web Page from the list, and click the Create button. A new, completely blank Web page appears, ready for your objects.

Converting a Print Pub to a Page

When you convert an existing pub to a Web page, the results are never perfect; you typically must do a substantial amount of editing and formatting in the resulting Web page to make it look the way you want it.

For that reason, the only time it makes sense to convert an existing print pub to a Web page is when the original pub contains so much content—text and pictures—that also belongs in the Web page. Cleaning up the Web page is often less work than starting over from scratch. Keep in mind that there is a happy medium: You can start a new Web page and selectively copy to it any text or pictures you want from the print pub.

The following To Do shows how to convert an existing print pub to a Web site.

When you convert a print pub to a Web site, you really create a copy of the print pub to use as a Web site—the original pub file is unaffected. When you save the Web site, give it a different filename than the pub from which it was created, so the Web page file doesn't replace the original.

To Do: Convert a Print Pub to a Web Site

1. Open the pub you want to convert to a Web site.

2. Choose File, Create Web Site from Current Publication. What happens next depends on the complexity of the original pub:

   For most simple, one-page pubs, Publisher designates it a Web site, makes no other changes, and displays a dialog box asking whether you want to run the Design Checker (to look for objects and formatting that won't work well on the Web). It's a good idea to run the Design Checker, and then preview the page to assess the situation before moving ahead to editing.

   For more complex pubs (especially multipage ones), Publisher displays the Convert To Web Site dialog box (see Figure 24.8). On the dialog box, choose Use the Web

▼   Site Wizard... to run the wizard (as described earlier in this hour) and let it rework your pub for the Web, creating a home page with a navigation bar leading to other pages. Choose Add My Own Hyperlinks... to simply designate the file a Web page, and edit it from there.

FIGURE 24.8

When converting a complex pub to a Web site, Publisher offers the option to call upon the wizard's design assistance.

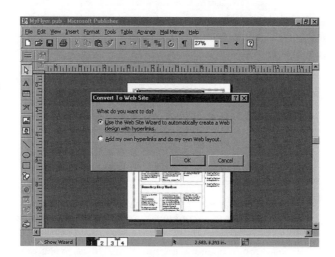

▲

24

Designing for Different Resolutions

By default, Publisher's Web pages are designed to look their best when the visitor's display is running in 640×480 resolution (the standard screen resolution for both Windows 95 and the Macintosh). This resolution is often called *standard VGA* resolution.

However, a growing number of computer users routinely use a higher screen resolution of 800×600 (called *SVGA* resolution), or even higher resolutions. Higher resolutions make graphics and some text appear smaller, altering the overall look of a Web page.

A page designed for VGA screens still looks pretty good when displayed on an SVGA screen, but the reverse is sometimes not true. A Web page designed for SVGA might be too wide for a VGA display, forcing the visitor to do a lot of annoying horizontal scrolling to see both sides.

On the Web, you'll get visitors using both VGA and SVGA resolutions. For that reason, I recommend sticking with the default VGA setup in your Publisher Web pages so they look good to everybody. But if you intend to publish on a company intranet where you might know that all your visitors will use SVGA resolution, you may choose to design your Web pages specifically for that resolution.

To design a page for SVGA, open the page in Publisher and choose File, Page Setup. On the Web Page Setup dialog box (see Figure 24.9), change the Page Width from Standard (VGA) to Wide (SVGA).

FIGURE 24.9

Use the Web Page Setup dialog box to create wide pages for 800×600 display.

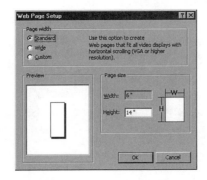

If you design pages for SVGA, you'll get an accurate preview on your PC only if your PC is configured for 800×600 resolution, too.

To configure Windows 95 for SVGA display, right-click an empty area of the desktop to open the pop-up menu, choose Properties, and then click the Settings tab on the Display Properties dialog box. In the Desktop Area part of the dialog box, drag the slider control to the right until it reads 800×600 Pixels.

Summary

At its heart, a Web page is a pub. But you can't control it quite as finely as you can a print pub. In a way, that sets you free. Use all your Publisher skills to make your pages shine, then trust Publisher to keep your work within the boundaries of Web formatting.

Q&A

Q I'm comfortable with Publisher and all that, but are there better programs for creating Web pages? Somebody told me I can actually use Internet Explorer or Netscape to write pages.

A When installed with their full installation options, both Internet Explorer 5 and Netscape Communicator include Web authoring programs. Internet Explorer's is called FrontPage Express (and is included with Internet Explorer on your Publisher 2000 CD-ROM), and Communicator's is called Composer. In addition to these easy-to-use, beginner's Web authoring programs, there are many other, more sophisticated programs, such as Microsoft's FrontPage 98.

Are they better than Publisher for creating Web pages? That depends. These programs let you work directly on the HTML file, and what you see while you work comes much closer to an accurate, WYSIWYG representation of the way the page will look online. On the other hand, switching to a new program forces you to learn a whole new way of working—you're already comfortable with Publisher.

So if you create many print pubs and only an occasional Web site, it's probably best to stick to Publisher. If you'll do a lot of Web authoring, it might be worth your while to learn one of these other Web-specific programs.

Q When you edit a Web site in Publisher, what are you actually editing?

A A pub file specially designed to generate a Web page file when you preview or publish. What you see in Publisher is a special pub file; the real Web site files are created only when you preview or publish, and are never seen in Publisher.

24

Appendix A

Small Business Tools

Office 2000 includes a group of tools designed to help small businesses get more out of the Office suite of applications. The tools are included in all editions of Office 2000, and they're not just useful for small businesses—large businesses, home offices, and individual users will all find something useful in one or more of the following Small Business Tools components:

- The Small Business Financial Manager
- The Business Planner
- The Direct Mail Planner
- The Small Business Customer Manager

To access these components click the Start button, and choose Programs. From the Programs list, select Microsoft Office Small Business Tools and then view the submenu and make your selection.

The Small Business Financial Manager

This small business tool adds a Financial Manager menu to your Excel menu bar, as shown in Figure A.1, although you can access it from the

Programs list in the Start menu as well. The Financial Manager menu offers a series of wizards to help you create reports, charts, and tools to assist you in making business decisions based on your worksheet data.

FIGURE A.1

If this menu doesn't show in your Excel window, choose Tools, Add-Ins, and click the Small Business Financial Manager check box.

Using the Import Wizard

The Import Wizard allows you to build a new database that is based on the data you've built using your accounting software. When you select Import Wizard from the Financial Manager menu, the wizard begins, as shown in Figure A.2.

FIGURE A.2

Build a database for use in creating reports and to begin using your worksheets as true analysis tools.

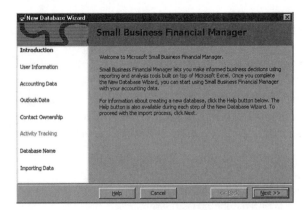

The New Database Wizard helps you extract data from your accounting software, such as QuickBooks or Microsoft Money. An Access database is created, although a knowledge of Access is not required to use the it.

After entering information about yourself (your name and an optional password of your choice), the Financial Manager searches your computer for accounting files. Once found, you choose which data to import, and your database is created. Figure A.3 shows an accounting database listing accounting categories.

FIGURE A.3

Collate pertinent accounting information into one database.

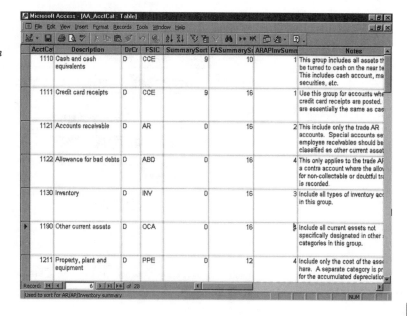

If you don't have any accounting software on your computer, choose the option to not import any data. As a result, a generic database is created, with many database tables into which you can manually enter your own accounting information. The process of building this generic database requires additional steps during set up, but saves you the wasted time watching your computer search for accounting data that isn't there.

Working with the Report Wizard

The Report Wizard makes it easy to create a variety of standard accounting reports, such as income statements, balance sheets, and trial balances. To activate the Report Wizard, choose Financial Manager, Report Wizard from the Excel 2000 Menu bar. The Small Business Financial Manager Startup Screen opens, as shown in Figure A.4.

*Click the Report
hypertext link to acti-
vate the Report Wizard.*

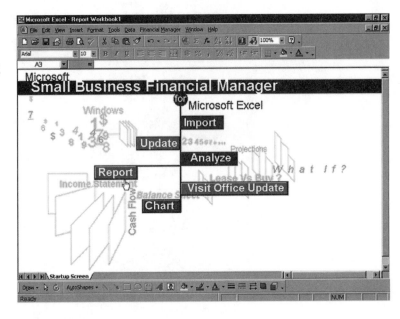

After selecting the Report link, the Create a Financial Report dialog box opens, as shown
in Figure A.5.

FIGURE A.5

*Choose from seven dif-
ferent reports and click
Next to proceed.*

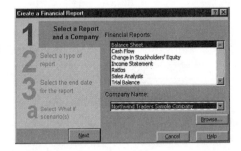

After choosing the type of report you want, the Financial Report Wizard asks you to
specify which variation you want to use. Figure A.6 shows the two different types of
Trial Balances you can create.

FIGURE A.6

The number of report variations depends on the type of report you selected.

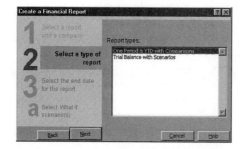

A series of dialog boxes follows, asking for further information. In the case of our sample Trial Balance, the next step in the process requires choosing the date of the report, as shown in Figure A.7.

FIGURE A.7

Make your date selection and click Finish to create the report.

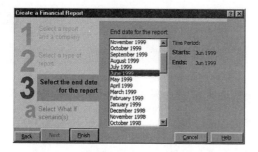

A

The Report Wizard then completes the report, based on your data, drawn from your accounting software files. For the purposes of this appendix, we're using the Northwind Traders database that comes with Office 2000. Their Trial Balance with Comparisons is shown in Figure A.8.

If you're not sure how you might use the Small Business Financial Manager tools, try running various reports with the Northwind Traders data—you'll have real data to look at, without spending time setting up your own information. The Sales Analysis and Cash Flow reports are two good choices for any small business—you'll see immediate uses for these reports in your own use of the Small Business Financial Manager.

FIGURE A.8

The finished report contains your data in all the right places, along with text and numeric formatting to give the report a pol- ished, professional look.

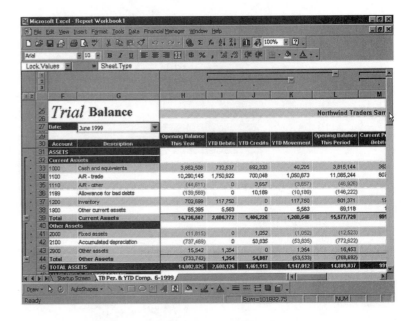

Using the Chart Wizard

Don't confuse this Chart Wizard with Excel's Chart Wizard tool. This wizard offers only business-related charts and does the charting for you, based on data you added to your database through the Import Wizard. Again, we'll be using the Northwind Traders sample database.

To run the Small Business Financial Manager Chart Wizard, follow these steps:

1. Choose Financial Manager, Chart Wizard.

2. Choose the type of chart you want from the Create a Financial Chart dialog box, shown in Figure A.9.

FIGURE A.9

Choose from four basic chart types.

3. Select the database you want to use from the Company Name dialog box and click Next.

4. Depending on the type of chart you selected, further questions and dialog box options appear in the next step. For this example, we're creating a Cash Flow chart and must choose the type of cash flow to include in the chart (see Figure A.10).

FIGURE A.10

How detailed should your chart be? Choose one or all of the options.

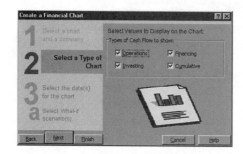

5. Click Next to choose a range of dates for the chart (see Figure A.11).

FIGURE A.11

Your starting and ending dates dictate the time over which the cash flow trend is tracked.

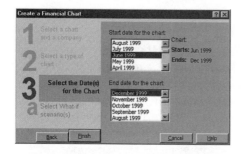

6. Click Finish to create the chart, which appears in Figure A.12.

The Small Business Financial Manager charts are especially useful in that they are created for you and don't require you to use Excel's standard charting tools—tools that require a greater starting knowledge of charting concepts and terminology. The charts you create through the Small Business Financial Manager can be copied and pasted as graphic objects into PowerPoint slides, Word documents, or a Web page you create with Word, Publisher, or FrontPage.

FIGURE A.12

The Chart Wizard selects the right kind of chart for the type of data being charted. A line chart is selected here to show trends in cash flow over time.

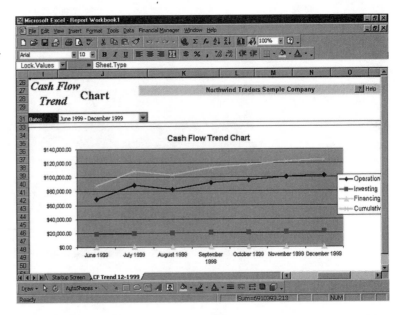

Selecting an Analysis Tool

The Small Business Financial Manager offers a tool for making decisions such as choosing whether to buy or lease an item for your business. Like the other Small Business Financial Manager tools, the analysis tool asks you a series of questions in a series of dialog boxes. To access this Small Business Financial Manager feature, choose Financial Manager, Select Analysis Tool. The first dialog box is shown in Figure A.13.

FIGURE A.13

Choose Buy Vs. Lease to ask the Small Business Financial Manager to help you make your decision.

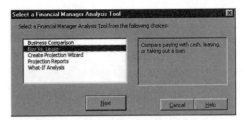

After selecting the Buy Vs. Lease tool, you are asked to give the Small Business Financial Manager more information about your intended purchase (see Figure A.14).

Enter the name, price, and tax amount for the item you're considering.

Click Next to proceed to the dialog box shown in Figure A.15. Here, you can give the Buy vs. Lease tool your purchase options—paying cash, taking out a loan, signing a lease, or other financing options.

FIGURE A.15

Document your purchase or lease options to help the Small Business Financial Manager analyze your alternatives.

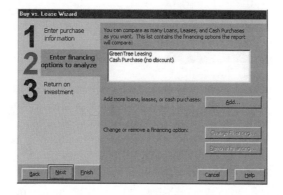

At this point, you can click Finish or Next. Clicking Next takes you to a final dialog box in which you can specify your tax bracket and any potential profit you'll make from the item (see Figure A.16).

FIGURE A.16

If you don't know your tax rate or there is no potential profit, leave the options blank and click Finish.

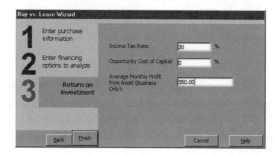

The resulting analysis appears on a formatted worksheet as shown in Figure A.17. Scroll through the report to view the various calculations and use the information to make your decision.

FIGURE A.17

Analysis reports are an excellent source of objective information—seeing the numbers on paper can help you make an unemotional financial decision.

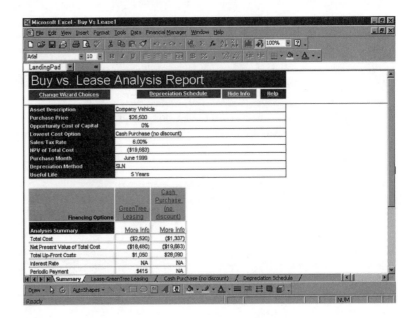

The Business Planner

Not all businesses have an actual business plan, but documentation of a plan for your business can be very useful when you're starting out or when you're going through normal growth phases in the life of your business. The Small Business Tools package gives you a tool for building a business plan, eliminating your need to know how such a plan is traditionally structured. Enter the requested information and let the Business Planner do the rest.

To use the Business Planner, follow these steps:

1. From the Start menu, choose Programs, Microsoft Office Small Business Tools. From the resulting submenu, choose Microsoft Business Planner.

2. The Business Planner window opens, displaying the Personal Interviewer Step 1 (see Figure A.18). The instructions tell you to scroll through the displayed text and answer questions about yourself and your business.

FIGURE A.18

Although you have to wade through a lot of text, you'll find much of it to be helpful in understanding business plans.

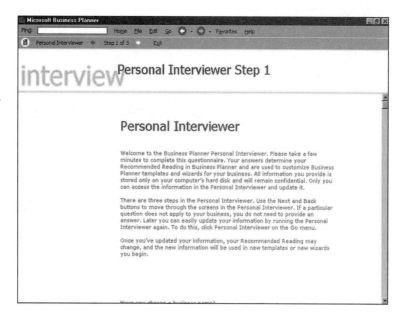

3. Answer each of the questions. Some questions require you to choose one of several options; others require you to type in text boxes (see Figure A.19).

FIGURE A.19

After you've entered your information, click the arrow to move to Step 2 of 3.

Click here to go back to a previous step.

Click this arrow to move forward through the Personal Interviewer.

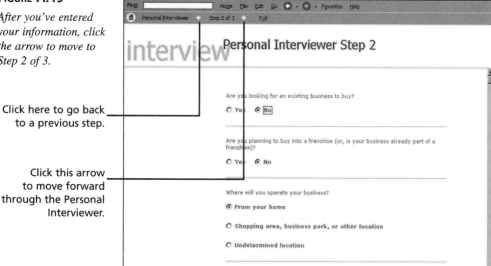

4. Answer the questions in Step 2 of 3, and click the arrow to proceed to the final step.

5. After answering the questions in Step 3 of 3, click the arrow again. The Business Planner displays a new window, as shown in Figure A.20.

FIGURE A.20

Follow each page of the Business Planner to answer questions and to get more information.

6. Click the Business Plan Wizard hyperlink.

7. The Business Plan Wizard window contains a series of seven hyperlinks (see Figure A.21). Click the History and Position to Date link to start.

Figure A.21

See the list of topic areas on which you'll read informative articles.

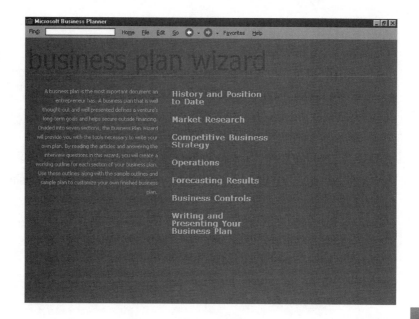

8. Read the first of 15 articles and click the right-pointing arrow to proceed (see Figure A.22). It's a good idea to read them all, clicking the arrow to move through the articles one by one.

A

Figure A.22

Move through the articles by clicking the right-pointing arrow when you're ready to go to the next one.

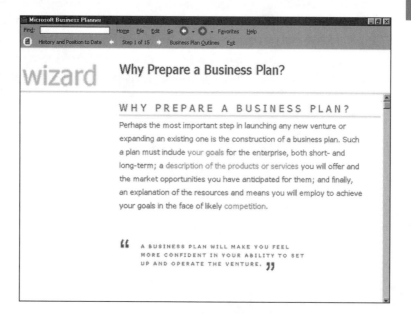

9. At Step 8 of 15, you are asked to name your business plan document in the dialog box shown in Figure A.23. Enter a name for your plan and click Save.

FIGURE A.23

Give your business plan document a name and choose a folder in which to save it.

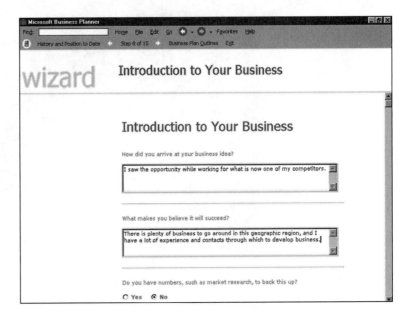

10. Step 8 of 15 continues by asking you to type answers to a series of questions (with intermittent option selections). After responding to all the questions, click the arrow to proceed.

11. At Step 10 of 15, questions regarding your Management Team are presented (see Figure A.24). Type your responses and click the arrow to move to Step 11 of 15.

FIGURE A.24

Describe your management team. If you're a very small business, this might be just you.

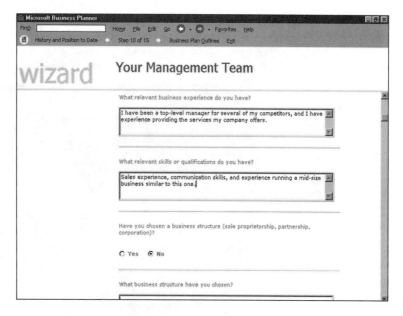

12. Articles appear in steps 11 through 15, at which point you are given a final set of questions regarding your Products and Services (see Figure A.25). Type your responses and click the arrow to proceed.

FIGURE A.25

Describe the products you sell or the services you provide.

13. An Action Plan page appears, which includes links to more articles and some Web pages with information that may be helpful to you in growing your business (see Figure A.26). Click any links that interest you.

FIGURE A.26

If you still want to know more about business plans, check these internal links and Web sites.

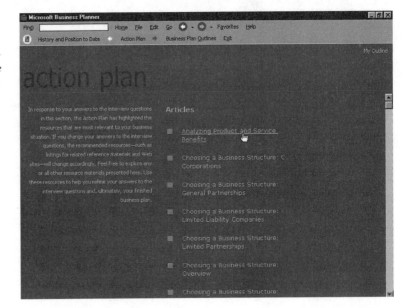

14. Click the Business Plan Outlines button and choose My Outline. An outline based on your entries to the questions posed throughout the previous steps appears (see Figure A.27).

FIGURE A.27

*View the results of
your Business Planner
labors in the form of
an outline.*

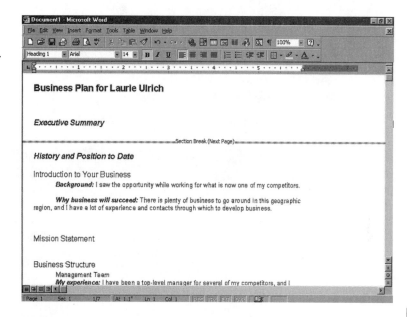

15. Replace the instructional sample text in the outline with your own text. After completing and customizing the outline, you can save and print it as you would any Word document.

Your Business Plan can be used in a variety of ways—as part of a package you supply to the bank or investors or as a reference for yourself to keep things on track as you grow your business. As your business grows and changes, run through the Business Planner again and see how the resulting outline changes to reflect your new answers.

The Direct Mail Manager

If your business does a lot of direct mail, you may find this Small Business Tools component very useful. The Direct Mail Manager performs the following tasks:

- Imports your address list—If you've already built an address list in another program such as Outlook, Outlook Express, Excel, or Access, you can access it through the Direct Mail Manager.

- Verifies your addresses—The Direct Mail Manager checks for and inserts missing zip codes, checks spelling, and deletes duplicate addresses. The verification process saves your time and supplies by eliminating incorrect addresses and redundant mailings.

- Prints envelopes, labels, and postcards—U.S. Postal Service guidelines have been built-in to the Direct Mail Manager to make sure the output meets federal requirements.

- Saves the updated database—Don't risk forgetting to save the imported and corrected records for your next mailing.

The Direct Mail Manager performs these tasks through a wizard, as shown in Figure A.28.

FIGURE A.28

Import, verify, print, and save your direct mail database with the Direct Mail Manager.

To access the wizard, start the Direct Mail Manager by following these steps:

1. From the Start button, choose Programs, Microsoft Office Small Business Tools, and then select Microsoft Direct Mail Manager.

2. After viewing the list of tasks the Direct Mail Manager will perform, click Next to get started.

3. Tell the Direct Mail Manager where to find your address list. Click the Browse button to navigate to the folder that contains the list and enter the path and filename into the File box. If your address list is stored in Outlook, click the Outlook Folder option and select the folder (see Figure A.29).

FIGURE A.29

Select your Personal Folder, which contains the contacts you've entered through Outlook.

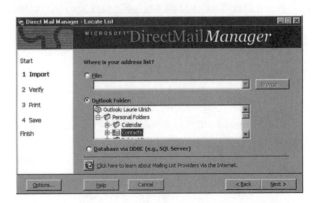

4. Click Next to proceed to the next step, wherein the Direct Mail Manager verifies the accuracy of your list and makes sure all your records are unique.

5. After verification, click Next to move on to the Print step. In the Print dialog box, choose the type of printed output you want for your mailing (see Figure A.30).

FIGURE A.30

Print the envelopes, labels, or postcards you'll be using for your direct mailing.

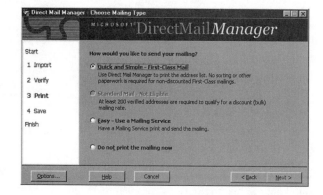

6. Click Next and choose how to Save your database. Your options are shown in Figure A.31.

FIGURE A.31

To save you from accidentally losing the changes made during the verification process, you are prompted to save your database.

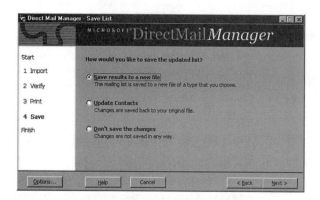

7. Click Next to create a form letter using Word or Publisher, or you can opt to skip this step entirely (perhaps you already have the letter or you're mailing a flyer). Make your selection and click Next.

8. If you chose to create the form letter, the Direct Mail Manager asks you to name your document (see Figure A.32). Click the Create button to build the letter.

A

FIGURE A.32

Build a form letter that will be merged with your database.

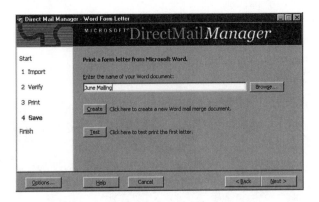

9. Choose the Letter Wizard from the Select a Mail Merge Template and follow the wizard's steps to create the letter.

After your letter is created, you can place the letters in your Direct Mail Manager-created envelopes and get the mailing out to your customers and prospects. The Direct Mail Manager can be run each time you do a mailing or just periodically as a means to verify the accuracy of your database.

For the Direct Mail Manager to verify your addresses, it must connect to the Internet and check phone and zip code databases there. If you would rather skip this step, click the Options button in the lower-left corner of the wizard dialog box and remove the check mark next to Run Address Verification. This step is skipped and you proceed to the Print stage.

The Small Business Customer Manager

You don't need to know how to use database software to query your list of contacts for specific records. If, for example, you need to see only your contacts in New Jersey, the Small Business Customer Manager helps you find them. In addition, the Small Business Customer Manager can be used to pull your contact information from popular accounting applications such as PeachTree, MYOB, and QuickBooks, or you can use your Outlook contacts folder.

To access and use the Small Business Customer Manager, follow these steps:

1. Open the Start menu and choose Programs, Microsoft Office Small Business Tools and then choose Microsoft Small Business Customer Manager from the submenu.

2. After starting the Small Business Customer Manager program, you are asked to select a database to use for your contacts (see Figure A.33). You can select one of the listed databases or click the Browse button to locate your file. For the purposes of this appendix, we'll be using the Northwind Traders sample database, provided by Microsoft.

FIGURE A.33

Choose the database you want to view and edit through the Small Business Customer Manager.

3. Click OK to close the Microsoft Customer Manager dialog box and open the Small Business Customer Manager main program.

4. A dialog box opens asking for your personal information—name, company name, and so forth. Fill this out and click OK to proceed.

The Small Business Customer Manager opens, displaying the selected database (see Figure A.34). A full set of tools for selecting specific records from within the database is offered, in the form of a menu bar, toolbar, and list boxes designed for use with your particular database.

You can insert, edit, and delete records from within the database and save your changes before exiting. You can also save your database with a new filename, creating a new version of the database file. The database can be used for direct mailings and reports through any of the Office applications, such as Word and Excel.

A

Click the Find button to search for a specific record based on key text.

Use the Ascending and Descending Sort buttons to change the order of your listed records.

FIGURE A.34

Click the Narrow Your Choice and Action list boxes to view only those records that match your criteria.

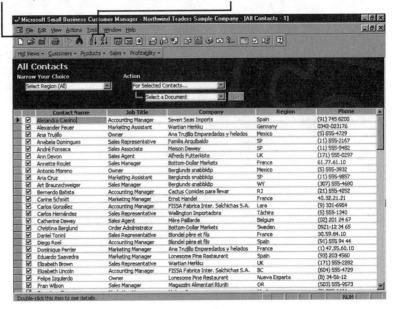

INDEX

Get FREE books and more...when you register this book online for our Personal Bookshelf Program

http://register.samspublishing.com/

SAMS

 Register online and you can sign up for our *FREE Personal Bookshelf Program*—immediate and unlimited access to the electronic version of more than 200 complete computer books! That means you'll have 100,000 pages of valuable information onscreen, at your fingertips!

 Plus, you can access product support, including complimentary downloads, technical support files, book-focused links, companion Web sites, author sites, and more!

 And, don't miss out on the opportunity to sign up for a *FREE subscription to a weekly email newsletter* to help you stay current with news, announcements, sample book chapters, and special events, including sweepstakes, contests, and various product giveaways.

 We value your comments! Best of all, the entire registration process takes only a few minutes to complete, so go online and get the greatest value going—absolutely FREE!

Don't Miss Out On This Great Opportunity!

Sams®is a brand of Macmillan Computer Publishing USA. For more information, visit *www.mcp.com*